Praise for *The Gaza Kitchen, Second Edition*

This book becomes more essential with every passing day. Not just a superb cookbook, a collection of vital recipes from a delicious yet often overlooked cuisine, but an argument for understanding. A classic of world food.

—ANTHONY BOURDAIN

It is a delight to be returning to this book—a real classic—in its second edition. The recipes and stories are magically woven together, inspiring to read, to cook, and to eat. Telling us about the food of Gaza is key to understanding the people's way of life, and this is what Laila and Maggie do so fantastically well.

—YOTAM OTTOLENGHI and SAMI TAMIMI
co-authors of *Jerusalem: A Cookbook*

The best cookbooks inspire you to be a better chef. This one can make you a better person. Laila El-Haddad and Maggie Schmitt guide readers through the rich, subtle and complex flavours, history and politics of the Jews, Christians, and Muslims of the Levant. Even if you never make any of these recipes—and you'd be depriving yourself of sublime taste if you didn't—your palate will grow through this excellent book. Part anthropology, part history, part politics, part biography, part geography, and always passionately intelligent, this is gastronomic writing at its finest.

—RAJ PATEL
author of *Stuffed and Starved: The Hidden Battle for the World Food System*

The Gaza Kitchen cookbook is a vital attempt to safeguard a rich culinary heritage that has existed in the Middle East for thousands of years. In documenting Palestinian recipes and food culture, despite the ravages of war, Laila El-Haddad and Maggie Schmitt have significantly succeeded in sharing their culinary travels while bringing dignity and pride to those who continue cooking traditional meals at home in Palestine. This book is an asset to those living in Gaza and to the rest of the world who would like to participate in protecting this rich cuisine.

—BARBARA MASSAAD
Lebanese author and photographer of the award-winning cookbooks
Man'oushé, Mouneh, Mezze, and *Soup for Syria*

Intriguing, homely, and delicious, the recipes are familiar as broadly Middle Eastern but they are distinctively Palestinian and many also uniquely of Gaza—with more pronounced flavours, more herby, spicy, peppery, lemony, than those of their regional neighbours. We also get from this very special book a rare insight into the intimate everyday lives of engaging people who grow vegetables and herbs and raise pigeons and rabbits on their rooftops even as they lament their predicament.

—CLAUDIA RODEN
author of more than a dozen books on Mediterranean cuisine

The
Gaza Kitchen

A Palestinian Culinary Journey

Second Edition

Laila El-Haddad & Maggie Schmitt

Just World Books

Charlottesville, Virginia

Just World Books
Timely Books for Changing Times

Just World Books is an imprint of Just World Publishing, LLC.

Interior design and typesetting by Diana Ghazzawi for Just World Publishing, LLC.

Cover photo by Maggie Schmitt.

Photo on p. 285 courtesy of Library of Congress #LC-DIG-matpc-11349.

Map on p. 45 courtesy of Linda Quiquivix.

Publisher's Cataloging in Publication

El-Haddad, Laila M., author.
    The Gaza kitchen : a Palestinian culinary journey /
    Laila El-Haddad & Maggie Schmitt ; foreword by Nancy
    Harmon Jenkins. -- Second edition.
        pages cm
        Includes index.
        LCCN 2016942730
        ISBN 978-1-68257-008-1

    1. Cooking, Palestinian Arab. 2. Cooking--Gaza
Strip. 3. Palestinian Arabs--Social life and customs.
4. Cookbooks. I. Schmitt, Maggie, author. II. Title.
III. Title: Palestinian culinary journey.

TX725.M628E44 2016   641.59'29274
                      QBI16-600092

Contents

Foreword

by Nancy Harmon Jenkins

A book about Gaza cuisine? Some cooks might be forgiven for thinking the concept is something of an oxymoron. After all, we know Gaza, don't we? That tiny, troubled sliver of the southeastern Mediterranean, the focus of seemingly unending struggle, uniquely both victim and perpetrator, injured and injurer, where bombs and rockets, stones and bitter invective, are hurled back and forth across the border with Israel and occasionally too with neighboring Egypt. Who could care about food in a context so contentious? Isn't that the very definition of frivolity?

Well, as it turns out, it's not. Not when the food is as delicious and exciting as this remarkable book reveals—from basic preparations like spicy meat broth and tahina sauce that are foundations for many other dishes, to lusciously buttery, citrusy, nutty pastries to end the meal—this is a cuisine of compelling flavors, substantial dishes, of traditions handed down from cook to cook over the generations. Gaza was an important station on the spice route, a link between southern Arabia and the Mediterranean, and spices from lands to the east continue to shape the cuisine to this day. At the same time, this patch of territory is also a repository of traditional foods and dishes from all over historic Palestine, a living legacy of the refugees who flocked here, driven from their homes in the north and the east.

If you believe, as I do, and as Laila El-Haddad and Maggie Schmitt so obviously do, that food—growing it, preparing it, sharing it with friends, family, and strangers—is a vital cultural marker, one of the most significant ways we have to identify ourselves as members of our own tribe and of the great tribe of humanity—if you believe that, then you will recognize that *The Gaza Kitchen* is not just a recipe book but a significant look at the people of this tiny corner of the world. Food, after all, is one of the most telling ways the people of Gaza have to say, to themselves and to their families, yes, this is who we are: Eat this because you are Palestinian, eat this in order to become more fully Palestinian, eat this to celebrate the memory of who and what we are. And what they eat in Gaza is delicious, even when, as so often, it is as basic as can be—like a traditional potato salad, sparked with chopped chilis and enriched with that very great Gaza specialty, red tahina made from dry-roasted sesame seeds, full of nutty fragrance.

It has to be understood that Gaza isn't just a narrow band of coastline with an unfortunate modern name—the Gaza Strip, as if it were merely the edge of some hapless suburban shopping mall. Gaza is also an integral part of Palestine, separated now from the other Palestine, the West Bank, by Israel's convoluted and unpredictable border controls. Today's Gaza, a mere 25 miles long and no more than 5 miles wide at its greatest point, is all that remains of what was historically, under the British Mandate, a much larger territory. In this place now nearly 2 million Palestinians are squeezed together, most of them refugees, or descendants of refugees, both from the original, much more extensive Gaza District, as well as from other parts of Palestine. All these historic aromas and flavors, then, have been absorbed into Gaza's own traditions to create a new and vibrant cuisine.

In many ways, food in Gaza is classic Palestinian, Middle Eastern cuisine, but it is unique with its own regional diversity, which includes a deep appreciation for the kick of red chili peppers, the zest of eastern spices (cardamom, cloves, cinnamon), and the soothing calm of fresh dill and dill seeds. You can see this immediately in Gaza-style falafel, those delectably crisp, deep-fried morsels of ground chickpeas with spices, universal street food throughout the Middle East, from Turkey to the banks of the Nile. In Gaza, though, the addition of chopped chilis and fresh green dill gives a special twist to falafel. (Only in Greece is dill used to the delicious extent it is in Gaza.) Or take stuffed grape leaves, *warak inab*, another classic of the eastern Mediterranean, filled with ground meat and rice or bulgur—in Gaza the filling is sparked with allspice, cardamom, nutmeg, and black pepper, a reflection of Gaza's great crossroads history, connecting southern Arabia and the Indian Ocean to the Mediterranean.

There are also special dishes here, ones you'd otherwise have to travel to Gaza to experience, which few of us are able to do. I think of the spicy roasted watermelon salad called *fattit ajir*, in which a whole, under-ripe watermelon is charred on the grill, then peeled, chopped and mixed with hot chilis and fresh dill, along with ripe tomatoes and torn bits of toasted Arab bread. Or *tabeekh baqla*, a stew of fresh purslane (*baqla*) with chickpeas and cilantro, sparked with pepper flakes and fragrant with olive oil. And I think especially of *sumagiyya*, which the authors describe as the quintessential Gaza dish, a basic meat stew with lots of tart-flavored sumac (hence its name), with the freshness of green chard and the heft of chickpeas, and of course with the ubiquitous dill and chilis, red and green alike. *Sumagiyya*, too, has that famous Gaza specialty red tahina, the endangered species of this fascinating kitchen.

Endangered species? Yes. And this is a place where politics enters the kitchen to unhappy effect. Unlike the familiar pale, creamy-colored Middle Eastern version, Gaza red tahina is made from toasted sesame, which gives it a richer color and flavor. Therein lies the problem: Since exports are forbidden, the market is strictly local, within Gaza itself. And since imports are controlled by Israel, most sesame seeds enter only through the illegal tunnels between Gaza and Egypt, driving the price way above that of Israeli-produced tahina—an import which is permitted. In a subtle but unmistakable undermining of local traditions, red tahina becomes part of the lethal games played in this part of the world—no longer affordable by the very people who invented it, relish it, identify with it, and now must substitute something lesser. It may seem slight in the great scheme of wrong-doing, but it is decidedly telling.

It should also be noted that, despite poverty and unemployment, despite reliance on hand-outs from UNRWA to eke out the family larder, Gazan cooks are resilient and exuberant. We could all take lessons from this healthful cuisine, much of it based on the goodness of legumes—chickpeas, lentils, and fava beans—on the deliciously smoky green wheat called *freekah*, and on fresh garden vegetables—onions, radishes, parsley and mint, squashes and a multitude of greens. Fish, once famously a part of the diet and of the economy, has been drastically reduced through Israeli-imposed fishing limits—another bitter example of how politics wreaks havoc with the food supply in a process the authors call, rightly, de-development, reducing a once productive and independent market economy to a network of dependence and uncertainty.

Laila El-Haddad and Maggie Schmitt understand right from the start that cuisine is something much more than a collection of recipes, no matter how delicious and varied—and the recipes in *The Gaza Kitchen* are indeed delicious. More than recipes, cuisine, taken as a whole as they have done in this book, is a singular expression of culture, of history—as painful as that has been—and of heritage—as important as it is for defining the future. So do leaf through this book, find recipes that attract you, try them out and then try them a second and third time, and as you do so, think about the place and the people and the way the cuisine reflects both.

But read the book too—the little essays on Gaza traditions, the profiles of cooks, farmers, fishermen, and food producers, the images of a still tormented history, all lend tremendous weight to its appeal. I guarantee you will come away with a renewed respect for the spirit and resilience of the people of Gaza. Not just a cookbook, *The Gaza Kitchen* is a reflection of a unique group of people at an important moment in their history. And as such, of course, it is a reflection of all of us, of our common humanity.

INTRODUCTION

The clamor of pots and pans, the rise and fall of a dozen voices laughing and talking, the neat clack of knives, the splatter of hot oil: This is the kitchen at the Olive Roots Cooperative in the Zeitoun neighborhood of old Gaza City. The tiny concrete-block room is dense with the warm, wheaty scent of steaming *maftool*, offset by the bright tang of lemon and fresh dill and the velvety perfume of cinnamon. Heedless of the 100-degree heat and the power outage, the cooperative's members peel pumpkins and marinate chickens, fry eggplants and crush garlic in a whir of activity. While all hands are at work, the conversation ranges from thyroid troubles to daughters-in-law, from the ravages of the most recent war to the correct candying of carrots.

And there we are in the midst of this savory maelstrom, with our camera and voice recorder, trying to take it all in.

We went to Gaza for these kitchen conversations because we intuited that they would allow us to tell the story of the place in a very special way. Nearly everyone in Gaza to whom we explained the project understood it immediately: To talk about food and cooking is to talk about the dignity of daily life, about history and heritage, in a place where these very things have often been disparaged or actively erased. Approached for an interview, Gazans braced themselves to explain one more time—gently, patiently—the impossible political situation of the Strip. When they discovered we did not want to talk about political parties or border crossings but about lentil dishes, there was a moment of astonished delight before they launched into the topic. Passersby crowded around, each proffering a hometown recipe: "No, no, it's much better if you add the onions at the end...." Food is a passionate subject.

We visited cooks—mostly women—of all different regions and social classes, prepared meals together, and listened to their stories. The conversations that take place in the kitchen are different from conversations anywhere else: more intimate, more leisurely. These conversations, and the recipes we learned through them, form the backbone of this book.

Additional context on the food system in Gaza is provided by interviews with economists, farmers, aid workers, nutritionists, and others. Learning where food comes from and what it costs reveals much about Gaza's labyrinthine economy, just as learning where recipes come from and how people learned to cook them reveals much about family histories and social structures. The recipes themselves, with their broad spectrum of tastes and techniques, provide a glimpse into the long and tumultuous history of this place.

The ones we have collected here range from the elaborate and luxurious rice dishes served on special occasions to simple family suppers made with the humblest of ingredients. In general, we have opted to present "home food," the traditional meals and preparations that are passed through families from generation to generation and are often very locally specific, rather than "restaurant food," which is much more uniform throughout the region. The recipes stand out for their bright and piquant tastes and their lavish use of the hot peppers, citrus, and aromatic herbs that so exuberantly grow throughout the Strip.

A sliver of green between the desert and the sea, Gaza and its environs have prospered since antiquity as a hub along essential transit routes—on the one hand, between the Levant and Egypt, and on the other hand, between Arabia and Europe. As well as its role in trade, most notably in spices, historic Gaza was a garden district, famous particularly for its orchards.

Today when we speak of Gaza we refer to the Gaza Strip, a miniscule enclave some twenty-five miles long and two and a half to five miles wide, within borders set in 1967. Historically, however, the greater Gaza District—one of the administrative districts of British Mandate Palestine and, before that, the Ottoman Empire—comprised a much larger region to the north and east.

The founding of Israel in 1948 changed the map radically and abruptly. A massive influx of Palestinian refugees displaced from neighboring towns and villages flooded into Gaza, their land and their homes suddenly inaccessible to them. What is now known as the Gaza Strip was carved out and separated from the rest of the Gaza District and historic Palestine under the Israel-Egypt armistice agreement. The enclave fell under Egyptian administrative rule until 1967, when Israel occupied the territory and cut it off from Egypt.

In 2005, Israel dismantled its settlement-colonies within Gaza while still maintaining control over all the territory's effective markers of sovereignty: its borders, its commerce, its population registry, its airspace, and its maritime access.

This geopolitical ping-pong, as well as the frequent closure of Gaza's borders, has isolated the Strip, obliging Gazans to adapt their cuisine—as well as all other aspects of their lives—to wildly uncertain economic and political circumstances.

In culinary terms, too, Gaza's location places it at a crossroads: While it forms part of the greater Mediterranean food universe of olives, fish, chickpeas,

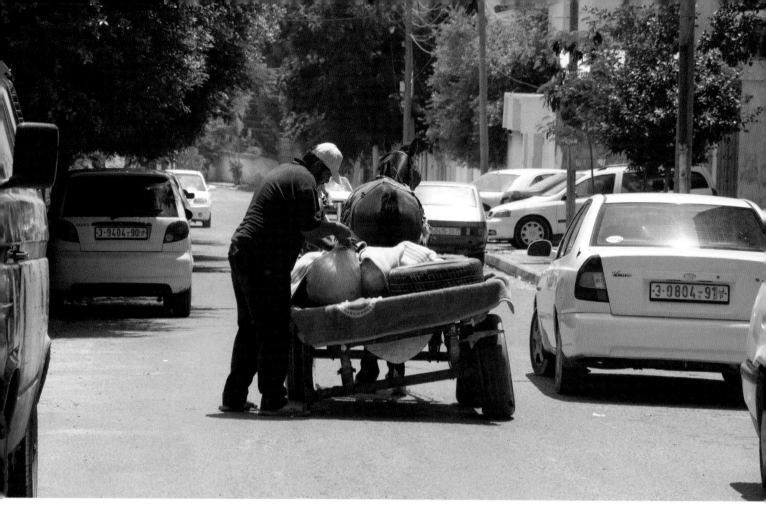

and garden vegetables, it is also a bridge to the desert culinary worlds of Arabia, the Red Sea, and the Nile Valley. Within the region, the cuisine of the urban coast—noted for its sophisticated seafood dishes—is clearly distinguishable from that of the farming interior, rich in vegetables and legumes.

The intense concentration of refugees from other parts of historic Palestine (80 percent of the current population of Gaza) makes Gaza an extraordinary place to encounter culinary traditions from hundreds of Palestinian towns and villages that now exist only in memory—having been depopulated and destroyed during the Palestinian exodus of 1948—as well as from Gaza itself.

Gaza's cuisine—like its culture and its political reality—is both inseparably linked to the rest of Palestine and very specific to local conditions. Our focus on Gaza should in no way be taken as participation in efforts to tear Gaza politically, economically, and symbolically from the rest of Palestine, deliberately fragmenting the Palestinian legacy. By focusing on

Gaza, we hope to contribute to the larger Palestinian narrative, as Gaza is often left out from anthropological and other studies of Palestine. We also like to think of Gaza as a case study of sorts: Understanding what happens to Gaza is key to understanding the conflict as a whole. In the words of the late Palestinian national poet Mahmoud Darwish, "Gaza equals the history of an entire homeland...it is the brutal lesson, and the shining example, for enemies and friends alike."

Gazans are consistently shown either as hapless objects of pity or as vicious objects of fear, but seldom as singular lives in a complex environment. The near-complete closure of the Strip has succeeded in isolating them, making it difficult to correct this misrepresentation. As for Gazan women, they're seldom represented at all, and their daily struggles to keep their families fed, clothed, healthy, and educated are almost entirely invisible from outside. One of the goals of this project is to give readers some sense of what households, families, and daily activities look like in Gaza, simply in order to recognize the humanity of those lives.

14

We would also like to suggest that Gaza can be seen as a hothouse laboratory for the kind of violent de-development that is occurring in many parts of the world. Gaza has been transformed from a fertile, productive, and sustainable territory into a radically impoverished political powder keg, with no autonomy and at the brink of ecological disaster, through a combination of physical violence and economic destabilization. While similar dynamics are at work in many parts of the formerly colonized world, Gaza is so tiny and its circumstances so extreme that it serves as an extraordinary illustration for understanding phenomena like agricultural dumping, aid dependence, and cash-crop farming. Its people have essentially been discarded as an exploitable work force; the Strip has been transformed into a cage full of consumers. A full development of this

idea may be beyond the scope of a cookbook, but we try to offer a few key insights.

In conclusion, this is a hybrid sort of book. It is mostly a cookbook that recovers and compiles both traditional and contemporary elements of a rich and little-known cuisine. But it also attempts to do a little ethnography, a little history, a little political analysis. Cuisine always lies somewhere at the intersection of geography, history, and economy. What makes it such a compelling subject is that it serves as a cultural record of daily life for ordinary people—traces of a history from below made palpable in something as evocative and delicious as a steaming plate of stew. Our hope in this book is to share this food with you and, in so doing, share something of the indefatigable spirit of the people we interviewed.

Notes on the 2016 Edition

A lot has changed in Gaza since we did the fieldwork for this book in 2010.

Readers should take this work as a snapshot of what Gaza was like three years into the suffocating economic blockade—at perhaps its most intense moment—and a year after the terrible attacks of 2008 and 2009 ("Operation Cast Lead"). Since then the inhabitants of Gaza have suffered two more major attacks, in 2012 ("Operation Defensive Pillar") and in the devastating summer of 2014 ("Operation Protective Shield"). Meanwhile, the blockade goes on, now in its ninth year, with parameters that have shifted slightly but not enough to permit any real economic recovery—much less prosperity.

Several of the individuals we interviewed in 2010 now form part of the 30 percent of the population displaced due to the destruction of homes in 2014. If agricultural land was scarce when we did our fieldwork, it has now been reduced by half due to the systematic targeting of farms and infrastructure. And if access to water and basic sanitation was already a crisis, after the destruction of some 80 percent of Gaza's water network, it is now a calamity. The burden of everyday survival in Gaza has multiplied in the years since this work was first published. Disenchantment with political actors on all sides is even more acute, and it is hard to imagine how ordinary people in Gaza avoid succumbing to despair.

Yet, somehow, they press on: By telephone and email, we hear from our protagonists who, like so many other Gazans, are rebuilding as best they can. They regroup, replant, and continue living and cooking, buoyed by the care and support of their families, their faith, and the importance of the legacy they bear. While some of the specific circumstances described here have changed, the stories and traditions at the heart of this book continue unaltered. For us, that is precisely the virtue of writing about food in so volatile a place.

For the 2016 edition of this book, we have updated general information about conditions in Gaza, but the near-total closure of the territory has prevented us from going back to visit our informants and provide a more extensive update. Laila did manage to return to Gaza in 2013 for one very brief visit, to guide chef Anthony Bourdain around the territory for his Israel/Palestine episode of *Parts Unknown*, but for the most part this edition's updates reflect statistics published by various NGOs and UN bodies rather than original fieldwork.

We have provided several new recipes, including some that were not included in the first edition due to space limitations and many others given to us by diaspora Gazans whom we met while presenting the first edition of this book in the United States and Europe. It was a tremendous honor for us to see the enthusiasm with which the book was received, especially by Palestinians from Gaza who felt the book provided—finally!—a nuanced and faithful portrait of a place they knew and loved and a record of the recipes that they grew up with. We started this project with no funding, no support, not even knowing each other personally; we just shared an idea and an intuition that it might work. The many and varied conversations this book has generated since its publication in 2012, including with individuals who would not have otherwise been inclined to learn about Gaza, have confirmed that intuition a hundredfold.

Again and again we have been asked whether food can somehow bridge differences and smooth asperities between what are perceived to be two sides in a conflict, a doctrine we have come to refer to as "Hummus Kumbaya." We laugh about it, but it's not an easy question to answer. On the one hand, the idea seems premised upon the mistaken notion that between Palestinians and Israelis (or Arabs and Jews) lies some essential, intractable, centuries-long enmity: that it is a matter of peoples who just can't get along, and that maybe food might span this unbridgeable gap. But this whole premise is false. Most Palestinian and Sephardic/Mizrahi families—including Laila's own—have fond memories of their Jewish, Christian, and Muslim neighbors before 1948. So it is not exactly a problem of "getting along." There are a lot of very real material things at stake: access to the land, to rights, to natural resources, to a future. Will a shared love of hummus solve this political problem? Not if it fails to confront the real bones of contention. The dispossession of the Palestinian people and the erasure of their history has become—over these few short generations—much more material than simple goodwill can remedy.

That said, our hope—because hope we must—is that understanding how people live, what they cherish, the stories they tell, and the sense they make of their lives may serve as a first step in a long and arduous process of change for the better, toward building a place where all can share the land and its resources—equally. That starts by re-engaging. Here, we do feel like food might make a modest contribution. Change is not a distant political horizon to be negotiated at faraway summits but a daily practice, weaving connections, creating solidarity, and a shared sense of the possible. We turn to the kitchen for these stories precisely because this is what happens in kitchens: Stories are transmitted, dignity is crafted, life is sustained. If hope is to be found anywhere, it is in the dogged persistence of ordinary people to continue living, loving, and supporting each other irrespective of the circumstances: in short, to stay human.

LAILA EL-HADDAD and MAGGIE SCHMITT

June 2016

FUNDAMENTALS: CONDIMENTS, BROTH, AND MORE

Certain building blocks of Gazan cuisine are repeated again and again throughout the book: a spiced broth key to nearly all the stews, a mix of spices used in most rice dishes, a chile paste used as ingredient and condiment. In this chapter, we provide these foundational recipes, as well as some pointers on technique.

Chickpeas: Many recipes call for this staple legume. We give measurements for dried chickpeas, which should be pre-soaked overnight and then boiled until just tender before use. You may also use canned, pre-cooked chickpeas: One 15-ounce can equals about half a cup of dried beans. If using canned chickpeas, strain and rinse several times before using.

Cucumbers: The cucumbers available in Gaza are the small, thin-skinned, and almost seedless Middle Eastern *khiyar*, sometimes sold in the United States as Lebanese, Persian, or "mini" cucumbers. Any burpless variety will do.

Cumin: Perhaps more than any other spice, ground cumin characterizes Gazan cooking. Cumin should ideally be toasted and ground immediately before use, otherwise the flavor dulls.

Dill: Fresh dill greens and dill seeds are both widely used in Gaza's cuisine. The seeds should be crushed in a mortar and pestle, using strong, circular strokes, in order to release their natural oils. "You'll know when it's enough," Laila's grandmother used to advise. "You can smell them!" Dill seeds can usually be found in Turkish or Polish markets; they are also readily available online.

Garlic: Rare is the Gazan dish that doesn't include garlic—often lots of it! Use fresh garlic, never jarred, pre-minced, or dried.

Green Chile Peppers: Fundamental to nearly all Gazan recipes, the local variety of green chiles is hot! Jalapeño or serrano peppers make a decent substitute; use hot Italian green peppers if you prefer less bite. Avoid Thai or bird's-eye peppers. Remove the seeds and membranes before using, and be aware of exactly how hot the pepper you're using is; they vary a lot.

Mastic: Also called "Arabic gum," mastic is the resin of a Mediterranean shrub. It is sold in small hard drops (or "pearls") and is used throughout Greece and the Middle East to season and thicken sweets. In Gaza it is widely used to perfume soups, as well as in many sweets.

Nigella Seed: The tiny, slightly bitter black seed of the *Nigella sativa* flower, often called "black cumin." It is used to flavor breads, cheeses, and pickles.

Red Chile Peppers: Used to make *filfil mat'hoon*, itself a basic ingredient. These chiles should also be hot, but not brutally so; mild red cayenne or serrano peppers would make a reasonable substitute. When preparing *filfil mat'hoon*, make sure you chop the peppers rather than using a food processor. Otherwise, the seeds produce a bitter taste.

Red Tahina: This brick-red Gazan variety of tahina is made by roasting sesame seeds in small batches over direct heat (for the more familiar "white" variety, the seeds are steamed). Add a little dark sesame oil to white tahina to achieve a similar effect, or make your own in a high-powered blender! Some health-food stores are now marketing a roasted-sesame tahina; this is very similar to the Gazan variety.

Squash: Several recipes call for *koosa*, small Middle Eastern squashes with pale skin, sometimes referred to as "grey squash" in Asian and Mexican markets. If this is not available, it is better to substitute yellow summer squash than dark-green zucchini.

Sour Plums: Extremely tart little dried plums, known as *arasiya*, are traditionally used to lend sourness to broths and stews. As these plums are now scarce, pomegranate molasses—available in Middle Eastern groceries—is a good substitute. We find that adding prunes and pomegranate molasses to recipes calling for dried plums is ideal: The prunes provide the sweetness, the pomegranate the sourness.

Maraqa

Basic Spiced Broth

Makes 5–6 cups (approximately 1.5 liters) of broth

For preparing the chicken
¼ cup (30 grams) flour
1 tablespoon salt
1 lemon, juiced, and rind reserved

For the chicken broth
Chicken parts, such as back, neck, and wings, or whole chicken cut
   into parts, skin removed
3–4 tablespoons olive oil
1 medium onion, chopped
2 dried bay leaves
1 cinnamon stick
1 teaspoon whole allspice berries
1 teaspoon cardamom pods
1 teaspoon whole black peppercorns
2 whole cloves
1 sprig rosemary
1 very small piece cracked nutmeg
2 pebbles of mastic, crushed with a little salt
2 teaspoons salt (to taste)

Clean chicken carefully in a bath of cold water, flour, salt, and lemon juice, then massage with spent lemon rinds as described in "Common Sense" on page 26. Rinse, then set aside in a strainer on top of a bowl for 10 to 15 minutes, until you see that bloody juices have run out of the chicken.

If so advised in the recipe you are using, brown the chicken pieces in a little oil for a few minutes on high heat.

Add 2 cups (480 milliliters) of water and bring to a boil, continuously skimming off any scum that rises to the surface. Add another 4 cups (1 liter) of water—enough to fully submerge the meat—along with the rest of the ingredients.

Bring to a boil again, then lower heat and simmer, partially covered, for 45 minutes to 1 hour. Discard spices. Strain and cool, reserving only meat and broth.

For beef, lamb, or goat broth
Follow the instructions above, substituting the specified quantity of meat from the recipe you are following, and substituting 2 tablespoons of white vinegar for the lemon juice. Strain the meat, then pat it dry or set it in the fridge to air-dry for 30 minutes. If you are cooking a vegetable stew, brown the meat first. Allow for 2 to 3 hours of cooking time on a stovetop or approximately 1 hour in a pressure cooker, until the meat is fork-tender.

A good basic broth, rich with spices, is key to some of Gaza's (and indeed the entire region's) most elaborate festive dishes like *fatta* or *maqlooba*. It also makes a delicious base for humbler fare like *mulukhiyya*, *fogaiyya*, or *shorabit freekah*.

For soups, this broth is often made with the less meaty parts of a chicken: the back, neck, and wings or head. For special occasions the whole animal is used to make the broth. The meat, tender and perfumed with spices after boiling, is served separately or incorporated later into the final presentation of the dish.

For some recipes, such as the many vegetable stews we feature in this book or some of the rice dishes, like maqlooba, we recommend browning the meat or chicken in a little oil before adding water. For other recipes, you can skip this step and proceed immediately to boiling the meat.

While starting with a basic homemade broth is best, the amateur cook should not be discouraged or dissuaded from trying recipes without it: use a good store-bought broth or natural bouillon paste and simmer with an assortment of the whole spices suggested below. Or consider making a large batch of broth and freezing portions in glass jars or resealable bags.

Placing the whole spices in a disposable tea filter or a piece of gauze tied together with kitchen twine makes it easier to fish them out and dispose of them when the broth is done. If unavailable, simply add spices and spoon or strain them out after cooking.

Common Sense

Rarely will you come across a cuisine that gives more importance to cleanliness. Arab cooks in general are very fastidious about the freshness and purity of ingredients—so much so that even in medieval times, the hallmark of a good cook was the gleaming cleanliness of his pots and pans. One of the secrets to the bright, vivid tastes of Gazan cuisine may be the scrupulousness with which meat and vegetables are washed, scrubbed, and purged of any grimy or gamey tastes. This is an accomplishment anywhere, but more so in the sweltering heat of a place where the electricity is cut more than eight hours a day and the coldness of refrigerators and freezers must be carefully preserved.

The result of this careful attention is a unique precision of flavor. Each thing tastes richly of what it is, with no smudgy indistinction. Broths are clear and golden; seafood is robust without low-tide murkiness. *Zanakha*, or gaminess, is considered the sign of a careless cook.

Every cuisine has its own "common sense": basic techniques that are automatic to the experienced cook and that in many ways define the taste of the food. This elemental vocabulary is largely learned by observation over time. For those who haven't imbibed these lessons at their mother's knee, here are some axioms of Palestinian cooking.

Meats

- Chicken, rabbit, red meat, and fish should be bathed in a bowl of cold water with a fistful of flour, a spoonful of coarse salt, and the juice of one lemon (or substitute 2 tablespoons of white vinegar for the lemon juice). Then massage the chicken, fish, or meat with the spent lemon rind. Remove all veins, blood, or scales, inside and out, then rinse the meat, chicken, or fish and leave it in a strainer—preferably in the refrigerator—to drain off the bloody juices for 10 to 15 minutes. Meat that is to be browned should be very fully dried after draining.
- If using a tough cut of beef or goat meat, soak it in white vinegar for 20 minutes, then rinse it well, pat it dry, and proceed with recipe.
- If you are cooking any meat in liquid, as in the preparation of a broth, first add just a cup or two of water and bring to a boil. This usually produces a scummy foam called *zafara*, which is considered utterly repulsive. Spoon this off continuously as it forms. When no scum remains, proceed to add the remaining quantity of water, onion, and spices. This results in a clean-tasting broth free of any gamey flavors.
- A chicken or rabbit boiled for broth may—after boiling—be rubbed with a halved tomato or lemon and then briefly placed in a broiler to brown. The meat will be tender and perfumed from the broth spices, but attractively crisp and brown for serving.

Vegetables

- Greens of all kinds should be first chopped and then submerged in a large bowl of water and swished around vigorously, then scooped out, not strained. Change the water 2 or 3 times and repeat until no grit remains at the bottom of the bowl, then strain the greens in a colander and dry on a kitchen towel or in a salad spinner.
- Most varieties of eggplant (except the Japanese type) should be salted before use. Sprinkle the eggplant slices with salt and leave them in a colander for 20 minutes until beads of moisture form, or else soak them in salted water then pat dry before proceeding. This is especially important for bitter or seedy varieties of eggplant. It also helps reduce the oil absorbed when frying.
- When tomatoes are in season, liquefy them in a blender (crush slightly with your hands first) or grate them with a cheese grater, then strain for use in stews. If tomatoes are not in season, substitute tomato paste diluted in water or unseasoned tomato purée.

Herbs and Spices

- Salt provides friction when you are crushing garlic or other ingredients with a mortar and pestle. Coarse sea salt is best, but regular table salt will do. When crushing mastic for use in sweets, a pinch of sugar serves the same purpose.
- Dried herbs should be crushed between the fingers to release their fragrance before use; dill seed should be crushed thoroughly with a circular motion in a mortar until fragrant.
- Many stews are finished off with a *taqliya*: Garlic or onion, fried crisp in plenty of olive oil or butter, sometimes with other aromatics like coriander, and added at the very end of cooking to provide a bright jolt of flavor

Filfil Mat'hoon/Shatta

Ground Red Chile Pepper Paste

Makes about 12 ounces (340 grams)

1 pound (approximately 500 grams) red hot chile peppers, stems removed
2½ tablespoons salt
¼ cup (60 milliliters) olive oil

First, prepare your storage containers or Mason jars. Sterilize the jars by boiling them in water for 3 minutes, then carefully remove them using tongs and allow to air dry completely before proceeding. Make sure there is no moisture inside or the pepper paste will spoil.

Next, hand-chop the peppers to a medium-coarse grind, or pulse them gently in a food processor until they are ground but not yet a paste. The seeds should remain whole and visible. Otherwise, the resulting paste will be bitter. Add salt. Mix well, then place the mixture in a strainer for 10 to 15 minutes, until an adequate amount of moisture has been drained and no more liquid is emerging. The less moisture, the longer you can preserve the pepper paste.

Pour the strained mixture into containers and cover with a generous layer of olive oil to prevent spoilage. Refrigerate. The paste may be used immediately.

فلفل مطحون/شطة

Unlike most chile paste recipes, this one calls for fresh, not dried, chiles. Called *shatta* in some families, it is ubiquitous throughout Gaza: as an ingredient in recipes, as a condiment to accompany meats, or mixed with feta cheese or *labna* and eaten with flatbread for a Gaza-style breakfast. Anaheim, Aleppo, or Korean red peppers work well here.

Daggit Toma u Lamoon

Hot Garlic and Lemon Dressing

Makes about ½ cup (118 milliliters)

6 cloves garlic
½ teaspoon salt
3 or 4 hot green chiles, finely chopped (adjust to taste)
Juice of 3 lemons

Using a mortar and pestle, crush the garlic cloves and salt to a rough paste. Add the chiles to the crushed garlic and pound slightly. Stir in the lemon juice and mix well, scraping in any bits of garlic from the bottom of the mortar. Increase the quantity as necessary.

دقة ثوم وليمون

This simple hot-and-sour dressing is served with innumerable dishes, from hearty stewed fava beans to eggplant salads.

"They make something like this in the rest of Palestine," many of the cooks we interviewed would say as they showed us how to prepare a favorite dish, "but we add hot chile peppers and dill."

Hot chiles and dill: the Gazan combination *par excellence*. How Gazans developed this love affair with the chile pepper is a culinary mystery for the ages. Whereas Lebanese cooks tolerate no spicy heat at all and cooks from other parts of Palestine and the greater region use spice in moderation, Gazan cooks (specifically those from Gaza City itself, as opposed to rural areas) make you sweat, whether using a local variety of fresh hot green chile peppers—generally crushed in a mortar with lemon and salt—or else ground red chile peppers conserved in oil and sold as a condiment and ingredient called *filfil mat'hoon*.

Ubiquitous dishes such as *tabeekh bamia*, okra stew with lamb, and *mulukhiyya*, green mallow soup, are served with a blaze of hot green chile and dill seed in lemon juice, cutting the dark, rich tastes with their brightness. Green chiles are ground with meat to make *kufta* and mashed in clay mortars to make *dagga*, Gaza's distinctive hot tomato salad.

The same peppers, ripened to fiery redness, are sun-dried for winter use in dishes such as *maftool*, a Gazan variety of couscous, perfuming the grains as they steam. In the summer, fields of bright red peppers—ripe for pickling and grinding—blanket what little remains of Gaza's seaside farmlands.

In fact, chile peppers play a nutritionally important role in Gaza. They grow fast and require little irrigation, making them a viable local product and very inexpensive in the market. For many of the poorest Gazans, nutritionally rich red chile provides some of the vitamins, iron, and potassium to which they do not otherwise have access, given the inflated prices of irrigated fruits and vegetables. Indeed, lunch for many schoolchildren in Gaza is a *filfil mat'hoon* sandwich.

Daggit Samak

Fish Dressing
Makes 2 servings

6 cloves garlic
½ teaspoon salt
1 green hot chile pepper, coarsely chopped
1 red hot chile pepper, coarsely chopped
2 tablespoons fresh dill
1½ teaspoons ground coriander
2 tablespoons extra-virgin olive oil

In a mortar and pestle, combine the garlic and salt and mash well. If you do not have a mortar and pestle, use the pulse function on a food processor. Add the chile peppers and pound (or pulse) them until well crushed. Stir in the dill, coriander, and olive oil and mix.

دقة سمك

Dagga refers to Gaza's famous hot tomato salad (see page 50), but it is also the general term for all manner of "pounded" dressings or sauces: "pounded" is the literal translation of the word. This one serves as a dressing or stuffing for fish of all kinds.

Salsit T'heena

Tahina Sauce
Makes approximately 1¼ cup (300 milliliters) of sauce

2 to 4 cloves garlic
½ teaspoon salt
½ cup (120 milliliters) tahina paste (available in specialty grocers, health-food stores, or online)
½ cup (120 milliliters) freshly squeezed lemon juice
¼ cup (60 milliliters) cold water (more as needed)

Using a mortar and pestle, thoroughly crush the garlic and salt to a paste. Stir in the tahina and lemon juice and whisk well until smooth. The mixture will become quite thick as it emulsifies. Bit by bit, add water and continue stirring until you have a smooth sauce of medium-thick consistency, similar to a chocolate sauce. Adjust the salt and lemon to taste.

صلصة طحينة

Whether used to smother fish *kufta*, to accompany falafel, or as a dressing for roasted cauliflower, this basic tahina sauce always strikes a marvelous balance between the mellowness of sesame paste and the bright tang of lemon. In the absence of a mortar and pestle, a high-powered blender works wonders to emulsify the sauce. It's a good idea to mash the garlic first, though.

A *zibdiya* is the most rudimentary and most precious kitchen item in every household in Gaza, rich or poor, urban or rural, as well as in Gazan Palestinian households in the diaspora. It is simply a handmade heavy unglazed clay bowl made with Gaza's rough, sandy clay, accompanied by a lemon-wood pestle. Though similar implements exist elsewhere in the region, the *zibdiya's* absolute omnipresence in the preparation and presentation of all manner of foods in Gaza makes it a key to the whole cuisine.

As you will see, there are few recipes in this book that don't begin "In a mortar and pestle, crush...." Crushing, pounding, grinding: the base of flavor for nearly every dish, and often the first thing a curious child will be asked to help out with. The many spices used in Gazan cooking are ideally ground in a *zibdiya*. Its rough walls are perfect for crushing garlic to a creamy pulp or for grinding dill seeds just until fragrant. It serves for mashing and mixing salad ingredients, then doubles as a handsome bowl to serve the salad.

But that is not all! It is also a vessel for cooking. The much-beloved *zibdiyit gambari* (see page 294) is a shrimp stew covered in pine nuts and baked in a larger zibdiya, known as a *kashkoola*, until crusty on the outside and meltingly delicious inside.

Local potters pile these simple bowls—as well as larger clay pots for *qidra*, Gaza's richly spiced meat and rice dish with garlic and chickpeas, and braziers for hot coals—in great mountains outside their kilns in the market area of Gaza. They cost about 50 cents each.

The modest price of the *zibdiya* makes it no less special. Several of the cooks we interviewed—from former government ministers to rural housewives—commented on their *zibdiyaat* with pride: several had seen twenty years of daily use and were regarded almost as family members.

For cooks who don't have a *zibdiya* from Gaza (they can be very difficult to obtain due to the ban on exports and near hermetic closure of the territory), any rough mortar and pestle with a wide base will serve. Mexican *molcajete*, South American *batans*, or Thai *kruk* mortars all work well. Avoid glazed or marble ones; they're too slippery for grinding.

Ibharat Qidra

Qidra Spices

Makes approximately 2 cups (250 grams)

½ tablespoon nutmeg
1 tablespoon ground red pepper
1 tablespoon cinnamon
2 tablespoons ground cardamom
2 tablespoons ground cloves
2 tablespoons dried lime powder (also known as *loomi*; the whole limes are readily available in Middle Eastern groceries)
½ cup (50 grams) ground allspice
½ cup (50 grams) ground black pepper
½ cup (50 grams) garlic powder
1 cup (100 grams) turmeric (if preparing for use in *qidra*)

This is a standard spice mix named for the rice dish in which it is most notably used. Individual cooks vary both the ingredients and their proportions, but the taste is always distinctive. With the turmeric omitted, this mix is used in a variety of other rice dishes, such as *sayadiyya*, *maqlooba*, and *mjadarra* and is known simply as *ibharat ruz* or rice spices. With turmeric, it is used exclusively for *qidra*.

Use the freshest spices available, grinding them yourself if possible. Store in an airtight container.

On Spices

Pepper, cinnamon, nutmeg, cloves...the spices that for centuries moved the world's economy in their storied transit from Southeast Asia to Europe all passed through Gaza. Its location, right at the narrow point between the Red Sea and the Mediterranean, put it on the key routes linking the trade coming by sea from Asia and by caravan across Arabia to the Via Maris and the network of Mediterranean ports. Its position at the crossroads between the region's major empires made it a nexus of trade from the Bronze Age on, as it weathered the rule of Egyptians, Persians, Greeks, Romans, Byzantines, Arabs, and Ottomans.

The tastes and customs of successive generations of rulers and traders were incorporated into local ways, making contemporary Gazan cuisine a tangle of many traces. While the humbler food of peasants and villagers has always relied upon what grows on the land, the richer and more luxurious dishes of wealthy urbanites make extravagant use of the exotic spices that once flowed through Gazan markets. Spiced rice dishes like *qidra* and *maqlooba* are inherited from the Abbasid Empire's courtly tastes, while spiced stuffed vegetables seem to have been popularized by Ottoman rulers.

If the standard Gazan spice combinations form part of a continuum with other parts of the region, Gazans' passion for dill and for hot peppers—introduced to the continent from the Americas via the Portuguese empire in the sixteenth century—is absolutely unique.

Dugga

Wheat and Spice Blend

Um Zuhair's Dugga (Gaza City version)
Makes approximately 3⅓ pounds (1½ kilograms)

5 cups (approximately 1 kilogram) wheat berries or whole wheat flour
1¼ cups (approximately 225 grams) brown lentils
½ cup (approximately 70 grams) cumin seeds
½ cup (approximately 50 grams) whole sumac berries (ground sumac may be substituted if milling at home)
¼ cup (25 grams) coriander seeds
¼ cup (25 grams) caraway seeds
½ cup (50 grams) dill seeds
5 dried red chile peppers (to taste)
¼ cup (75 grams) salt
1 teaspoon citric acid or sour salt
Toasted sesame seeds

Toast the wheat berries, lentils, and spices individually on medium heat in a large skillet, stirring constantly until golden and fragrant, taking care not to let them burn. If using the flour, toast this separately. Mix and grind in small batches using a spice grinder or high-powered blender. Stir in the salt and citric acid, mixing well. Store in sealed containers. Before using, add 1 tablespoon of toasted sesame seeds per cup of *dugga*.

Um Hana's Dugga (Bedouin version)
Makes approximately 4½ pounds (2 kilograms)

6 cups (approximately 1¼ kilograms) wheat berries (substitute whole-wheat flour if making at home)
1¼ cup (250 grams) dried chickpeas (substitute gram/chickpea flour if making at home)
5 dried red chile peppers
½ cup (50 grams) dill seeds
½ cup (100 grams) red lentils
½ cup (50 grams) cumin seeds
¼ cup (25 grams) coriander seeds
¼ cup (25 grams) whole sumac (ground sumac may be substituted)
1 tablespoon whole cloves
1 small bunch high-quality sun-dried basil
½ cup (40 grams) dried *zaatar* or oregano leaves
1 whole nutmeg
1 teaspoon citric acid or sour salt
½ cup (100 grams) salt
Toasted sesame seeds

دقة

Dugga, not to be confused with the spicy tomato salad *dagga*, is an intensely nutritive blend of roasted and ground grains, legumes, and spices. It is eaten with olive oil and bread, baked on *manaeesh*, sprinkled on sliced oranges, or, in some modern kitchens, used as a seasoning for chicken or meat.

While each cook has her own variation of *dugga*, what is unique about the Gazan blends is their dazzling array of ingredients, including more pulses, herbs, and spices than in recipes from Egypt, where *dugga* is also consumed. Here are two varieties, one more urban and the other more Bedouin in style.

Gazan families generally roast up enough ingredients to fill a sack, which they then take to the community mill. There it is ground into a fragrant powder that can be stored in airtight containers for some months. If you don't happen to have a community mill, grind the mix yourself in a spice grinder: substitute the wheat berries in this case for whole-wheat flour, toasted carefully in a skillet on a stovetop until golden. You can also substitute lentil flour for the lentils, or else bake them in a 400°F (200°C) oven for 10 minutes, then transfer them to a food processor and pulse till powdery. You can also try asking a natural-foods store to mill it for you.

Take care to stop the food-processor blade as soon as you have a uniform, loose powder. If it starts to become a paste, you've gone too far.

Um Hana grows and sun-dries her own basil in her rooftop garden. You can substitute high-quality dried basil instead.

Toast the wheat berries and chickpeas (or flours) in a pan in the oven, or in a large skillet over medium heat, until fragrant and golden. Set aside. Then toast the peppers, dill seeds, cumin seeds, coriander seeds, sumac, cloves, and *zaatar* one by one on low heat, being careful not to burn them. Combine all of the ingredients and add the basil, nutmeg, and salts.

Grind this mixture to a fine powder in a high-powered spice grinder or blender. Seal in airtight containers, adding 1 teaspoon of toasted sesame seeds to each cup of *dugga* just before consuming (sesame seeds spoil quickly and should not be added before use).

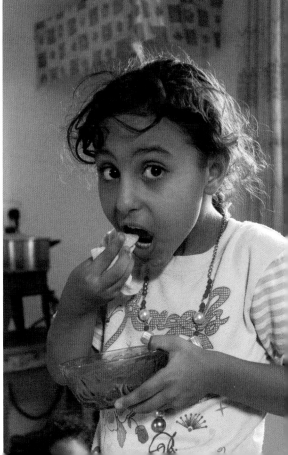

Some households have a lightness and a joy to them that you feel the moment you walk in. Maybe it is the brightly colored posters on the wall or the tidily raked courtyard blooming with herbs. Maybe it is the eager faces of the six little girls who come out to greet you, shiny black braids hanging down their backs as they run up the stairs ahead of you. For whatever reason, Um Hana's household in the northern town of Beit Lahiya is a tangibly happy place, and this probably has a lot to do with Um Hana herself.

We have come to her house to see how she prepares *dugga*, a powdery mix of toasted wheat, legumes, and spices that many Gazan families prepare in bulk. The little girls crowd around, giggling and sneaking tastes of the toasted wheat. Some are Um Hana's daughters; some are the daughters of her husband's second wife. He married a second time, she tells us, winking, in hopes of having a son. More girls ensued. All seem to live together in unusual harmony.

Up on the building's roof, Um Hana shows us the planters she made from halves of oil-drums, now vivid with flowering basil plants, as well as the hutches in which she raises rabbits and the dovecote where the second wife raises pigeons. Both the rabbits and pigeons serve to supplement the family's diet; occasionally they sell a rabbit for extra cash.

From the rooftop one can see across devastated fields and heaps of rubble all the way to the border with Israel and the smokestacks of the Ashkelon power plant. Beit Lahiya was badly hit during the attack in 2008 and 2009; Um Hana grimaces recalling how white phosphorus rained down over the neighborhood, how the whole family hid in the storeroom throughout the twenty-two days of madness. Thank God, she says, all of us are all right and our house was not destroyed. Others were not so lucky.

But the girls continue to cavort on the rooftop, and the rabbits need to be fed, and somehow the sheer vitality of the household pushes onward.

Jibna Baladiyya

Fresh White Farmer's Cheese

Makes approximately 11 ounces (300 grams) of cheese

جبنة بلدية

2 cups (approximately 260 grams) powdered milk

6 cups (approximately 1½ liters) of water, boiled then left to cool until warm

½ tablet of cheese-grade rennet (available in natural food stores)

5 tablespoons salt (for brine—add more if needed)

1 tablespoon dill seeds

1 teaspoon dried red pepper or 1 fresh green chile pepper, deseeded and chopped

Combine the water with the milk powder in a blender; make sure the water is not too hot or else the cheese will coagulate too quickly. Dissolve the rennet tablet in a little water and add, mixing well. Pour this into a large tray until about 2 inches deep and cover, or ball up in a cheesecloth and set aside in a strainer. After 1½ hours, the mixture should have partially solidified. Cut it into even squares or pieces.

If the cheese is in a tray, gently pour out the excess liquid, then flip or gently transfer the pieces onto a cheesecloth. Cover it with another cheesecloth or kitchen towel to absorb excess moisture. Put a heavy tray on top of the cheesecloth and leave it for 30 minutes.

Meanwhile, prepare the brine: Bring 5 or more cups of water to a rolling boil. Remove it from the heat, and stir in a tablespoon of salt for each cup of boiling water. Let the salt dissolve well and allow the solution to cool completely. Stir in the dill seed and dried red pepper flakes or fresh green chile peppers. Gently transfer the cheese to the cooled brine. Store for at least a week before consuming.

One of the ration items that has been distributed by donor organizations for decades now is powdered milk. While only young children drink milk in Palestinian society (as in many Middle Eastern societies, yogurt is the go-to dairy product), everyone recognizes the nutritional importance of dairy and finds ways to use powdered milk to make more familiar products. Among them is this fresh cheese made by local farmers and sold at public markets as *jibna baladiyya* (country cheese). It is often eaten for breakfast with bread and olives, and is particularly well suited as a topping for *manaeesh* and as a stuffing for savory cheese pastries.

In the highlands of Beit Lahiya, we stop at a tiny family-run dairy farm to inquire about the dairy industry. Nafi Attar, who runs the farm with his father, receives us.

He explains that their family has farmed for generations. In the past, they had a large piece of land where they raised sheep and cows, but that land became part of the Israeli-imposed buffer zone, inaccessible to many. They now keep a small herd of Dutch dairy cows in a stable in a largely residential area. Nafi explains that his father learned this kind of dairy farming while working at a large industrial dairy in Israel. Before that, his grandfather had farmed the old way, raising a hardier local breed and grazing them freely.

Raising the productive Dutch cows in a barn was very profitable, says Nafi, as long as feed was inexpensive. But prices on imported feed have risen, from 7 shekels before Operation Cast Lead to 25 after, forcing the prices of both locally raised milk and meat to go up accordingly.

Moreover, with the current electricity outages, people are buying less fresh milk because it will not keep without reliable refrigeration. Instead they're depending more upon powdered milk rations or Israeli dairy, which is often allowed in when Palestinian dairy is not. When electricity was not such an issue, says Nafi, his neighbors would buy six or seven liters a week; now they buy one half-liter.

For the moment there is still a local market for milk used to make butter and cheese, and one frequently sees dairy farmers such as Nafi selling their products in the city of the back of a donkey cart, although as the border selectively opens to manufactured products, this too may disappear when the market is confronted with cheaper imports.

Kishik

Fermented Wheat and Yogurt

Makes approximately 2 quarts (1¾ liters)

2 pounds (approximately 1 kilogram) spring wheat berries, soaked in water for an hour

4 cups (approximately 1 kilogram) whole-milk yogurt or buttermilk, left at room temperature overnight, more as needed

5 tablespoons salt

3 tablespoons dill seeds (optional)

4 tablespoons red-pepper flakes (optional)

Wheat bran, for coating

Pick through the wheat berries, rinse, and strain well. Crush the wheat berries coarsely using a heavy mortar and pestle, or pulse several times in a food processor; the idea here is to release some of the natural starch. Don't be alarmed if the wheat berries do not actually crack.

Mix the wheat with yogurt or buttermilk. Adjust the quantity of yogurt or buttermilk to achieve a dough-like consistency.

Cover with plastic wrap pierced with holes. Set aside to ferment for three days, preferably outdoors or by a window that has been slightly cracked open. In a pinch you can also just let the mixture sit in a bowl on a countertop.

Knead the mixture daily. Once it has fermented, add the salt, dill seeds, and red pepper flakes. Divide it into palm-sized patties, then dust these with wheat bran or flour and leave them to dry on a clean cheesecloth in direct sunlight or indoors in a sunny location. If you decide to make the liquid form of *kishik*, as described in the introductory paragraph, then add 2 cups more buttermilk.

Tip: An aunt from Laila's extended family in California informed us that instant dry yeast can also be used to speed the fermentation process. Simply soak the crushed wheat berries in a bowl full of water. Sprinkle with a generous pinch of yeast (but don't mix it in). Set this aside for several hours, then strain the wheat, discard the water, and mix in the yogurt or buttermilk as above. Cover with perforated plastic wrap and set aside for seven days, then freeze or use immediately.

Before refrigeration was available, throughout the Middle East and Central Asia, *kishik* was a means of conserving milk for later use: a fermented paste of yogurt and grains, formed into disks and dried in the sun. The disks could be stored all year and then crumbled or ground for use in salads, stews, and savory pastries.

In Gaza, *kishik* is traditionally made with sheep's-milk yogurt and flavored with dill seeds and red pepper flakes.

Instead of sun-drying, some families now make a liquid version of *kishik* that may be frozen and then defrosted for immediate use. To do this, add 2 cups more buttermilk and set aside in a bowl covered with a perforated plastic wrap to ferment for 7 days, then freeze in resealable bags or jars. This is the method we kitchen-tested, with excellent results.

Palestine forms part of a broad cultural continuum that stretches across the lands once known as *Bilad il-Sham*, the Levant. Its cuisine, therefore, has much in common with other cuisines from this region, between what is now Turkey and the edge of the Nile. Birthplace of the olive tree, Palestine has a rich indigenous food heritage. Moreover, the many civilizations that have contended for this storied corner of the world have all left their mark on its cuisine: the perfumed rice of the Persians, the date preparations of the Arabs, the yogurt dishes of the Turks.

Palestinian cuisine can be divided into urban, rural, and nomadic variants, with distinctions between the northern, southern, and coastal regions. Northern Palestinian cuisine relies heavily on yogurt-based sauces and tart flavors and shares much with Lebanese and Syrian food, whereas the south tends to use tomatoes as a base for stews and meats. The coastal areas of Palestine, from Haifa down to Gaza—more urban and sophisticated—were known for their seafood and use of exotic spices, while the farming interior relied principally on seasonal agricultural products, wild greens, lamb, sheep's milk, and grains such as barley and *freekah*.

Gaza's cuisine once fit more tidily into this geographically defined continuum, but the massive influx of refugees in 1948 from neighboring areas changed its culinary habits. Now in Gaza one finds a little of the coast and the greater Mediterranean, a little of the farming regions, a little Egyptian influence, and a little influence from migration to the Gulf, all mixed up with the native Gazan love for dill, hot pepper, fresh herbs and earthy spices. In the end, the commonalities with broader Palestinian cuisine remain strong: stews and stuffed vegetables for family meals, rice and meat for festivities, elaborate sweets for special occasions, and of course, that quintessential combination of *zaatar* and olive oil at any time of the day or night.

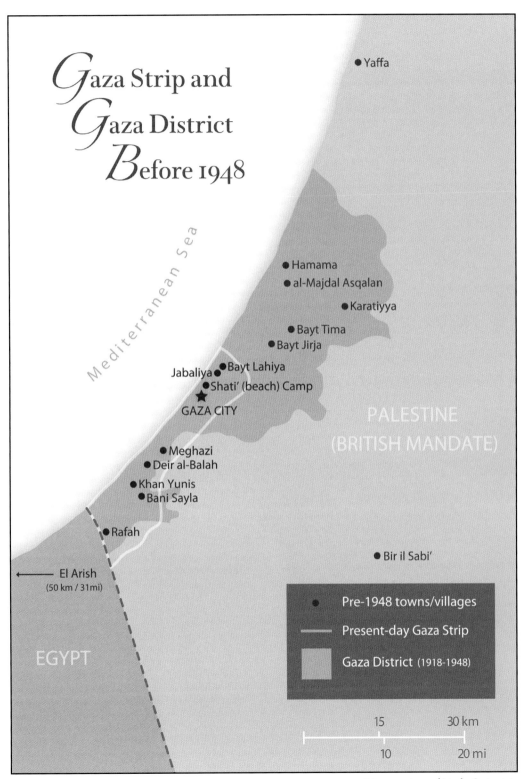

Gaza Strip and Gaza District Before 1948

Yaffa

Mediterranean Sea

Hamama
al-Majdal Asqalan
Karatiyya
Bayt Tima
Bayt Jirja
Bayt Lahiya
Jabaliya
Shati' (beach) Camp
GAZA CITY

PALESTINE
(BRITISH MANDATE)

Meghazi
Deir al-Balah
Khan Yunis
Bani Sayla

Rafah

Bir il Sabi'

← El Arish
(50 km / 31mi)

EGYPT

- Pre-1948 towns/villages
— Present-day Gaza Strip
Gaza District (1918-1948)

15   30 km
10   20 mi

Map courtesy of Linda Quiquivix

45

SALADS

Rare is the Palestinian meal that does not include a salad. Whether served as an accompaniment to a main dish or as part of an array of mezze, Gaza's salads are notable for their vibrant flavors and brilliant colors.

Dagga (Salata Ghazawiyya)

Gazan Hot Tomato and Dill Salad

Serves 2–3

½ teaspoon salt
2 cloves garlic, peeled
2 to 3 hot green chile peppers (to taste), coarsely chopped
¼ cup (10 grams) finely chopped fresh dill
3 ripe, flavorful medium-sized tomatoes, coarsely chopped
2 tablespoons high-quality extra-virgin olive oil

Using a mortar and pestle, mash the garlic and salt into a paste. Add the chile peppers and crush until they are tender, followed by the dill. Using a circular motion, gently muddle the dill until fragrant. Add roughly chopped tomatoes and pound until the salad reaches a thick, salsa-like consistency. Mix the entire salad with a spoon, then drench it with extra-virgin olive oil. Serve with *Khubz Kmaj* (page 100) on the side for scooping it up.

Variation

Substitute 1 tablespoon of dill seeds for the fresh dill and 2 tablespoons of finely chopped or grated onions for the garlic. The dill seeds should be ground thoroughly in the mortar in a circular motion, along with some salt, before adding the onions. Finish the dagga *with a squeeze of fresh lemon. Top generously with olive oil.*

دقة (سلطة غزاوية)

This is the most basic and most frequently served salad in Gaza, with a hot bite that makes it a fantastic accompaniment to meaty stews or rice dishes. *Dagga*, which is a variation of the word meaning "pounded" in Arabic (an irony that is not lost on Gaza's inhabitants), is commonly scooped up with Arabic bread and has a consistency similar to that of a Mexican salsa.

As with many other recipes in this book, there are hotly contested variations. Many friends and family members insist that authentic *dagga* should only be prepared with dill seeds and onions, while others argue that fresh dill and garlic are the essential components and that the color should be greener than it is red. While the origin of these elemental allegiances remains a mystery for the ages, one thing is clear: *Dagga*, no matter how it is prepared, is always a winner, "the centerpiece of the Gazan dinner table" as Laila's late maternal grandmother used to put it. Here, we include the recipe Laila grew up with.

Salatit Abu Safiya

Abu Safiya's Salad

Serves 2–3

½ teaspoon coarse sea salt
1 tablespoon dill seeds
3 cloves garlic
2 to 3 hot green chile peppers, chopped
1 shallot, finely diced
2 tablespoons chopped green onions
½ cup (12 grams) finely chopped herbs (any combination of fresh parsley, mint, dill, cilantro, or basil)
3 very ripe, flavorful tomatoes, chopped
Juice of one large lemon
2 tablespoons tahina
Extra-virgin olive oil

In a mortar and pestle, roughly grind the dill seeds along with the salt, using strong circular motions, until fragrant. Add the garlic and mash it to a smooth paste. Next add the chiles, green onions, and shallots and crush well. Add the herbs, muddling with the rest of the ingredients until well incorporated. Stir in the chopped tomatoes and mash until a salsa-like consistency is achieved.

In a separate bowl, whisk together the lemon juice and tahina until they are emulsified, then mix this into the salad. Flatten the top of the salad, then finish it with a generous drizzle of olive oil on top. Serve with *Khubz Kmaj* (page 100).

سلطة أبو صفية

Yousef Abu Safiya is the former minister of the environment. He is also a zealous ecologist, amateur nutritionist, innovative cook, and tinkerer. Eager to tell us about his adventures in the kitchen, he shared this recipe for a cousin of *dagga* that has been in his family for generations, since before they fled to Gaza for safety from the village of Hamama in 1948. He makes it, with great pride, in the same twenty-seven-year-old *zibdiya* his father used.

"We ate this salad for any meal of the day, even for breakfast, particularly in the 1950s and 1960s when we refugees didn't have much else. Most of the time it was made without the herbs, sesame paste, and olive oil, which were too pricey."

Salata Khadra Mafrooma

Gaza "Confetti" Salad

Serves 4–6

سلطة خضراء مفرومة

3 firm, flavorful tomatoes
4 Middle Eastern cucumbers, or 1 English cucumber, peeled
1 bunch green onions
1 yellow bell pepper
1 orange bell pepper
3 green chile peppers (to taste), seeds removed
¼ small head red cabbage
1 bunch fresh mint, leaves picked
1 bunch fresh parsley, thick stems removed
1 garlic clove
Rind of one lemon, finely chopped
½ teaspoon salt
¼ teaspoon fresh black pepper
Juice of 2 lemons
3 tablespoons extra-virgin olive oil

This bright and spicy salad is often served alongside *maqlooba* or other similar rice dishes. The dedication of the cook is revealed by how finely she chops her vegetables.

Finely chop the tomatoes, cucumbers, onions, peppers, and cabbage into equally sized small bits. Toss them together in a bowl. Wash and towel-dry the herbs well, chop to a medium-coarse consistency, and add them to the mix.

Mash the garlic to a paste with a ¼ teaspoon of the salt using a mortar and pestle. Stir the garlic, along with the lemon rind, into the salad.

Just before serving, season the salad with the remaining salt and the pepper. Drizzle with lemon juice, followed by olive oil. Toss to combine. Adjust the dressing to taste: the salad should not be soggy.

Serve with rice-based main dishes such as *maqlooba* or *qidra,* or with stews (*tabeekh*).

Variations

• *Add one avocado, chopped into ½ inch cubes. Omit the mint.*

• *Substitute minced green dill for the mint and parsley.*

Every once in a while, you meet someone who is absolutely radiant with conviction, pleased with his work and the place he has made in this world. Abdel Munim Ahmed, co-founder of the Gaza Safe Agriculture Society in Beit Hanoun, is one of these people. He shows us around the Society's tiny organic model farm, gleefully explaining the ingenious harmony of birds and beneficial insects that keep the farm free of pests. "We send them written invitations," he says, pointing to a ladybug. "Of course, whenever they find any place without vicious pesticides, they come inhabit this niche, produce eggs, and multiply. Whenever you apply something poisonous, this repels everyone, even people. It's a very simple idea. The ideas here are very simple ones."

Abdel Munim founded the Society in 2001, when he returned to Gaza after studying landscape architecture in Egypt and organic farming methods in Italy.

Initially, the idea was to provide technical support to farmers interested in applying organic techniques. Local farmers were interested, but didn't feel they could take any risks and stuck to using pesticides. In 2005 the Society began a demonstration farm to show that organic methods really would work.

At first the farm covered seven hectares (about seventeen acres), producing more than enough to supply an all-organic store in Gaza City. But when the siege began in 2008, fuel prices skyrocketed and they could no longer pump water for irrigation nor get their products to market. Like so many of their neighbors, they had to reduce the land under cultivation radically. Now the farm is less than one hectare (about two and a half acres): a verdant oasis climbing with garden vegetables, aromatic herbs, and a fishpond for collecting winter rainwater.

Most of the Society's business now comes from local consumers, who come to the farm to purchase pesticide-free produce.

As for spreading the gospel of organic farming, many of the neighboring farmers admire the work the Society does and have adopted some of the organic techniques. For several months the siege blocked access to all chemical fertilizers, and there was a surge of interest in the organic compost that the Society produces. But now fertilizers and pesticides are entering the Strip again on a limited basis.

Many farmers acknowledge that compost helps retain groundwater better than chemical fertilizers and that pesticides represent a futile race against increasingly resistant infestations. Even so, their economic needs are immediate, and without ongoing support, they cannot begin to make the slow transition to organic methods. Moreover, as the whole border area has been stripped of all tree cover in successive Israeli incursions, it becomes harder and harder for beneficial birds and insects to find their way across that wasteland to whatever little piece of land is hospitable to them. As Abdel Munim explains:

> This is a small place to be a habitat for such a number of birds and bugs. We lost a lot of beneficial insects with the war. Especially when big trees were destroyed. Can you imagine a big tree like this one, how many birds and insects are living in it? It is a skyscraper for beneficial insects. And when a bulldozer comes and eliminates this tree, of course the ecological balance is destroyed. Can you imagine the buffer zone, the whole eastern part, totally destroyed? You cannot find any living thing there now. And it is not only the birds and insects, but also the land through erosion.

It is no surprise, then, that many farmers overuse pesticides: With all means of natural pest control annihilated, how else are they to produce enough to stay afloat, especially when they've lost acres of land to the buffer zone? This phenomenon has only increased since 2010, with recent spraying of broad-spectrum herbicides throughout the Israeli-imposed "no-go zone" and further razing of all vegetation in the area.

57

Salatit Beit Jirja

Beit Jirja Salad

Serves 2–3

½ tablespoon dill seeds or ¼ cup (5 grams) fresh green dill
1 garlic clove
2 hot green chiles (to taste)
3 ripe tomatoes, chopped
Juice of a half a lemon
1 small Middle Eastern cucumber or half a hothouse cucumber, finely chopped
¼ packed cup (5 grams) of parsley, finely chopped
1 tablespoon red tahina or 1 tablespoon regular tahina mixed with ¼ teaspoon toasted sesame oil
Extra-virgin olive oil
Salt to taste

Grind the dill seeds with ½ teaspoon salt in a mortar and pestle until fragrant, or else muddle the finely chopped fresh dill. Add the garlic, mashing well, followed by the chilies. Crush well.

Add the tomatoes and lemon juice and pound slightly until just incorporated.

Stir in the finely chopped cucumbers and parsley. Mix in the tahina until it is uniformly spread. Adjust salt to taste. Flatten the top of the salad, and drizzle generously with olive oil . Serve with *Khubz Kmaj* (page 100).

سلطة بيت جرجا

Salatit Beit Jirja is typical fare from a village—now disappeared—that was just north of the present-day Gaza Strip. For the many refugees in Gaza originally from the Beit Jirja area, this is the basic salad that accompanies most meals.

Salatit Jarjir

Arugula Salad

Serves 2–3

1 small onion, thinly julienned
1 bunch arugula (approximately 2 to 3 cups, or 60 grams), coarsely chopped
2 tomatoes, finely chopped
Juice of 1 lemon
Salt and pepper to taste
Extra-virgin olive oil

Rub the julienned onion with the salt and pepper. Toss with the chopped arugula and tomatoes. Season with olive oil and lemon juice.

سلطة جرجير

Peppery arugula (also called rocket) is one of the most common greens in Palestine and is particularly popular in Gaza and neighboring Egypt. The leaves are often served whole with white cheese and other mezze for supper, or chopped into a simple salad, like this one.

El-Manar Tahina Factory, Zeitun

The sliding metal door of the El-Manar Factory opens to reveal a large aluminum warehouse with rows of hoary steel machines humming and grinding, making one of Gaza's best-known brands of tahina. Sacks of sesame seeds are piled at one end of the factory, and the finished product waits in plastic tubs for distribution on the other end.

Twenty-year-old Yusuf Al-Dirawi, who works here at his family's factory while finishing his university degree, hurries over to show us around.

The raw sesame seeds come from various countries: India, Somalia, Sudan. For the moment, Yusuf says, there is no problem getting them in through the Israeli border, although in the past years there have been periods when this was impossible and the sacks of sesame had to enter through the tunnels, driving the prices through the roof.

The seeds are first soaked until the skin comes off, then rinsed several times and drained. They are then transferred to one of two different roasting machines: one that roasts with steam heat, for making the "normal" kind of tahina known all over the

Middle East, and the other that roasts with direct heat, toasting the seeds to make Gaza's own particular "red tahina," which has a nuttier, richer sesame taste.

Once roasted, the seeds are ground "the old way," between two great millstones, which Yusuf says produces a better taste than any of the modern machines they've tried over the years. After milling, the paste is bottled for local distribution.

El-Manar does not export; none of the nine small-scale tahina factories still operating in Gaza do. Even if Israel did not ban nearly all exports from Gaza, they could not compete with tahina made elsewhere, due to the exorbitant price of importing the raw material—sesame seeds—into Gaza. Ninety percent of the factories active in Gaza before 2007 have already gone under due to this impossible balance of trade. Like all the other manufacturers that have survived, the owners and workers of the El-Manar factory watch the borders anxiously. At the time of our visit, Israel was allowing some manufactured goods (like tahina) to enter the Strip, where

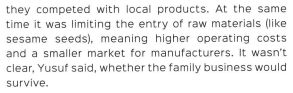

they competed with local products. At the same time it was limiting the entry of raw materials (like sesame seeds), meaning higher operating costs and a smaller market for manufacturers. It wasn't clear, Yusuf said, whether the family business would survive.

As of 2016, Israel has begun to allow some manufacturers from Gaza to market their goods in the West Bank. It remains to be seen if this window of opportunity will be sufficient to keep these companies on their feet.

Salatit T'heena

Tahina Herb Salad

Serves 3–4

1 medium tomato
½ cup (12 grams) finely chopped dill or parsley
1 quantity *Salsit T'heena* (page 30)

Finely chop and de-seed the tomato. Gently stir the chopped tomato along with the herbs into the prepared *salsit t'heena*. Transfer to a small flat bowl and garnish with fronds of dill or parsley. Serve accompanied with warm *Khubz Kmaj* (page 100).

سلطة طحينة

Though delicious on its own scooped up with Arabic bread, this salad is commonly served alongside fried fish or *sayadiyya* (page 280).

Mareesa

Kishik and Hot Pepper Dip

Serves 2–3

1 round of hard *kishik* or 3 tablespoons powdered or 5 tablespoons
　liquid *kishik*
½ teaspoon salt
1 teaspoon dill seeds (optional)
2 hot green chile peppers, chopped
Juice of one lemon
Olive oil

If the *kishik* is hard, break it into small pieces and moisten with a few spoonfuls of water. Allow it to absorb the liquid for a few minutes, and then pulverize it in a food processor or blender or by hand in a mortar and pestle until a paste, similar in consistency to hummus, is achieved. (If you are using powdered *kishik*, moisten with water as above and mix by hand. If you are using liquid *kishik,* skip this step.)

In a mortar and pestle, crush the dill seeds with salt, using a strong circular motion, until fragrant. Add the peppers and pound until soft. Stir in the lemon juice and mix well.

Add the *kishik* paste and stir. If the mixture appears too thick, add a bit of water or more lemon juice until the consistency is that of a dip. Spread it out in a small flat or oblong serving platter and drizzle it with olive oil. Serve with *Khubz Kmaj* (page 100).

مريسة

Check Middle Eastern markets for *kishik* or make your own (see page 42). In southern Gaza, each town or region has its own way of using this traditional fermented dairy product; we have included two here.

Salatit Kishik u Bandora Meshwiya

Charred Tomatoes and Kishik

Serves 2–3

سلطة كشك وبندورة مشوية

This *kishik* salad is typical of Garara, an agricultural region in the central part of the Gaza Strip.

1 round of *kishik* (page 42) or 3 tablespoons powdered or 5 tablespoons liquid *kishik*
7 cherry tomatoes or 4 to 5 small tomatoes
¼ teaspoon salt
2 cloves garlic
1 tablespoon olive oil
1 tablespoon chopped fresh dill

Moisten and crush the *kishik* as described in the previous recipe. If you are using powdered kishik, mix it with about 5 tablespoons of water until a smooth, thin paste forms. If you are using liquid *kishik*, you may skip this step.

Pierce the skins of the tomatoes and broil them in an oven until limp (you can also skewer them and roast them over a gas burner or grill). Allow to cool, then peel and transfer to a serving plate.

In a mortar and pestle, crush the garlic and salt until smooth. Add oil and mix well. Meanwhile, crush the tomatoes gently with a fork, so they don't totally lose their form. Drizzle the liquefied *kishik* on top, then sprinkle with the chopped dill. On top of this, spread the garlic-and-oil mixture. Serve with *Khubz Kmaj* (page 100).

Samira Hamdan shows up to do her shopping at the Gaza Safe Agriculture Society Farm in Beit Hanoun while we are interviewing the farmers. She jokes and laughs with them while she selects her vegetables, and her kids run off to play with theirs: She is clearly a regular client. We ask her why she shops at the farm, and she explains that she had started to notice lots of people getting sick for no reason and wondered why. She herself survived breast cancer after a mastectomy, and when two of her kids fell terribly ill to watermelon poisoning—a very common problem in Gaza—she decided something was not right. She asked around and came across the organic farm, not far from her home. "I love this place," she says, as her kids romp among piles of pumpkins. "We eat these vegetables and we know what is in them, we know they are good for us, not like others."

Unfortunately, eating quality organic products is no guarantee of health in Gaza. The uncontrolled use of pesticides that once entered through the tunnels to circumvent the Israeli blockade—some of which have been banned internationally due to their high toxicity—is just one of many sources of environmental illness in the territory. The depleted uranium, white phosphorus, and harmful metals present in the weapons used in repeated Israeli attacks on the territory have left the soil dangerously contaminated. Moreover, many families are rebuilding damaged homes with recycled rubble, meaning that the toxic metals and radioactive waste found at impact sites come to form part of their everyday living spaces. The consequences—in terms of birth defects and the proliferation of cancers—have yet to be fully measured, though studies have begun to demonstrate clear correlations.

Samira Hamdan shakes her head. "Everything here is poisoned. But we have to eat, we have to breathe air and drink water.... All we can do is try the best we can to stay safe and pray to God to protect us." Then, grinning, she hoists up her heaping bag of fresh greens, whistles to her boys, and heads home.

Salata Milaaha/Fatt Malaahi

Sailors' Salad

Serves 3–4

1 small round of day-old Arabic bread, toasted (see *Khubz Kmaj*, page 100)
½ teaspoon salt
2 to 3 hot green chile peppers, to taste
1 packed cup (about 25 grams) fresh basil, torn
4 green onions, finely chopped
2 Middle Eastern cucumbers or half a hothouse cucumber, finely chopped
3 medium-sized tomatoes, finely chopped
¼ cup (60 milliliters) red tahina or regular tahina whisked well with 1 teaspoon dark sesame oil
Juice of 2 medium lemons
Radishes, pitted green olives, and pickled peppers, to garnish

Break the toasted bread into small pieces. Set aside.

Chop the chile peppers, removing some of the membranes and seeds if you prefer less heat. With a mortar and pestle, pound the peppers along with the salt until soft. Add the basil and muddle in a circular motion to extract the flavor. Add the green onions and crush well, followed by the cucumbers. Finally, stir in the tomatoes and mash. Mix the entire salad to incorporate all ingredients.

In a separate bowl, whisk the tahina with the lemon juice until it is emulsified. Immediately before serving (not earlier, or the bread will get soggy), mix the tahina sauce and bread pieces into the salad. The juices from the tomato will thin out the tahina and soak into the bread. Transfer to a serving dish and flatten the top. Drizzle the surface of the salad generously with olive oil.

To finish, garnish with pitted green olives, pickled peppers, and radish slices.

سلطة ملاحة/فت ملاحي

Basema Abu Daff and her son Sami Zaharna, Gazans living in the United States, explain that sailors (*milahee*) would make this salad when they didn't have much on hand except hard bread. "They would mix it with tahina and anything else in season, such as tomatoes, cucumbers, or basil. *Ya salaam!*" explained Sami, an engineer, part-time imam, and self-described "*fatt malaahi* evangelist." Basema showed Laila how to make the irresistible salad at her brother-in-law's house in Edgewater, Maryland.

Another source in Gaza City, Refaat Alareer, reports that "the best thing about it is that, according to my grandma, all the farmers would bring whatever they had available, put it in the mix, and eat it together, always with their hands. And of course olive oil! It was like the second most important ritual after prayer."

Salatit Batata

Garlicky Potato Salad

Serves 2–3

A very Gazan twist on the potato sal-ad; makes a great picnic food.

1 pound (500 grams) new potatoes
Olive oil
Salt and black pepper
½ quantity *Daggit Toma u Lamoun* (page 28)
2 tablespoons red tahina or 2 tablespoons regular tahina whisked
   thoroughly with 1 teaspoon toasted sesame oil

Wash and scrub the potatoes well, leaving the skins on. Cut them into halves or quarters. Boil them until they are just tender, drain well, then pan-fry or sauté them in a little olive oil until they turn golden. Alternately, you may oven-roast the potatoes with some olive oil.

Season the cooked potatoes with salt and black pepper. Transfer them to a serving platter, then dress them with garlic and lemon dressing and drizzle with the tahina.

Variation

Boil 1 pound (500 grams) baking potatoes with skins until tender; cool and peel, then mash well or press through a food mill. Add Daggit Toma u Lamoun *(page 28), salt, and red tahina. Mix well and serve.*

Of all the terrifying aspects of life in Gaza, perhaps the most ominous of all is the water crisis. Less visible than the repeated assaults, less likely to make headlines than the political impasse, the depletion of Gaza's aquifer is an inexorable countdown that threatens every single one of the territory's 1.8 million inhabitants. Not in some remote future—now.

In 2013, the UN issued a report affirming that by 2016 there would be no more potable water in Gaza, and that by 2020 damage to the aquifer would be irreversible. That was before the 2014 assault left 80 percent of the territory's water networks destroyed and its damaged sanitation network leaking raw sewage into farmland and the sea. More than a hundred thousand people don't have running water at all; those who are connected usually have water in their taps for just a few hours every three or four days. The water they receive is, by all international standards, undrinkable. Those who can afford to pay for privately distributed drinking water often spend up to a third of their family income on water alone.

How has it gotten to this point? The dice were loaded from the start: Israel uses the vast majority of the water from the Mountain Aquifer—in principle shared by Israel and Palestine—as well as the surface water of the Jordan River and does not allow the transfer of any of this water to Gaza, even though the West Bank and Gaza are formally considered a single entity. The Israeli military, in fact, granted itself authority in 1967 over all water-related issues in the occupied territories. In tune with this, it diverts most of the surface water, which flows from the Hebron Mountains into Wadi Gaza, into a reservoir just before this water reaches Gaza. The result: While Israel has a water surplus, Palestinians are resorting to over-extraction, drilling, and other unregulated means to slake their thirst.

Thus Israel holds the water—an absolutely key element of survival in the region—and uses it as a bargaining chip in its relations with the Palestinians. In 2015, Israel began to fulfill an obligation acquired in the Oslo II Agreements (in 1995!) to pump water into Gaza, but just months before, it had bombed the reservoir intended to hold this water. Since the 2014 bombings, the various infrastructures needed for water storage and distribution have been so severely damaged that a significant percentage of the precious stuff is lost or contaminated along the way. Municipal workers race around madly trying to patch, mend, and redirect these leaky pipes.

Plans to ensure more sustainable access to water—and make that access less subject to Israeli political whims—are not lacking: There are plans for desalination plants, rainwater catchment, wastewater treatment and recycling, and so on. Critics argue that Gaza doesn't need radical solutions, only equitable distribution. Until this happens, such plans could give the aquifer a needed rest and allow it to regenerate. But any of these plans, like the urgently necessary overhaul of the whole water network, would require a degree of political stability and cooperation and, of course, building materials and electric power—all of which are presently nowhere in sight. Meanwhile, the clock keeps ticking.

SOUPS, DIPS, AND SPREADS

This chapter features soups—usually eaten on their own as a light evening meal or to break a day of fasting during Ramadan—as well as dips and spreads, which are more often served as part of an array of light dishes or mezze, to be scooped up with fresh bread.

Shorabit Adas

Red Lentil Vegetable Soup

Serves 4–6

2 tablespoons olive oil plus 2 tablespoons vegetable oil

1 medium onion, chopped

4 cloves garlic, peeled and chopped in half

1–2 stalks celery, chopped

2–3 carrots, peeled and chopped

1 medium-sized *koosa* or other firm squash, chopped, or *koosa* pulp
   (approximately 90 grams)

8 cups (2 liters) water or broth (Laila's mother uses 2 bouillon cubes or
   paste)

1 cup (approximately 200 grams) red lentils, rinsed

1½ teaspoons salt, to taste

1 teaspoon cumin

¼ teaspoon turmeric (optional)

¼ teaspoon ground coriander (optional)

¼ teaspoon red pepper flakes (optional)

2 tablespoons chopped parsley

Lemon wedges

شوربة عدس

This recipe is from Laila's mother, who, being of mixed diasporic ancestry (partly Kurdish Damascene, partly Circassian, partly Palestinian), inherited an amalgamated culinary repertoire. It is her most requested recipe. Here, we provide a slightly adapted version. The secret is to take the time to caramelize the onions first before proceeding: Don't be tempted to skip this step or the soup won't come out the same. The soup makes good use of the pulp of a cored *koosa* (a light-skinned Middle Eastern squash), an example of how nothing goes to waste in the Palestinian kitchen. While chronic power cuts in Gaza prevent regular use of major appliances, the pulp does freeze extremely well. Feel free to substitute any locally available summer squash.

Warm the oil in a medium-sized pot. Add the onions and sauté them until they turn golden and caramelized, stirring every few minutes and taking care not to burn them. This will take about 10 to 12 minutes.

Add the garlic and cook until it is slightly charred, then add the celery, carrots, and fresh squash (if you are using fresh). Sauté an additional 5 minutes or until lightly golden. Then add the broth (or water with bouillon cubes) along with the lentils. Bring to a boil, then stir in the frozen squash pulp (if you are using frozen). Skim any foam that rises to the surface.

Reduce heat and simmer, partially covered, for about 40 minutes or until the vegetables and lentils fall apart easily. Stir in cumin and salt, along with turmeric and coriander if you are using them, and mix well.

Let it cool slightly, then puree until smooth using an immersion blender or in small batches in a high-powered standard blender. For a silky soup, whisk the blended soup through a mesh strainer and discard the residual pulp.

Ladle the soup into bowls and garnish with chopped parsley and red pepper flakes. Serve with lemon wedges.

Variation: Fatt Adas

To make this heartier version, which is often served as a complete meal in fall or winter, do not blend the soup after cooking. Instead, leave chunky and stir in (or "fitt") a handful of toasted bread pieces. This makes good use of leftover or stale bread.

Shorabit Freekah

Fire-Roasted Green Wheat Soup

Serves 4–5

1 cup (approximately 200 grams) cracked *freekah*, carefully picked over
6 cups (1½ liters) *Maraqa* (page 24)
2 tablespoons olive oil
1 medium yellow onion, finely chopped
1 carrot, finely chopped
1 tomato, peeled and finely chopped
Salt and pepper to taste
Juice of ½ lemon
1 tablespoon chopped parsley

Wash the *freekah* well in a bowl of cold water, rinsing several times and discarding the small flakes that rise to the surface. Strain.

If you made *maraqa*, pick the chicken or rabbit meat off the bones and reserve it. Discard the bones.

Sauté the onion in the olive oil on medium heat until deeply golden. Add carrot and stir for several more minutes. Stir in the *freekah* along with salt and pepper. Add the broth and bring to a boil.

Simmer gently for 15 to 20 minutes, or until the grains are plump and slightly chewy. Add the tomatoes and reserved chicken or rabbit meat and heat through for 5 minutes. Adjust seasonings. Add the lemon juice and the parsley. Stir and serve hot.

شوربة فريكة

Look for *freekah* in your local Middle Eastern market. It comes in two varieties: whole and cracked. This recipe requires the latter. Make sure to pick it over for any small stones.

If you don't have time to make *Maraqa* (page 24), use packaged broth and add the spices listed in the broth recipe (tied in a piece of gauze or cheesecloth for easy disposal) to this soup while it cooks.

About Freekah

Freekah is an extraordinarily nutritious green wheat product traditionally used in rural areas throughout Palestine and the greater Levant. It has recently enjoyed a boom of popularity in the West, being called "the next supergrain." In Australia, "Green Wheat Freekeh" has even recently been trademarked!

Making *freekah* requires harvesting wheat in the early summer while the grains are still milky, before they dry. The green sheaves are dried in the sun for just a few hours, then burned in a highly controlled and rapid fire. The charred chaff is then winnowed away, leaving greenish grains imbued with a rich, smoky flavor. These can be left whole or coarsely milled.

Rice was introduced to the Middle East in the Hellenistic period, but remained a luxury product in most of the region until the mid-twentieth century, when bulk imports lowered prices. Many of the dishes now prepared with rice were originally made with bulgur or *freekah*.

The grains are often cooked with meat or chicken, requiring approximately 1½ parts liquid to 1 part *freekah* for a chewy, rice-like consistency. *Freekah* is also used in a variety of different soups and can also be cooked as a meal in its own right, as rice would be, and topped with poached chicken and an assortment of fried nuts.

You can find *freekah* in most Middle Eastern grocery stores. Palestinian fair-trade *freekah* is available via Canaan Fair Trade in the United States and Europe and via Zaytoun in the United Kingdom.

Shorabit Jarjir

Arugula Soup

Serves 3–4

1 medium onion, chopped
2–3 tablespoon olive oil
2–3 carrots, chopped
2 medium potatoes, chopped
1 Middle Eastern squash (*koosa* or similar summer squash), chopped
8 cups (2 liters) *Maraqa* (page 24)
4 packed cups (approximately 100 grams) arugula (salad rocket),
   coarsely chopped
2 tomatoes, peeled and finely chopped
Salt and pepper to taste
Juice of 1 lemon

In a large saucepan, sauté the onions in olive oil on medium heat until they are partially caramelized. This will take about 10 minutes. Stir in the chopped carrots, potatoes, and squash and sauté for 5 more minutes. Add the broth and bring it to a boil. Gently stir in the arugula, a handful at a time. Simmer for 10 to 15 minutes or until the vegetables are tender. Stir in the tomatoes and cook for an additional 2 to 3 minutes. Season with salt and pepper and finish with the juice of one lemon. Adjust the seasonings to taste.

شوربة جرجير

Peppery arugula is widely available in Gaza, and fresh leaves are often served to accompany meals. Um Sultan provided the recipe for this nutritious soup as she showed us the mountains of fresh-cut arugula her sons were preparing to take to market. If you don't have homemade broth on hand, use packaged broth or else some bouillon and add an assortment of whole spices tied in a disposable tea filter, as instructed in *Maraqa* (page 24). Make sure to chop your vegetables into evenly sized pieces.

Shorabit Halayone

Asparagus Rice Soup

Serves 4–6

شوربة هليون

1 medium-sized onion, finely chopped
2–3 tablespoons olive oil
1 pound (approximately 500 grams) fresh white or green asparagus, trimmed of dry stalks and finely chopped
1 teaspoon salt
¼ teaspoon ground black pepper
½ teaspoon cardamom
⅛ teaspoon cinnamon
8 cups (2 liters) *Maraqa* (page 24)
⅓ cup (approximately 65 grams) short-grain rice
Filfil Mat'hoon (page 28), for garnish
Lemons, for garnish

Sauté the chopped onions in olive oil on medium heat until golden. Add the asparagus to the onions and cook for about 5 minutes or until the asparagus softens. Mix in the spices and stir well, then add the broth. As soon as the soup comes to a boil, add the rice and reduce the heat to medium. Simmer until the rice is tender. Adjust seasonings to taste.

Garnish with a teaspoon of *Filfil Mat'hoon* (page 28) in the middle of each soup bowl, along with a twist of lemon peel.

Asparagus grows wild between prickly-pear cactus plants in the southern Gaza District, where this soup comes from. Mediterranean wild asparagus has a strong and aromatic taste that is quite bitter; the stalks must be blanched or soaked in salted water and lemon juice overnight to rid them of their unpleasant taste. For this soup, any store-bought asparagus will do and won't require soaking. Again, if you don't have time to make the basic broth, use packaged broth and add the whole spices listed in the broth recipe to this soup while it cooks.

This easy and delicious recipe is from Shafeeqa El-Farra, from the village of Garara.

Imtabbal Abucado

Spicy Avocado Dip

Serves 2–3

½ teaspoon salt
2 cloves garlic
1 green chile, chopped
2 small ripe avocados, peeled and seeded
Juice of 1 lemon
1 tablespoon yogurt
Extra-virgin olive oil, for garnish

Pound the garlic and chile pepper with salt in a mortar and pestle. Add the avocado, yogurt, and lemon juice and mash until smooth, stirring the bottom of the bowl to make sure all the garlic is mixed in.

Swirl the top of the salad with the bottom of a spoon in a circular motion, creating a small canal, then drizzle with olive oil. Decorate with paprika and cumin as follows: Wet your thumb with some water, place it in a bowl of paprika, then press down on the edge of the bowl, leaving a red fingerprint. Repeat procedure, alternating paprika with cumin, all around the bowl. Garnish with thinly sliced lemon.

Serve with *Khubz Kmaj* (page 100).

متبل أبوكادو

Avocados are not native to the Middle East; rather comically, as the Arabic alphabet doesn't have the letter *v*, they are referred to in Gaza as *Abu Cado*—that is, "the father of he who annoys others."

Avocado trees were introduced by Israeli settlements occupying Palestinian land in Gaza in the 1980s. The settlers have since gone, but the avocados have been adopted with enthusiasm. They grow in great abundance, particularly in the rich agricultural land of central Gaza. Avocado dip is an elegant starter, part of the new Gazan repertoire.

Imtabbal Ari'

Autumn Squash Dip

Serves 2–3

2 cups (410 grams) butternut squash, chopped into medium-sized
   chunks
½ teaspoon salt
2 cloves garlic
1 hot green chile, chopped
1 tablespoon yogurt
Juice of 1 lemon
Extra-virgin olive oil, for garnish

Boil the squash pieces until they are tender. Strain them, then set aside
to cool completely.

Meanwhile, mash the garlic and chile with salt in a mortar and pestle.
Add the lemon juice and mix well, scraping in any bits of garlic from the
bottom of the mortar. Reserve half of this mixture for garnish. Stir the
other half into the butternut squash, mashing with a fork until smooth
(you can also pulse it gently in a food processor).

Test for salt: Depending on the sweetness of the squash, you may want
to add more. Stir in yogurt. Swirl the top of the salad with the bottom
of a spoon in a circular motion. Drizzle with olive oil and top with remaining garnish. Sprinkle with chile powder. Serve with *Khubz Kmaj*
(page 100).

متبل قرع

In Gaza this spread or dip is made
with a gourd from the pumpkin family that is not at all stringy. In terms of
consistency, the closest gourd available in North America is the butternut
or kabocha squash, which we have
used here. Any orange-fleshed winter gourd will do.

Imtabbal Bitinjan

Hot Charred Eggplant Dip

Serves 2–3

متبل باذنجان

1 large eggplant (aubergine) or 2 smaller ones (1 pound or 500 grams)
1 tablespoon tahina
1 tablespoon yogurt
½ tablespoon pomegranate molasses (optional)
½ quantity *Daggit Toma u Lamoun* (page 28)

Puncture the eggplant's skin and roast whole on a grill, in a 400°F (200°C) oven, or directly on your (gas) stovetop, until the skin is well charred and blistered. Let it cool, then peel and discard the skin. Split the eggplant in half lengthwise. If it has large seeds, remove them with a spoon.

If you are short on time, you can omit this step by using jarred, preroasted eggplant pulp, available at Turkish markets. Proceed as follows.

Combine roasted eggplant pulp, tahini, yogurt, and molasses, along with half the dressing in a food processor and pulse a few quick times, until well combined but not totally pureed. For a chunkier salad, mash with a fork.

Transfer to a serving platter and spread evenly, up to the edges of the plate. Then, using the back of an oiled spoon, make a circular indent around the middle of the salad. Drizzle some olive oil here and garnish with the remaining dressing. Adorn with pomegranate seeds and parsley.

Serve with warm *Khubz Kmaj* (page 100).

Versions of this popular eggplant spread appear all over the Levant. Better known in the West as *baba ghanooj*, it is marvelously rich and smoky. *Imtabbal* literally means "marinated" or "dressed." This dish differs from most *baba ghanooj* in that it includes yogurt. The Gazan version is also, characteristically, a bit spicier than others.

Hummus Bil T'heena

Chickpea Spread

Serves 9

1½ cups (280 grams) dry chickpeas (garbanzo beans), picked over and rinsed
½ teaspoon baking soda
3–4 cloves garlic
1 teaspoon salt
Juice of 3 lemons
6 tablespoons tahina
2 tablespoons strained yogurt (optional)
1 teaspoon cumin
Daggit Toma u Lamoon (page 28)
Paprika and cumin, for garnish
Extra-virgin olive oil

Soak the dried chickpeas overnight. Strain, then rub them with baking soda to remove the skins and soften them. Rinse well. Boil the chickpeas in a large pot for 1 to 2 hours with enough water to cover them amply, or else cook them in a pressure cooker or slow cooker overnight until they are very soft. Strain them, making sure to reserve the cooking liquid. Set aside a small quantity of the chickpeas for garnish.

Pound the garlic with salt in a mortar and pestle until it is very smooth. Puree the remaining chickpeas in a food processor or blender with the mashed garlic, lemon juice, tahina, yogurt, and cumin. Pulse until smooth, adding ¼ cup reserved cooking liquid, or more if the mixture seems too thick. Adjust the seasonings to taste.

Transfer the hummus to a serving platter, creating a small moat around the edges and a small mound in the middle with an oiled spoon. Drizzle the garlic and lemon dressing on top of the prepared hummus. To finish, drizzle some extra-virgin olive oil all around and sprinkle some paprika, cumin, and the reserved chickpeas on top.

حمص بالطحينة

Known the world over, with hotly contested rights of political "ownership" (including a petition by the Association of Lebanese Industrialists to grant it protected status), hummus is a centuries-old regional staple that you will always find at the breakfast and supper table in Gaza, more often purchased at street-side stands than made at home. In Khan Younis, there is a hole-in-the-wall hummus shop that has lines around the block every day of the week. The owner, a native of Lydd and relative of the late abstract artist Ismail Shammout, is reputed to make the best hummus the whole Strip over.

Adding a dollop of this or a handful of that transforms hummus into other dishes: *imsabaha, fattit hummus*.... Here we provide the basic recipe.

In January 2012, an article in *Haaretz* described the latest food craze in Israel: *freekah*, the roasted green wheat that has been a staple of the Palestinian diet for centuries. The article said it had been introduced by chef Erez Komarovsky, who learned of it from "Arabs living in the Galilee," as though they were some hitherto undiscovered species inhabiting the land.

Another article in the *Atlantic* claimed that "*freekah* is mainly a symbol of Israel's growing awareness of local food traditions, customs, and ingredients." *Whose* food traditions and customs, we are never told. Palestinians are not mentioned once in the article; they are absent altogether from this historical narrative. The Mizrahim, Jews native to Arab lands who share many Arab culinary traditions, are also whisked right out of existence.

The same story is repeated on city streets, supermarket shelves, and food magazines around the world: falafel stands hawk "authentic Israeli food," hummus is branded with etymologically ambiguous and often orientalist names, articles expound upon "Israeli foods" like *zaatar* or *shakshuka,* and food magazine editors are head over heels for Israeli celebrity chefs. (Laila was once told by a magazine editor with whom she was corresponding that the magazine had covered Palestinian cuisine…but from the trending Israeli food perspective.)

Palestinians take great offense at such attempts at cultural appropriation—in fact, erasure of their very existence—viewing them as yet another form of colonization.

Food is more than just nourishment; it is highly political, emotional, and symbolic. How it is marketed and spoken about is a means of propagating stories and perpetuating histories. In his *Wretched of the Earth*, Frantz Fanon argues that colonizers and occupiers make a determined effort to devalue or render invisible the histories of the native people they control, and thus those populations' hope of a future national culture. In this way, says Israeli writer Yahil Zaban, "hummus, tahina, and falafel were turned into symbols of Israeliness, while their Arab heritage was repressed and obliterated."

Appropriation "erases not only Palestinians, it also erases the bitter ways in which the state of Israel erased the Arabness of its Mizrahi Jews," argues Laleh Khalili, a scholar of Middle Eastern politics, in a conversation with the authors.

Yael Zerubavel, a scholar of Israeli culture at Rutgers University, gives another explanation. "Politically, the Zionists ignored the Arabs, but culturally, they romanticized and tried to imitate them. This imitation didn't seem like theft," she explains, "but localization, a process of putting roots in soil."

The key here is context and intent. Everywhere the history of cuisine is one of borrowing, adapting, transforming: that is not the problem. It would be a far different script if Israeli chefs were to acknowledge the heritage of the "new foods" they are just now discovering, rather than quietly rebranding them as Israeli. But when so much of what was once Palestinian is now Israeli—the land, the water, the towns and houses and orchards—it stands to reason that Palestinians should resist the colonization of this last frontier of Palestinian identity.

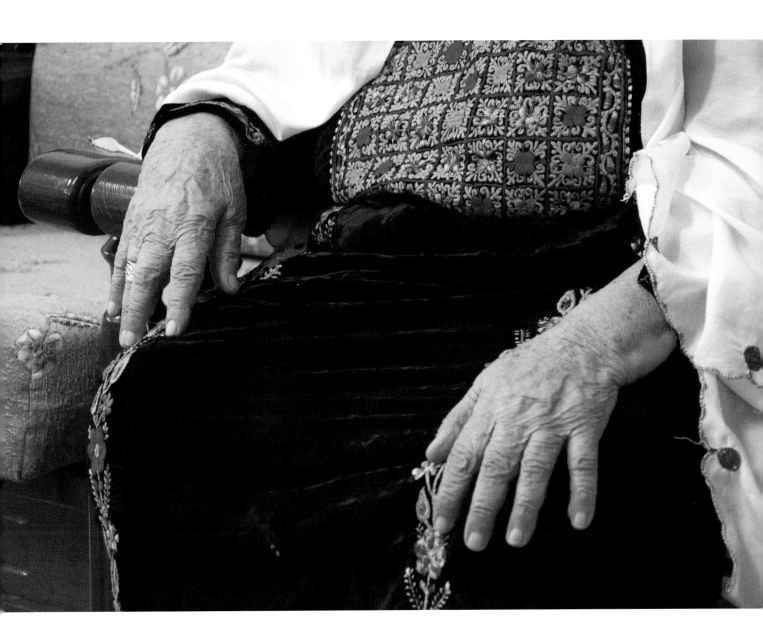

Bisara

Fava Bean Spread

Serves 3–4

1 cup (approximately 200 grams) skinless fava beans (*fool majroosh*), rinsed
2 teaspoon red pepper flakes
5 garlic cloves
1½ teaspoons salt
½ cup (about 40 grams) dried *mulukhiyya* leaves
1 teaspoon coriander seeds
1 tablespoon dill seeds, crushed with a pinch of salt in a mortar and pestle
1 teaspoon ground cumin
1 onion, chopped
2 tablespoons olive oil
6–7 cups (about 1½ liters) water
Lemon wedges
Filfil Mat'hoon (page 28)

Boil the skinless fava beans in 6 to 7 cups of water (just under 2 liters), partially covered, removing any scum that rises to the top. Add the pepper flakes and cover, cooking until tender. This should take no more than 20 minutes. Add more water if necessary; there should be a little liquid visible around the beans. Set aside to cool slightly.

Meanwhile, grind the dill seeds with a pinch of salt in a mortar and pestle using a strong circular motion until fragrant. Transfer to a pinch bowl. Add the garlic to the mortar and pestle along with ½ teaspoon of salt and mash well. Set aside.

Mash the cooked fava beans, along with any remaining liquid, using a mortar and pestle, or potato masher, or press through a food mill, or food processor. The beans should be tender enough that this will not require much effort. Return them to a clean pot, then stir in the dried *mulukhiyya*, salt, coriander, dill seeds, cumin, and half the crushed garlic. Allow to simmer.

The mixture should have approximately the consistency of loose mashed potatoes: Cook down or add a little water if necessary to achieve this.

In a separate pan, fry the onion and remaining garlic in 2 tablespoons of olive oil, then add this to the *bisara* pot and mix well.

Pour the mixture into bowls and cool completely. Squeeze a lemon wedge onto the *bisara* and serve with *Filfil Mat'hoon* (page 28) or freshly cracked black pepper. *Bisara* should be scooped up with *Khubz Kmaj* (page 100), like a dip.

بصارة

This nourishing vegetarian dish is popular with people of all backgrounds and social classes in Gaza, including Gaza's Christian population during Lent. You can find both skinless fava beans and dried *mulukhiyya* leaves at almost any Middle Eastern market.

Um Zaher

Um Zaher has a small house in a modest walled lot in Garara, in the central Gaza Strip. Several similar houses cluster around a dirt road; beyond lie agricultural fields with tidy rows of eggplants and chile peppers growing under the blazing summer sun. Inside the gate, a haven of green: figs and pomegranates, hibiscus and palms grow thick around the house. Chickens scratch in the shade of a grapevine. And there is Um Zaher: vital, energetic, commanding, overseeing every detail of her tiny domain with almost uncanny efficiency. Immediately after greeting us and while still making small talk, she hoists herself into the fig tree to pick burstingly sweet fruit to eat with our tea.

The kitchen is separate from the house, a little outbuilding with a shady entrance where Um Zaher sits to chop chard and onions for *fogaiyya* while she tells us about her youngest son, who has just graduated with honors from the university and is about to marry. There is much laughter and some perplexity as she confesses that, while she herself went to great lengths to finish high school and worked hard to make sure her daughter could finish university, she is happy to have found a sixteen-year-old bride for her son: "Has she studied? No, no! I want a girl who will only be a great wife for him!"

In the tiny kitchen lined with plastic jars of homemade pickles and her prized 150-year-old stone grain mill, passed down to her through the generations, she prepares several different meals at once: *fatta* for the workers who are helping rebuild a damaged room in her house, *fogaiyya* for us, *bisara* for a neighbor.

All of this with a sort of effortless coordination, while chatting about families and recipes. Nothing goes to waste: Vegetable scraps are taken out to the chickens, coffee grounds fertilize a small bed of garden vegetables irrigated with gray water, lemon rinds are reused for scrubbing meat.

Has her diet changed since the siege? "No, people waste a lot, but there are rations and vouchers, and if you don't mind buying frozen meat instead of fresh, there's not that much difference." But then, this is Um Zaher, home economist *par excellence*, a no-nonsense, "let's get on with it" kind of person who refuses to so much as entertain notions of victimhood.

Fool Imdammas
Smothered Fava Beans
Serves 7–8

Base recipe

2 cups (approximately 400 grams) small dried fava beans (available in most Middle Eastern grocers)

⅓ cup (approximately 65 grams) dried chickpeas

½ cup (approximately 65 grams) skinless fava beans (*fool majroosh*)

¼ cup (approximately 50 grams) red lentils

1 tomato

Seasoning (per 2 cup serving of fool)

2 cloves garlic

2 hot green chile peppers

½ teaspoon salt

1 teaspoon cumin

Juice of 2 lemons

Pick through the legumes and rinse them all well. Soak the fava beans and the chickpeas in water for 16 hours, or until small bubbles begin to rise to the surface. Change the water several times over this period. Drain and rinse well under running water.

Place the soaked beans and chickpeas, skinless fava beans, lentils, and tomato in a slow cooker (this is best), pressure cooker, or large stockpot and cover fully with water. Bring to a boil, then lower heat and simmer for several hours—overnight, if you're using a slow cooker—until the legumes are completely soft and falling apart. Add water as needed to prevent burning, and remove any scum that rises to the surface. Let cool, and (if desired) divide into servings of 2 cups each and freeze in sealable bags or storage containers.

When ready to use the *fool*, prepare the seasoning: Crush the garlic, hot peppers, and salt in a mortar and pestle, then stir in the lemon juice. Reserve a quarter of this dressing for garnish, and combine remaining dressing with about 2 cups of prepared *fool*. Add cumin. Pound the *fool* mixture gently in a mortar and pestle (traditional) until partially mashed or else mash gently with a fork, though the beans should be falling apart and will not require much mashing. This is a matter of preference: Some prefer their *fool* chunky, others mashed to a smooth paste.

Spoon into serving platter and make a circular indentation in the surface of the *fool* with the back of an oiled spoon. Drizzle some olive oil in this "moat." Garnish the "island" with remaining dressing.

Serve with Arabic bread. A complete breakfast or *suhur* spread would include *Filfil Mat'hoon* (page 28), white onion wedges, sliced tomatoes and cucumbers seasoned with salt and black pepper, baby arugula, feta cheese, boiled eggs, and olives.

فول مدمس

While *fool imdammas* is best known as an Egyptian staple, it is equally popular in neighboring Gaza. Along with hummus, *fool* is the food of choice for *suhur*, the pre-fast morning Ramadan meal, because it "sits in your stomach." Canned varieties abound but cannot compare to this slow-cooked homemade version. Palestinians prefer their *fool* lighter in color and add chickpeas and lentils. Sometimes a few spoonfuls of prepared *hummus* (page 85) are mixed in with the *fool*, and some chickpeas added on top for garnish—a combination known as *imsabaha*.

Many families prepare a large quantity of the base *fool* recipe, freeze it, and then season it just before serving; this is how we have organized the recipe.

Adas Imdammas

Smothered Lentils

Serves 6–8

3–4 cups (approximately 800 grams) brown lentils, picked over and
    rinsed well
1 large onion, chopped
½ teaspoon cumin
1½ teaspoons salt
2 tablespoons tahina (optional)
Daggit Toma u Lamoon (page 28)
Extra-virgin olive oil

Submerge the lentils in a large bowl of hot water and soak them for half
an hour. Strain and transfer them to an oven-resistant pot, preferably
an unglazed clay or other earthenware one. Add the chopped onion,
cumin, and enough water to completely cover the lentils. Cover and
bake at 300°F (148°C) for several hours, or else cook in a slow cooker
overnight. Check periodically and add more water if the lentils are
drying up. It should be somewhat stewy, not dry or thick like hummus.

Before serving, stir in the tahina, if desired, then pour the lentils into
individual bowls and garnish with the *Daggit Toma u Lamoon*. Drizzle
generously with olive oil.

Serve with *Khubz Kmaj* (page 100), olives, white cheese, and jam.

عدس مدمس

This comforting and surprisingly simple dish, prepared in the same manner as *fool*, is particularly popular
in the winter months. Um Ibrahim
shared it with us, and explained that
some people add *tahina* to lighten
the color and mellow the flavor of the
final dish. It has since become a favorite in both of our households.

In 2013, Laila had the opportunity to return to Gaza to guide chef and food critic Anthony Bourdain while he filmed the episode that covered Jerusalem, the West Bank, and Gaza for his wildly popular series *Parts Unknown*. Bourdain's team had tried unsuccessfully in previous years to enter Gaza, but this time the stars aligned: The border was—under the short-lived Egyptian Morsi government—relatively open, allowing Laila passage. Bourdain and his team managed to secure a Gaza entry permit from Israel, and after filming in Jerusalem and the West Bank, Bourdain arrived in Gaza flabbergasted at the sheer disparity of what he had witnessed along the way.

It was the first time a mainstream American television program had been to the besieged Strip for a cultural feature like this, and it did something few such programs have achieved: it showed Palestinians as people. Viewers laughed with Um Sultan and her exuberant family, waited in anticipation as the whole Sheikh clan prepared *Fattit Ajir*, and heard about the precarious situation of Gaza's fishermen from the fishermen themselves. In a frank manner, with no histrionics, the episode showed the impact of the blockade on the daily lives of ordinary people.

This show was broadcast the world over and into the homes of millions of Americans. Many viewers have told us that it was the first time they had ever seen Gaza in this light, through this lens: families were who were, well, normal. Human. Gaza has a cuisine? A sense of humor? A culture? Yes, as it turns out, it has all these things and more! It is a sad testimony to the situation that such an obvious fact needs to be stated. But in a day and age when dehumanizing media coverage can have a very real, even deadly impact on people's lives, it is crucial to provide other images. This unique episode, while not perfect, was groundbreaking in this sense, even more so as it still ranks among CNN's most popular.

BREADS, BISCUITS, AND SAVORY PIES

In Egyptian Arabic, bread is often called *aish*, or "life." It is that important. Throughout the region, bread forms a central part of most meals, from the humblest to the most spectacular. Fluctuations in bread prices have driven revolutions; access to bread is the prime vector of well-being. Bread is often used in place of a utensil, for scooping up thick dishes and mopping up soupier ones. In Gaza, many families cannot afford to buy store-bought bread anymore, so they make it at home with their flour rations. In this chapter, we provide recipes for the two main kinds of bread consumed, as well as a variety of other dough-based snacks and pies.

Khubz Kmaj

Arabic Bread

Makes approximately 16 rounds of bread

1¼ pounds (approximately 4 cups or 625 grams) soft (sometimes known as "white") whole-wheat flour or a combination of wheat and barley flours
8 ounces (approximately 1½ cups/250 grams) white bread flour
2 teaspoons salt
2¼ teaspoons active dry yeast
1 teaspoon sugar
2 to 2½ cups (480 to 600 milliliters) warm water, more or less as needed
Olive oil, as needed

Proof the yeast if necessary: Dissolve it in a tablespoon or two of warm water and ½ teaspoon of sugar. Set this aside for about 10 minutes until it is frothy.

Mix all ingredients, including the proofed yeast, adding the water slowly along with 2 tablespoons of olive oil. Knead well, either by hand or with a mixer on low speed for about 10 minutes, until the dough forms an elastic ball and does not stick when pressed with a finger. Shape it into a taut ball and pat the surface with olive oil.

Cover the dough and let it rise in a draft-free place for 2 hours or until it has doubled in volume.

Punch the dough down and knead it once again, then divide dough into 3-inch balls and set aside on a well-floured surface. Cover the dough with a clean kitchen towel and let rest for half an hour.

Roll out each ball, forming flat loaves approximately 6 inches (15 centimeters) across and ⅛ inch (3 millimeters) thick. Let the rolled-out rounds rest for at least 30 minutes (they can be left to rest as long as overnight).

Prepare the baking sheets or ceramic baking tile (the latter works best, as it will not warp under high heat) by sprinkling them with a little flour, wheat bran, or fine semolina. Preheat your oven to 500°F (260°C) or the highest available setting, then place the prepared baking sheets inside. Switch the oven to broil. At the same time, preheat an electric or stovetop griddle to medium-high heat. If you do not have a griddle, heat a heavy skillet on medium heat.

Begin by placing the rolled-out dough on the griddle or skillet on medium heat. Wait about 30 seconds until the underside of the dough begins to set. Before it browns, quickly transfer the dough to the preheated baking sheets or stones in the oven. Broil for a few minutes, until the bread puffs up and is slightly golden on top. Take the bread out and cover with a towel or sheet. There is nothing quite like warm *kmaj* with olive oil and *zaatar*!

The standard Palestinian bread—eaten with almost every meal—is related to the bread called "pita" in the United States, but it is a far cry from the wan rounds you'll find at the supermarket. These round loaves have more texture and more flavor, and are slightly thicker than their Lebanese cousins.

Traditionally, bread in Gaza, especially in the farming interior, was made with a mixture of barley and wheat. Part of the naturally fermented dough was always reserved for the next batch of bread, and part of it was distributed to neighbors. The rolled out rounds were sometimes left to "rest" overnight, developing flavor, then were baked at dawn; this is what Laila's paternal grandmother, Hoda, always did.

The resulting rounds were more flavorful and more nutritious than the white bread that has replaced them.

In Gaza, bread is most commonly baked in small, pot-shaped aluminum electric ovens or in small gas ovens often reserved specifically for this purpose. The rounds of dough are first heated on a griddle, a skillet, or the hot surface of the oven, then baked under a broiler until they inflate, forming hollow loaves.

Through trial and error, we have found the method outlined here to be the most reliable one in modern kitchens. The bread may also be baked directly on preheated ceramic tiles or cookie sheets, although it may or may not puff correctly this way.

Khubz Saj

Griddle Bread

Makes approximately 6 large portions

4 cups (500 grams) bread flour (ideally, use half soft whole-wheat and
   half white flours)
1 teaspoon salt
1½ cups (360 milliliters) water, more or less as needed

Mix all ingredients until incorporated; the dough should be elastic but
not dry, and need only be kneaded until it is springy and uniform. Set it
aside to rest for 20 minutes, then divide it into lemon-sized balls.

Flatten each ball with the palm of your hand, then roll it out on a floured
surface until very thin (almost translucent), making a large circle.

Some cooks prefer to roll out all the dough pieces partially with a rolling
pin and then do the final stretching by hand, gently, resting the flattened
dough on their fingertips and slowly stretching it out right before cooking. This takes practice, but is more reliable and makes the process of
transferring the dough to the *saj* surface much easier.

Heat your *saj,* wok, or skillet to high and carefully stretch the thin dough
over it. It should cook very quickly: just a minute or so on each side.

Remove and wrap in a cloth to keep warm while you cook the remaining
pieces. Don't worry if the resulting bread is not uniformly browned or is
irregularly shaped—this is quite normal!

This very thin bread is baked on a *saj*, a metallic dome constructed of sheet metal or cast iron, heated over coals or a gas burner. The curved surface helps keep the bread stretched out for uniform thinness.

A carbon-steel wok flipped upside down on a gas range works well for this (but don't put your wok upside down on a burner if it has any kind of anti-stick coating!). If you don't have any kind of curved surface, this bread can also be made on an ordinary grid-dle or in a skillet.

Many Middle Eastern markets will carry this bread in their freezer sections, sometimes referred to in Lebanese shops as *markouk*.

UNRWA and Food Aid

In 1948, hundreds of thousands of Palestinians found themselves homeless, many with little more than the clothes on their backs. Fearing imminent attack by Zionist militias and often under heavy bombardment, they were expelled or fled for safety to neighboring countries like Lebanon, Syria, and Jordan, but also internally to what would become the West Bank and the Gaza Strip.

All believed that the conflict would end shortly and that soon they would return to their homes and lands. Sixty-eight years later, numbering some five million people, they comprise the largest group of refugees in the world.

The influx of refugees to Gaza tripled the enclave's population overnight. The first to set up emergency relief were the Quakers. When it began to be clear that the plight of the refugees would be prolonged, the United Nations Relief and Works Agency for Palestine Refugees in the Near East (UNRWA) was established by the General Assembly to take charge of

their needs. UNRWA has been serving the Palestinian refugee population and their descendants ever since.

Today, refugees comprise roughly three-quarters of the population in Gaza. Their education, health, and social services are provided by UNRWA, whose mandate is renewed by the UN every three years. Many consider the behemoth of an organization to be a government on its own, without which the society would surely collapse. Others argue that it, along with the dozens of other aid organizations operating in Palestine, has bred a culture of dependency.

We spoke with director of UNRWA Gaza operations Christer Nordahl. Here is an excerpt of that 2010 interview:

> Right now, with unemployment above 42 percent, some 80 percent of refugees are food insecure and without the food rations they would be starving. That is a figure which has been climbing upwards since 2001. Then with the blockade, job opportunities inside Gaza

have disappeared. All these people need support.

It would be so easy to reduce the number of aid recipients. It would just be a matter of lifting the blockade and so many jobs would crop up! For example, in the construction sector: There are thousands of projects on hold, and people waiting for work in construction. The day the blockade is lifted, the food aid dependency will go down immediately. What is strange is that we have a lot of donor countries that are supporting the blockade or else doing nothing about it. In these countries, taxpayers are paying money for us to feed people in order for the blockade to continue.

Here you don't see kids with blown-up bellies like in some parts of Africa; here they are not starving. But if you do a little research on the medical side, you will find that there is malnutrition and a very high prevalence of anemia, which has to do with the diet. We would be delighted if we could give more complete rations. We give them 60 percent [of what they need]. We can't afford more. Then they have to find the other 40 percent. And of course fruits and vegetables and all that. It is very tight. It means that those who are keeping a very good household economy are eating perhaps one meal a day. Many families are eating every two days. But nobody is starving. Everybody is hungry; nobody is starving.

In 2015, five years later, little of what Nordahl describes has changed. Certain elements of the blockade have eased slightly: For example, since 2014, some agricultural, textile, and furniture exports have been permitted to leave Gaza for markets in the West Bank and Israel. There was also a slight uptick in the import of desperately needed construction materials after an agreement between Israel and the newly

established State of Palestine—but these exports and imports are still a shadow of what Gaza exported before the blockade, and Palestinians still have no say over what exactly is allowed out and when.

Such minor gains in employment barely make up for the massive and systematic destruction wrought by the 2012 and 2014 assaults on Gaza, which killed 2,200 Palestinians and left some 90,000 homeless. The rate of unemployment still hovers around 42 percent (60 percent for young people, who comprise half the population), and around 70 percent of the population depend on humanitarian aid to fulfil their daily caloric needs.

As a well-informed taxi driver explained to Laila during her 2013 visit, using a familiar Arabic expression— *"Min barra, hallah hallah! Min juwa, yi'lam Allah!"*— appearances can be deceiving. Many families that seem to be doing okay have actually have resorted to taking loans that they are now unable to pay back, and are mired in debt.

Ajeenit Iqras

عجينة أقراص

Basic Savory Dough

6 cups (820 grams) all-purpose flour
6 heaping tablespoons powdered milk
1½ tablespoons active dry yeast
1 teaspoon baking powder
2 teaspoons salt
1 tablespoon sugar
¾ cup (180 milliliters) olive oil
1 egg (optional)
2 cups (480 milliliters) warm water, more or less as needed

This reliable dough is used for all manner of little savory pies and stuffed breads. Again, we have found that most instant yeasts don't need proofing, but if the yeast available in your locale requires it, then add this step.

If necessary, proof your yeast by dissolving it in a bit of water and a pinch of sugar and set it aside for 10 minutes until it becomes frothy. Knead all ingredients well, using a mixer or by hand, until dough is elastic and no longer sticky to the touch. Shape into a ball and pat with a little olive oil. Cover and let rise in a draft-free place for 1½ hours or until doubled in volume. Use in recipes as directed.

Iqras Sabanikh
Savory Spinach Pies
Makes approximately 30 pies

أقراص سبانخ

1 quantity *Ajeenit Iqras* (page 107)

2½ pounds (approximately 1 kilogram) fresh (or good-quality frozen) spinach or greens, thoroughly washed and dried

2 or 3 medium onions, finely chopped

2 teaspoons salt, more for sprinkling

½ teaspoon ground black pepper

⅛ teaspoon allspice or cinnamon

4 tablespoons ground sumac

¼ cup (60 milliliters) extra-virgin olive oil

2 tablespoons *Filfil Mat'hoon* (page 28)

Juice of one fresh lemon

1 teaspoon lemon zest

1 tablespoon pomegranate molasses (optional)

1 egg

Preheat your oven to 450°F (230°C).

Finely chop the spinach, then sprinkle it with some salt and place it in a strainer for 10 to 15 minutes, allowing the moisture to seep out. To get rid of excess moisture, squeeze the spinach by hand in batches, repeating several times until nearly no liquid remains, or use a salad spinner if you have one. You can also try transferring the spinach to a large skillet on low heat and stir until it is just barely wilted, about 30 seconds. Remove it from the heat and transfer to a strainer immediately. Drain well, squeezing out any liquid by pressing with the back of a spoon. This step is important to prevent the dough from getting soggy once stuffed. Set aside.

Rub the chopped onions with salt, pepper, and allspice. Mix this into the spinach, then add the sumac, lemon juice, olive oil, *filfil mat'hoon*, and lemon zest. Taste the mixture; it should be very tart. You can adjust the flavor by adding more sumac or a tablespoon or two of pomegranate molasses.

Separate the dough into golf-ball sized pieces (or larger, if you prefer bigger pies), cover them, and allow to rest for 10 minutes. Roll out each piece to less than ⅛ inch (approximately 3 millimeters) thickness.

In the center of each round, place 1 tablespoon of the spinach mixture. Fold three sides of the circle up to cover the spinach, creating a triangle, and pinch the dough together at the seams, leaving a small opening in the center. You can also simply fold the three sides over each other and place the pies seam side down in the pan.

Make an egg wash: beat the egg well with a little water, then brush it over the surface of the pastries to assist browning.

Delicious savory pies that are easy to make in advance and freeze. We have found that using a good-quality frozen chopped spinach works just as well as fresh for these pies, and will save you time and much squeezing by hand. Set the frozen spinach in a colander to thaw to room temperature, then proceed with the recipe as written. The intrepid may wish to use a variety of edible wild greens, finely chopped, blanched, and drained.

The pomegranate molasses is a Syrian twist, but we find it adds tang without making the pies overly soggy.

108

Transfer the pastries to a baking sheet on the bottom rack (seam side up, if leaving a small opening; seam side down, if not) and bake for 10 to 15 minutes or until golden.

Variation: *Iqras Jibna u Zaatar (Cheese and Zaatar Pies)*

Shred a combination of partially de-salted Nabulsi cheese and Monterey Jack or another semi-salted white cheese that melts well (like the white farmer's cheese on page 40). Mix in a few tablespoons of extra-virgin olive oil and finely chopped fresh or dried zaatar, oregano, parsley, or mint. To differentiate between your pies when baking, you can keep the spinach ones open and seal the cheese ones.

Nutrition

She pauses to describe to us the steady increase in cases of malnutrition in Gazan children: Anemia is endemic, and bone disease is frequent due to lack of calcium. Ard el-Insan supports breastfeeding and trains mothers in childhood nutrition to help them make the most of the food that is available, but Najah admits with a sigh that ultimately it is a question of the families' economic possibilities: If there is no money for overpriced fruits and vegetables, the children do not get the vitamins they need.

Until 2000, she says, they had few cases of malnutrition. But during the Second Intifada, when the borders closed to the more than 100,000 men who worked in Israel every day, many families' household economies collapsed and nutrition became a widespread problem. Since then, each subsequent blow to the Gazan economy has been reflected in children's health: the repeated attacks on agricultural lands, the closure of borders in 2006, and of course the bombardment of the Strip in 2008 and 2009.

When we interviewed Najah in 2010, she said the organization was overwhelmed by cases of undersized and sickly children. Now, after the devastating attacks of 2014, the NGO American Near East Refugee Aid (ANERA) affirms that nearly 40 percent of Gazan children continue to suffer from iron-deficiency anemia—and access to nutritious food is more precarious than ever.

The food aid provided by UNRWA and various international NGOs is sufficient to keep people from starving, but does not provide the vitamins they need to prosper. The rations set for Gazans are defined by world-standard criteria for emergency areas: 2,100 calories a day. But "emergencies" are supposed to be short-term, contingent situations, not the permanent status of a population for generations. Rations consist of flour, sugar, pulses, powdered milk, and oil, and therefore don't include the vitamins and minerals only fresh food can provide. Some families sell part of their rations to buy fruit and vegetables, but this is often insufficient. Likewise, the enriched biscuits and vouchers some NGOs distribute are just enough to offset the problem, but not enough to resolve it.

Najah Zohod is the director of the Children's Food and Nutrition Program at the Palestinian nongovernmental organization Ard el-Insan. She is also a lactation consultant: another one of Gaza's many unsung heroes. A crowd of mothers with small children wait in the hall outside her office as she painstakingly trains a young mother with an inverted nipple how to extract her breastmilk using a syringe.

Fatayer Saliq u Lahma

Chard and Meat Pies

Makes 20 pies

2 quantities *Khubz Saj* bread dough (page 102)
1½ pounds (680 grams) green chard, thick stems removed
1 medium onion, finely chopped
½ pound (250 grams) extra-lean ground beef
1 teaspoon allspice
1 teaspoon salt
½ teaspoon black pepper
½ teaspoon cardamom
⅛ teaspoon nutmeg
Olive oil

Preheat your oven to 450°F (230°C).

Finely chop the chard, then sprinkle it with a little salt and set it in a strainer for 10 to 15 minutes. Squeeze the chard by hand, in batches, to get rid of excess moisture, or transfer to a large skillet on low heat and stir until it is barely wilted, for about 1 minute. Return it to the strainer, squeezing out any liquid. This step is important to prevent the dough from getting soggy once stuffed.

Divide the dough into egg-sized balls and set aside for 20 minutes on a tray or cookie sheet greased with olive oil.

Meanwhile, sauté the onion in a little olive oil until it is soft. Add the ground beef and spices and cook until the meat browns. Remove from heat and mix with the strained, chopped chard. Set aside.

Warm about a cup (236 ml) of olive oil in a bowl. Dip the palm of your hand in some of the warmed olive oil, and use it generously to flatten each dough ball into a very thin, almost translucent circle on a well-greased surface. You might also try dipping the entire dough ball in the oil first. Place about 1 heaping tablespoon of the chard-meat mixture in the middle.

Fold in two sides of the circle to the center to form a rectangle, then fold the remaining two sides (the short ends) of the rectangle over the stuffing to form a square and flatten it slightly with your hand.

Arrange the pastries on a greased baking pan or cookie sheet. Bake for about 20 minutes on the lowest rack, until lightly golden.

These pastries are a favorite of the Palestinians of Karatiya and neighboring villages off Gaza's eastern borders. They use an unleavened dough that must be spread very thin by hand on a well-greased surface.

Manaeesh
Open-Faced Pies

To make *manaeesh*: Make *Ajeenit Iqras* (page 107). Allow the dough to rise as directed. Punch down, then divide the dough into lemon-sized balls and let them rest, covered with a kitchen towel, an additional 20 minutes. Pat down the balls with the palm of your hand or use a rolling pin to roll them out into rounds about ¼ inch thick.

Preheat your oven to 450°F (232°C). Brush two or more baking sheets with a little oil. Transfer the flattened rounds of dough to the baking sheets, then cover them with any one of the toppings listed below.

Once the topping is spread across the surface of the dough, gently press your thumb along the perimeter of the dough, making shallow indentations in it, then pierce the surface of the dough with a fork. This will help hold the topping on and prevent puffing.

Bake for 5 to 7 minutes. Serve hot out of the oven!

Manaeesh are irresistible at any time of day or night. While elsewhere in the Levant they are often sold on the street, in Gaza they are mostly made at home, and on a thicker dough. We list the most typical toppings here; feel free to experiment with others. Make sure to place the rolled-out dough on your baking pan before adding the toppings, as moving them once topped will be a messy affair.

Toppings

Zaatar
You can purchase fair-trade Palestinian *zaatar* (a widely available spice mixture of dried and ground wild mountain thyme or oregano rubbed with olive oil, sumac, and sesame seeds) online from many vendors, including Canaan Fair Trade and the Palestine Online Store, and the Zaytoun and Hadeel non-profits in the UK. Check to make sure the mixture you are using does not include wheat (a common filler) as an ingredient or vegetable oil instead of olive.

Mix approximately one part *zaatar* to one part extra-virgin olive oil. Stir well and apply this mixture with a spoon, spreading over the surface of the dough.

Cheese and Zaatar
In Gaza, *Jibna Baladiyya* (page 40) is commonly used. Feel free to substitute partially de-salted Nabulsi, or another white semi-salty melting cheese such as Monterey Jack or fontina. We find that a combination of more than one cheese works best. Crumble the cheese into a bowl and mix well with a little olive oil. Add dried or fresh *zaatar* or oregano leaves and a bit of black pepper. Mix and apply to the dough.

Hot tomato and onion
Finely chop one small onion or two shallots. Rub with a little salt and black pepper. Mix the onions, 2 to 3 tablespoons of tomato paste, and a teaspoon of *Filfil Mat'hoon* (page 28) with 2 tablespoons of olive oil. Spread across the surface of the dough.

Aluminum Pot Ovens

For baking, broiling, and toasting, many Palestinian kitchens use *tanajir kahraba*: small countertop aluminum pots with heating coils under the top cover. These locally made devices, which sell for about US$15, can be found in kitchens all over Gaza and the West Bank. Though they only cook two bread rounds at a time (one on the oven's top, as on a griddle, and one inside, as under a broiler), their quick and even heating makes them practical in a place with extraordinarily high electricity rates and frequent blackouts.

Cooking gas is much too expensive to use for daily baking, especially since most of the smuggling tunnels through which gas was provided have been destroyed. Though traditional wood-burning clay ovens enjoyed a brief revival in the most restrictive years of the siege, and continue to be used in more rural areas, their use in dense urban areas is not realistic. Some believe residents make wide use of *tanajeer kahraba* ovens because most cannot, and therefore simply do not, pay their electric bills. So these peculiar electric pot-ovens serve a thousand and one uses, from baking bread or *manaeesh* to roasting nuts to browning chicken just before serving.

Halazonia

Coiled Meat Pies

Makes 10 to 12 pies

Dough
4 cups (500 grams) flour
¼ cup olive oil, warmed
1 cup warm water, more or less as needed to reach a pliable dough
½ teaspoon salt

Filling
1 pound (approximately 450 grams) lean ground beef
1 onion, chopped
1 teaspoon salt
1 teaspoon sumac
½ teaspoon black pepper
½ teaspoon cinnamon
1 teaspoon *qidra* spices (page 34)
Olive oil

Knead the ingredients for the dough until well incorporated, about 2 minutes, then shape the dough into a ball and set it aside to rest for 20 minutes.

Meanwhile, prepare the filling. Warm 2 tablespoons of olive oil in a skillet. Add the onion and cook until soft. Stir in the meat, breaking up any large lumps, followed by the spices. Cook the meat until it is no longer pink, about 7 to 8 minutes. Remove from the heat and set aside to cool.

Drizzle a generous amount of olive oil on an upside-down round baking pan or tray, a granite countertop, or another very smooth surface. Divide the dough into equal fist-sized balls. Dip each ball into a bowl of olive oil then transfer to the greased surface.

Preheat your oven to 450°F (230°C).

Using the palm of your hand, spread the dough ball into a large, thin, almost translucent rectangle. Divide this into 3 equal parts, cutting along the longer edge of the rectangle. In each part, line the length of one edge with the ground beef filling. Pinch the dough closed over the meat, then gently roll into a log with the meat inside. Next, starting with one end, roll the log up into a coil, like a snail's shell. Repeat this process with the remaining dough balls. Transfer the meat pies to a well-greased baking pan and bake on the lowest rack of your oven until golden, flipping over halfway through the baking process if necessary.

حلزونية

These unleavened meat pastries, also known as "snail pies" in Gaza, are easier to make than they appear. They are served with salad and yogurt.

115

On Olive Oil

Olive oil used to be the principal cooking oil used in Gaza, as in all of Palestine. Some dishes, especially the winter stews of the rural interior, were traditionally prepared with lamb tail fat or clarified butter, but otherwise both rich and poor cooked nearly everything with the lush green olive oil harvested from the region's indigenous olive trees, famed for producing some of the world's best oil.

Today, olive oil is a luxury that very few can afford. A little drizzle is reserved for salads, to give them flavor, but even the wealthy seldom use it for cooking. In fact, several of the home cooks we spoke to in Gaza were incredulous at the thought that olive oil might have ever been the main fat in many of the traditional recipes, savory or sweet. Nearly all of Gaza now relies upon donor-distributed jugs of oil (usually soy). Those fortunate enough to still have access to family olive groves carefully distribute small bottles of oil to family and friends, like a treasure.

The destruction of olive trees through Israeli attacks on Gaza has been prodigious: The Ministry of Agriculture estimates that 20,000 have been uprooted or destroyed in the last ten years just in Gaza. The numbers jump to half a million if we include incursions and tree-burning rampages by Israeli settlers in the West Bank. By some estimates, 800,000 Palestinian olive trees have been destroyed by Israeli authorities and settlers since 1967. Because trees take approximately eight years to bear fruit after planting and increase in productivity with age, this represents a major long-term agricultural setback.

Many farmers are opting to replace the destroyed olive trees with faster-growing crops to guarantee some kind of immediate income. Since the olive tree is a rain-fed crop and does not rely on irrigation for good yields, however, the current administration, along with many donors, are taking measures to support farmers while they replant.

Bascote Zaatar

Savory *Zaatar* Biscuits

Makes 24–30 biscuits, depending on size

1 cup fresh *zaatar* (you can substitute oregano)
3 cups all-purpose flour
½ teaspoon salt
½ teaspoon baking powder
½ teaspoon baking soda
⅓ cup (80 milliliters) olive oil
⅓ cup (80 milliliters) corn or other vegetable oil
¼ cup sesame seeds
1 cup (240 milliliters) water

Preheat your oven to 375°F (190°C).

Wash the *zaatar* well, selecting only the green leaves and discarding any stems. Set it aside to dry on a kitchen towel, then chop finely.

Combine the flour with the other dry ingredients. Gradually mix in the oils, along with the water. Knead in the chopped *zaatar* and sesame seeds. If the dough appears too dry, add a little more water, a spoonful at a time. Spread the dough evenly across the bottom of a 12 inch (30 centimeter) baking pan by hand and score into diamond shapes. Bake until lightly golden, about 10 to 12 minutes.

Serve with sage-scented tea.

بسكوت زعتر

A savory biscuit with a flaky bite: very addicting, especially with a cup of *shai bil maramiya* (sage-scented tea). Fresh *zaatar*—a wild-growing thyme typical of Palestine and the Levant—has become expensive and hard to come by in Gaza, since the uncultivated hills where it grows are now largely inaccessible due to the Israeli "no-go" zone along the border.

This recipe is from Laila's mother's friend Yosra, may she rest in peace. We have also tried using entirely olive oil (rather than a mix of olive and corn oils) with excellent results.

It's nearly sunset in Gaza City's bustling commercial center, the end to another oppressively hot summer day. The clocks strike eight, and suddenly the city is consumed by darkness. After a brief pause, a cacophonous motorized symphony fills the night; backup generators have been switched on almost in unison. The air grows thick with carbon monoxide fumes and the whir is deafening.

During the field research for this book, electricity was being rationed in eight- to twelve-hour blocks, driving the wealthy to rely on generators burning diesel smuggled in through tunnels (which at that time were operating full-tilt: no longer) and leaving everyone else to study and cook and dine by candlelight or in darkness. Now access to electricity has become even more precarious, with the lights coming on for only an unreliable four to six hours at a time.

The outages affect everything: water pumps to fill storage tanks on rooftops, refrigeration in homes, shops and pharmacies, and water treatment plants which—overwhelmed—end up spewing raw sewage into the sea. Hospitals frequently cannot afford the thousands of dollars a day it would cost to keep their generators going, meaning that doctors operate in the dark, and incubators and life-support machines are at risk of shutting off. There have also been several tragic incidents of children burning to death in fires caused by the candles used to light crowded houses.

Israel's 2006 punitive bombing of Gaza's sole power plant left its turbines crippled and only partially operational. It has never been fully rebuilt due to a subsequent Israeli ban on the import of the factory components needed to do so. Matters are further complicated by the fact that restrictions on fuel supplies force the plant to operate only part-time.

Hence the blackouts that have become a fixture of daily life in Gaza, waxing and waning in frequency and length over the past few years. Access to fuel has become a matter of hot political contention both internally and with Egypt and Israel, and the tangle of tax, payment, and bill-collection issues deriving from the fuel crisis between the Palestinian Authority caretaker government in Ramallah and the de facto Hamas administration in Gaza aggravates an already explosive political environment.

Various alternatives have been proposed: Some NGOs, as well as crowdfunded grassroots projects, have started setting up solar panels to take advantage of Gaza's 320 sunny days a year to power both homes and hospitals. This is a very promising option, but relies on Israel's permission to allow materials and batteries into the territory. On the other hand, a major Qatar-funded project to bring a natural gas line into Gaza is presently being discussed, though the political implications and motives of the initiative are generating much controversy.

The Israeli organization GISHA–Legal Center for Freedom of Movement asserts that responsibility lies with Israel: "As the occupying power in the Gaza Strip, it is incumbent upon Israel to provide for the regular supply of electricity to residents there."

But the brunt continues to fall upon ordinary people, who scrabble for just enough fuel to continue cooking for their families and conserving precious foodstuffs from the withering heat of summer.

LITTLE DISHES: EGGS AND HOT MEZZE

This chapter brings together a variety of different "little dishes," any of which might serve as an appetizer, a snack, or a light evening meal on the Palestinian table. Several might be served together as an elegant and varied spread.

Ujjit Zahra (Imshatt)

Cauliflower Fritters

Serves 10

1 head cauliflower, chopped into small florets
2 teaspoons cumin
1½ teaspoons salt
1 onion, chopped
½ teaspoon allspice
½ teaspoon black pepper
5 garlic cloves
2 hot green chile peppers
½ cup plus 2 tablespoons flour (130 grams)
½ teaspoon baking powder
½ cup milk or water (120 milliliters)
5 eggs
½ cup (15 grams) chopped parsley
½ cup (15 grams) chopped dill
Vegetable oil for frying

Boil the cauliflower florets with cumin and ½ teaspoon salt for just a few minutes, until slightly tender. Strain and set aside.

Rub the chopped onion with the allspice, black pepper, and ½ teaspoon salt. In a mortar and pestle, crush the garlic and chiles with the remaining salt and add to the onions. Add the flour, baking powder, milk or water, and eggs. Mix well until no lumps remain. Stir in herbs.

Fried version: Coarsely chop boiled, strained cauliflower florets and stir into the egg batter. If necessary, add more flour until the batter reaches a medium consistency, more or less like pancake batter. Using 2 large serving spoons—one to scoop out of the bowl and the other to scoop into the oil—fry batches of the *ujja* batter in hot vegetable oil until golden. Each fritter should be approximately 3 inches (about 7 centimeters) in diameter. Strain on a paper towel and serve with *Khubz Kmaj* (page 100), olives, *Filfil Mat'hoon* (page 28) and other mezze.

Baked version: Pour the mixture into a large, well-greased baking pan, then bake in a 400°F (200°C) oven for 15 to 20 minutes or until the eggs are cooked through. Drizzle the *ujja* with a little oil, then switch the oven to broil for about 5 minutes or until the top is slightly golden. Cut into squares and serve.

عجة زهرة (مشاط)

Ujja, often translated somewhat erroneously as "omelettes," refers to a whole category of egg-based dishes that can be adapted to include all manner of leftover vegetables, such as eggplant, asparagus, or squash. They can be fried like fritters or baked in a skillet or casserole dish like frittatas (a practice Laila's mother has popularized in her family). For a nice brunch presentation or even for school-lunch snacks, you might also try baking them in a muffin pan.

Halayone u Bayd

Spicy Asparagus Scramble

Serves 2–4

1 hot green chile pepper, chopped (optional)
1 small onion, finely chopped
½ pound (approximately 250 grams) asparagus, trimmed and finely chopped
5 eggs
Salt and black pepper
Olive oil

Crush the chile peppers in a mortar and pestle with a little salt. Sauté the onion on medium heat in 2 tablespoons of olive oil until it turns lightly golden. Add the finely chopped asparagus and the chile and continue to cook for about 5 minutes, until the asparagus is bright green but still slightly crisp.

Reduce the heat to low and stir in the eggs until they set. Do not overcook. Remove from heat and season with salt and black pepper.

هليون وبيض

A simple way to prepare wild asparagus, common in southern Gaza.

Bayd Marit

Egg and Parsley Salad

Serves 2–3

1 chile pepper, seeds removed
4 eggs, hard-boiled and cooled
2 tablespoons extra-virgin olive oil
2 tablespoons chopped fresh flat-leaf parsley or thyme
2 green onions, thinly sliced
1 teaspoon salt
¼ teaspoon freshly cracked black pepper
¼ teaspoon allspice

In a mortar and pestle, coarsely crush the chile peppers with ½ teaspoon of salt. Finely chop the eggs or mash them using a fork. Combine with the olive oil, parsley or thyme, green onions, crushed chile, remaining salt, allspice, and pepper. Serve with olives, *Fool Imdammas* (page 92), and other mezze.

بيض مرت

A quick preparation that transforms plain boiled eggs into a colorful and delicious breakfast dish.

Batata u Bayd

Potato Chile Scramble

Serves 3–4

2 large potatoes, peeled and diced
5 cloves garlic
2 hot green chile peppers, crushed
1 heaping tablespoon fresh *zaatar* or oregano, finely chopped
6 eggs
Olive oil
Salt and black pepper to taste

Fry the potatoes in 4 to 5 tablespoons of olive oil on medium heat until golden brown, stirring occasionally to ensure even browning and prevent burning. Meanwhile, crush the garlic and peppers in a mortar and pestle along with ½ teaspoon salt. Add the garlic and chiles, along with ¼ teaspoon black pepper and *zaatar* or oregano to the potatoes. Stir well and heat through. Reduce the heat to low. Add the eggs, stirring gently to combine, and remove from heat. Adjust the seasonings. Serve with olives, *Khubz Kmaj* (page 100), and an assortment of other small dishes.

بطاطا وبيض

A guaranteed crowd-pleaser, frequently made for brunch or a light supper. You can substitute dried *zaatar* if fresh is unavailable; just make sure to rub it between your fingers to extract its flavor first. You can also try using dill.

Restless and anxious to learn, Um Salih (Kiyaan El-Najjar) has clearly read up on health and nutrition; her kitchen conversation is scattered with opinions ranging from her wariness of plastic and wooden cutting boards (fragments of the board's material might enter the food) to her enthusiasm for medicinal herbs and light, fresh, mostly vegetarian cooking.

She has adapted several classic Gazan dishes to her family's more modern and health-conscious tastes. Her daughter, who comes to chat with us in the kitchen while we're cooking, says she doesn't know how to cook anything; she is busy with her studies at the university and isn't really interested. "But she looks up recipes for me on the Internet!" says Um Salih proudly.

Her house, a simple but spacious apartment in Gaza City, is impeccably appointed, but Um Salih longs for broader horizons:

Take me, for example. Here I am, a forty-six-year-old mother whose daughter is now at the university. I have a lot of spare time on my hands. In my opinion, the best thing to do would be to keep busy and invest my time in something useful for me. Like what? Something to give back to the community. Last year I took a course on techniques of reading the Quran, but my husband did not like me leaving the house because I have responsibilities here. This idea [of an older woman going back to study] doesn't appear to be acceptable in our culture; if I were to try, I think I would be stopped and be put down. Anyhow, I believe I will find the time and energy to do what I want.

I believe my children are set once they finish high school. My daughter knows how

to program a computer, and she taught her brother. I would love to take a course in computer skills, to keep up with modern technology.... Also, I watch programs about history and travel on television. I love to learn about other parts of the world.

The political closure of the territory's borders may be the overwhelming fact of daily life in Gaza as a whole, but there are many other, subtler borders as well. And wherever there is a border, there is someone figuring out how to get around it. One gets the sense that one way or another, Um Salih will not be so easily contained.

Imfarrakit Koosa

Spicy Sautéed Squash

Serves 2–3

2 cloves garlic
1 teaspoon salt
1–2 hot green chile peppers, chopped
1 small onion, chopped
1 cup (approximately 120 grams) squash pulp or 1 cup shredded
    summer squash
¼ cup (8 grams) chopped green dill or parsley, or 2 tablespoons dried
    mint
¼ teaspoon black pepper
¼ teaspoon allspice
4 eggs
Olive oil

Crush the garlic and the peppers with ½ teaspoon of salt in a mortar and pestle. Set aside.

Next, sauté the onion in 2 tablespoons of olive oil on medium heat until golden. Add the squash and cook until tender, 5 to 7 minutes. Stir in the chopped dill or other herbs, then season with ¼ teaspoon of salt and half the pepper and allspice. Reduce the heat to low. Add the eggs, one at a time, if using. Sprinkle with the remaining salt, pepper, and allspice.

You can leave the eggs whole and cook until just firm, or scramble them gently on low heat for 10 to 15 seconds. Serve with *Khubz Kmaj* (page 100), pickles, and an assortment of other small dishes.

مفركة كوسا

This is one of several dishes that make use of the pulp left over after hollowing out a squash for *Mahshi* (page 212). Finely chopped summer squash of any variety works just as well. You may also prepare this dish with seasoned ground beef or with the squash alone. Simply omit the eggs, in either case.

Imfasakh Bitinjan

Spicy Eggplant Salad

Serves 4–5

2 large or 5 small eggplants, peeled and cut into ½ inch (1 to 2 cm)
    slices
1 to 2 tablespoons salt
1 cup extra-virgin olive oil
1 quantity *Daggit Toma u Lamoon* (page 28)

Sprinkle the eggplant slices with salt and set aside in a colander for 20 minutes, or soak in a salt-water bath for 20 minutes, then rinse and pat dry with a kitchen towel.

Next, fry the eggplant slices in small batches in very hot oil until brown. Transfer to a paper-towel lined plate. Set aside to cool slightly. If you prefer not to fry them, the eggplant slices may be generously coated

مفسخ باذنجان

This simple and delicious dish consists of slices of fried or roasted eggplant, cooled and then torn into shreds and doused with spicy garlic-lemon dressing. Beachside kiosks often put this in sandwiches as a cheap and delicious meal.

with olive oil and roasted using a panini press or other indoor grill with equally delicious results.

While the eggplant is cooling, prepare the *Daggit Toma u Lamoon*. Tear the slices of eggplant into rough strips and arrange on a serving platter. Drizzle with the dressing.

Serve with *Khubz Kmaj* (page 100). This salad also makes a magnificent vegetarian sandwich.

Variation: Samak al-Armala (The Widow's Fish)

This same dish prepared with potato serves as a poor man's substitute for much more expensive grilled fish (or a widow's, as an indication of the poverty and economic exclusion that too often afflicts female-headed households in Gaza). Fry the eggplant as indicated above. Then, in the same oil, fry an equal quantity of thinly sliced potatoes until they are golden and cooked through but not crisp. On a serving tray, arrange the eggplant and potato slices in alternating and overlapping layers, then drizzle with Daggit Toma u Lamoon.

Mayit Bandora u Bayd

Tomato Rice and Poached Eggs

Serves 2–4

مية بندورة وبيض

This is a popular and inexpensive meal from the rural villages in eastern Gaza.

1 medium onion, chopped
3–4 tomatoes, liquefied in a blender, then whisked through a strainer
¼ cup (50 grams) rice, washed and strained
¼ teaspoon cumin (optional)
½ teaspoon salt
¼ teaspoon black pepper
5 eggs
1 piece *Khubz Saj* bread (page 102) or other thin flatbread, torn into pieces
1 cup (240 milliliters) *Maraqa* (see page 24) or other broth, warmed
1 tablespoon butter, melted
Olive oil

In a high-rimmed frying pan or skillet, sauté onion in 2 to 3 tablespoons of olive oil on medium heat until golden. Add the liquefied tomato, rice, salt, cumin, and black pepper and cook, partially covered, until rice is *al dente*.

Meanwhile, dip the torn bread quickly into the broth, then spread the moistened bread on a round serving platter or divide into individual serving bowls. Drizzle melted butter over the bread.

Reduce the heat. Make small hollows in the tomato-rice mixture and carefully crack the eggs into the hollows, making sure not to break the yolks. Cover and cook until the egg whites are set but the yolks are still runny, about 3 minutes.

Carefully slide the rice and eggs out of the pan and onto the bed of buttered bread. Serve with pickles and olives.

Variation: Maya u Basala (Poached Eggs and Bulgur)
Omit the tomatoes and torn flatbread and substitute bulgur for the rice.

Shakshuka

Eggs in Hot Tomato Sauce
Serves 2–4

2 garlic cloves
1 hot green chile pepper, chopped
¾ teaspoon salt
1 onion, finely chopped
4 tablespoons olive oil
4 very ripe tomatoes, chopped
4 eggs
⅛ teaspoon allspice
⅛ teaspoon black pepper

In a mortar and pestle, crush the garlic and chile pepper along with ½ teaspoon of salt. Set aside.

In a high-rimmed frying pan, brown the onion in olive oil on medium heat until golden. Add the garlic and chiles and sauté for about 3 more minutes or until the garlic is fragrant and the chiles are wilted. Add the tomatoes and stir for approximately 5 minutes or until the tomatoes have softened and fused. Reduce the heat to low.

Crack each egg, one by one, into a bowl. Here you have two options: leave the eggs whole or stir them to creaminess.

If you are leaving the eggs whole, slide them onto the surface of the tomato mixture and cook slowly until the whites are set and but the yolks are still quite runny. Remove from heat. Sprinkle the remaining salt, pepper, and allspice on top.

If you prefer to stir the eggs, slide them whole onto the surface of the tomato mixture and cook until the whites are almost but not quite set, then remove from heat and sprinkle with the remaining salt, pepper, and allspice. Stir just the eggs with a spoon, leaving the tomatoes below in place. The eggs will become creamy and finish cooking with the heat from the pan.

شكشوكة

Shakshuka is one of those dishes that everyone claims: Tunisians, Algerians, Lebanese, and Palestinians all have variations of it and call it their own. Then, adding to the confusion, Moroccans make a different dish by the same name, and Turks make the same dish by a different name. That said, it is extremely simple and totally satisfying, perfect for a hearty breakfast or light supper. For a somewhat more substantial dish, additional vegetables may be added to the tomato sauce. The Gazan version is—no surprise—somewhat spicier than most others.

In the summer of 2010, the Hamas government released a Ten-Year Plan for Sustainable Development Strategies, outlining an agricultural policy that would emphasize Gazan self-sufficiency to the extent possible, including rain-fed agriculture, energy independence, and strategic local production to fulfill basic needs.

To some extent, the plan is a reflection of the current siege reality; imports are sporadic and unreliable and exports are all but completely blocked, so it doesn't seem a bad idea to push hard for self-reliance and minimum consumption of scarce resources. What Gaza needs, says the government, is to create a viable internal economy, producing and processing for its own basic needs for as long as the siege lasts.

Critics say this is a fantasy born of an "Iron Curtain mentality." Gaza has neither the land nor the water to sustain itself; even if it could, accepting its current isolation as a permanent situation would be geopolitical suicide. What Gaza needs, they say, is trade, economic relevance, and a vital commercial relationship with the rest of the world. That is, an end to the siege.

In the meantime, the blockade continues, waxing and waning in intensity and changing in form each year. Each family and each project attempts to find a way between the immediate necessity of self-reliance and the desired horizon of connection to the outside world.

According to agriculture minister Mohammed Al Agha:

Sustainable agricultural development is the vision. The mission is to enforce sustainable economic and social development in the whole of the agricultural sector, making better use of resources, developing the agricultural economy, improving the standard of living of the farmers. One of the important ways to do this is creating what we call a marketing environment here in Gaza by preventing imports of some types of crops from Israel. Our farmers have been happy in the last two years. They've started depending on themselves and on the local market. Yes, Israel has prevented us from exporting, especially vegetables, even to the West Bank, but we have made some replacements, planting things we were importing from Israel before.

We are not talking about full self-sufficiency. We know where we are and where we are going. We are talking about relative efficiency, relative self-sufficiency. It's more of a strategic shift. When we say that we change the emphasis from citrus and vegetables as big consumers of water to dates and olives that consume less water, this marks a major strategic shift. Of course it takes time. This is why we call it strategic. It takes time.

Our strategy is flexible. We can make some kind of accommodation to export if the Israelis allow it, especially of vegetables and some other things. And if they don't, then we will continue in our policies here.

Omar Shaban, economist and director of the PalThink think-tank, says:

First of all, Gaza will never be sustainable. Who is self-sustaining? China? America? Not even. So, self-sustaining, no. What is the problem with Hamas? It is not that they are bad; it's that they are not aware. You can't talk about schnitzel with someone who doesn't know what schnitzel is. They don't know about international relations, GATT, America, Europe—they don't know this system. They don't want to. And they think—this is the dangerous thing—that they can live without it. Of course not! Sustainable Gaza? With what water? We don't even have enough for drinking! Even if we could, I'm not interested. I want a relationship with Israel in which Israel sees the benefit in me so they will keep me alive. If no one cares about me, then everybody wants me dead. Why is Gaza not important? Because we have no oil. But if they came and built a big refinery then they would say, "Oh, that's our gas, let's be careful with those people, let's not kill them." If there were branches of ten Israeli companies here, they would say, "Hey, that's our people there." Why do the British send ambassadors to Africa? Because they have interests like Shell and British Petroleum. Not because they like Chad.

Thus the tension between giving priority to local sustainability and participation in the global economy plays out in Gaza, much as it does in so-called developing countries all over the world. It is perhaps illuminating for people outside of Palestine to see these debates within Gaza. Far from obsessively discussing the ideological foundations of their relationship to Israel, as international media would suggest, Palestinian political forces are debating specific policies regarding how best to live within the given circumstances, with ramifications as material as whether to plant dates or strawberries.

Allayit Bandora

Fried Summer Tomatoes

Serves 2–3

4 large, flavorful tomatoes, cut into thick slices
4 cloves garlic, peeled
2 hot green chile peppers, chopped
½ teaspoon salt
3 tablespoons olive oil
3 tablespoons vinegar
2 tablespoons freshly snipped basil

In a mortar and pestle, crush the garlic, chile peppers, and salt together. Fry garlic-chile mixture in olive oil for about 30 seconds on medium-high heat until the garlic is fragrant.

Add the tomato slices and fry, uncovered, for 2 minutes without stirring. Lower the heat and cover the pan. Let simmer for about 10 minutes. Uncover, then drizzle with vinegar. Remove from heat and sprinkle basil on top. Serve with Arabic bread.

قلاية بندورة

Vinegar and basil round off this summertime favorite. Use good, flavorful ripe tomatoes.

Yousef Abu Safiya's Allayit Bandora

Yousef Abu Safiya's Fried Summer Tomatoes

Serves 2–3

4 large, firm tomatoes
Salt
2–3 hot green chile peppers, chopped
5 garlic cloves, peeled
1 tablespoon ghee
2 tablespoons dill seeds, crushed until fragrant in a mortar and pestle

Slice each tomato in half and remove seeds, sprinkling each half with a little salt. Lightly crush the chile peppers and garlic with a little salt in a mortar and pestle, then brown them in the ghee over medium high heat. Add the dill seeds and sauté half a minute more. Add the tomatoes, cut side down. Do not stir. Lower the heat and cover until the tomatoes are heated through and their skin begins to curl. Carefully peel the tomatoes and squeeze whatever ghee clings to the skins back into the pan. Simmer until the tomatoes are saucy, about 10 minutes. Serve with *Khubz Kmaj* (page 100).

Variation
Once the skins peel away, add two beaten eggs and slices of white cheese (such as halloumi); allow to set around the tomatoes.

قلاية بندورة يوسف
أبو صفية

Yousef Abu Safiya gave us very precise (perhaps obsessively precise) instructions on how to prepare his famous fried tomatoes.

Falafel

Spicy Chickpea Croquettes

Serves 4–5 (makes about 24 falafel balls)

2 cups (approximately 400 grams) dry (not canned) chickpeas, soaked in cold water for 16 hours
¾ packed cup (approximately 30 grams) fresh cilantro
½ packed cup (approximately 12 grams) fresh dill
1 packed cup (approximately 25 grams) fresh parsley
7 garlic cloves
5 hot green chile peppers (to taste)
1 tablespoon cumin
1 tablespoon cilantro
1 tablespoon black pepper
2 teaspoons salt
½ teaspoon nutmeg
1 teaspoon baking soda
2 tablespoons toasted sesame seeds
Water, as needed
Oil for frying

For toppings
Thinly julienned onions rubbed with 2 tablespoons sumac
Thinly sliced and quartered tomatoes
Salsit T'heena (page 30)
Filfil Mat'hoon (page 28) or other hot sauce
Chopped parsley
Assorted pickles (such as cucumbers and turnips)

Strain the chickpeas well. Using a meat grinder (preferably) or a food processor on pulse, pulverize all ingredients except the baking soda and sesame seeds, starting with the chickpeas. Mix well and set aside for 2 hours for the chickpeas to absorb the liquid.

Immediately before frying, add baking soda and sesame seeds to the batter and mix well. Shape the mixture into small patties (dip your hands in a little water if necessary to prevent sticking) or use a falafel mold, then deep-fry them in plenty of very hot vegetable oil. Fry a few sacrificial falafel patties first: If they fall apart, your batter is too dry. In this case, add a little more water to the batter, a couple of tablespoons at a time, and try again. Set the fried falafel on a paper towel to absorb excess oil.

Serve with *Khubz Kmaj* (page 100) and the assortment of condiments and toppings listed above.

This jewel of a fast food is beloved to all—rich and poor, urban and rural—throughout much of the Middle East. Gazans, never satisfied with the mild, add hot green chile peppers and a generous bouquet of green herbs: dill, cilantro, and parsley. The resulting bite-size marvels have a bright green interior bursting with flavor.

This particular recipe is in memory of Laila's mother's friend Yusra "Um Khaled" Ashour, who passed away from cancer in the middle of so-called Operation Cast Lead.

The *falaheen* of the Gaza region omit the cilantro, garlic, and nutmeg, and substitute onions in their place.

For a smoother batter, add ½ teaspoon of baking soda to the soaking water of the chickpeas, then rub the chickpeas between your palms and rinse well before removing the husks.

A few street stalls in the town of Khan Younis in southern Gaza make a special variation, drawing a reliable crowd. Julienne an onion, rub the slices with sumac, and set aside. Shape the falafel batter into logs, make an indentation in them with your pinky, and stuff each log with a bit of sumac-onion mixture. Seal them up and fry: stuffed falafel!

Kibda Maqliya

Spicy Fried Liver

Serves 2–3

1 pound (approximately 500 grams) sheep or chicken liver
1 onion, chopped
7 cloves garlic, crushed
2 tablespoons *Filfil Mat'hoon* (page 28)
1 teaspoon ground allspice
Salt and pepper to taste
Sliced cucumbers, radishes, and olives (for serving)

Olive oil

Wash the livers well with a little bit of salt, flour, and vinegar. Rinse and pat them dry.

Next, slice the livers (if using sheep liver) into slices approximately ½ inch (1¼ centimeters) thick by 3 inches (7½ centimeters) long. Pan-fry the slices in olive oil until they are browned on all sides, then add enough water to fully submerge the livers. Bring the water to a boil, then reduce the temperature and simmer until tender for about 20 minutes. (If using chicken livers, simply slice them and brown them—no need to simmer.)

Drain and season with allspice, salt, and pepper. Set aside.

Fry the onions in a little olive oil until golden. (If you are using sheep liver, you can do this while the liver is simmering.) Add the garlic and stir until opaque, about 1 minute. Add the fully cooked liver and stir well over low heat for about 5 minutes or until reheated. Transfer to a serving platter. Spread *filfil mat'hoon* over the liver. Serve with fresh sliced cucumbers, radishes, olives, and *Khubz Kmaj* (page 100).

كبدة مقلية

One frequently sees street vendors pushing brightly decorated push-carts through the streets of Gaza City selling trays of spicy sheep liver and other organs covered with a thick layer of brilliant red *filfil mat'hoon*.

For quicker preparation, this recipe can be made with chicken livers. They do not require pre-boiling.

In Palestine, as in most of the Middle East, there is a very clear difference between the foods you eat in public—in restaurants, cafes, or street stalls—and the foods made at home. The Middle Eastern foods now familiar around the world—hummus and falafel, shawarma and kebab—are all restaurant fare. While these foods may also be made at home, traditional home foods, like the hearty vegetable stews, little dishes, and one-bowl meals we feature in this book, are almost never made at restaurants and are therefore quite unfamiliar to Western audiences.

Home foods are almost exclusively prepared by women and are closely associated with the intimacy and integrity of the family. Some feel it would be a violation of that intimacy to offer home foods in a restaurant context. In Gaza, restaurant food is nearly always prepared by men, and its sharp distinction from home food may have as much to do with conserving the masculine character of restaurant cooking as respecting the terrain of home cooks.

Restaurants in Gaza range from street carts selling falafel to international-style fast-food joints selling hamburgers, from modest family places offering hummus and kebabs to elegant restaurants serving elaborate Continental cuisine. Some of the wealthier and more cosmopolitan families also prepare European foods at home, though never to the exclusion of traditional Palestinian dishes.

This cookbook collects almost exclusively the home foods made by generations of Palestinians from Gaza. While we include a few new recipes that point to the ongoing creative updating of Gazan cooking, our emphasis is on the traditional meals that everyone we spoke to proudly hailed as part of their heritage. These dishes continue to form the base of Gazans' diet. We present these foods not without some trepidation: Palestinians have seen their heritage and history intentionally erased and their traditional foods appropriated and lucratively marketed as "Israeli." There is some fear that the same thing might happen with these home foods.

ONE-BOWL MEALS: PULSES, GRAINS, AND GREENS

This chapter features some of the dishes most characteristic of traditional Gazan home cooking. These meals make use of inexpensive and widely available seasonal ingredients in creative ways, endowing them with a surprising and delightful spectrum of flavors. Many, like *fogaiyya* and *sumagiyya,* are quite unknown outside Gaza. These dishes are generally served in bowls at room temperature as a complete meal, to be scooped up with Arabic bread. While traditionally made with meat broth, a vegetable broth or even water can easily be substituted to make vegetarian versions.

Sumagiyya

Sumac-Infused Chard and Lamb Stew

Serves 5–6

1½ pounds (750 grams) boneless beef or lamb, cut into 1 inch (2½ centimeters) pieces
1 large onion, chopped
10 packed cups (approximately 360 grams or two large bunches) finely chopped chard, trimmed of thick stems
½ cup sumac berries or ground sumac
3 heaped tablespoons flour
1 tablespoon dill seed
5 garlic cloves
1 teaspoon dried red pepper flakes
1 hot green chile pepper, chopped
2 teaspoon salt
1 teaspoon ground coriander seeds
½ cup (100 grams) dried chickpeas, soaked and precooked, or a 15 ounce (425 grams) can, strained and rinsed
3 tablespoons red tahina or 3 tablespoons standard tahina whisked with 1 teaspoon roasted sesame oil
Olive oil

Prepare the meat according to the instructions in the *Maraqa* recipe (page 24), without browning. Strain, discarding the spices and reserving the meat and broth separately.

Warm 2 to 3 tablespoons of olive oil in a skillet on medium heat. Add the onion and sauté it until translucent, then stir in the chopped chard. Cook until the chard wilts, about 5 minutes, then set aside.

In a small saucepan, submerge the sumac berries in water and boil them gently for 10 minutes. Strain and reserve the liquid. Allow the liquid to cool to room temperature. If you are using ground sumac, simply steep it in hot water for 10 minutes in a bowl, then strain well. Squeeze the strained sumac by hand or press down onto the sieve with the back of a spoon to extract any remaining liquid. Cool.

Add the flour to the cooled sumac infusion and whisk well until it has dissolved.

In a mortar and pestle, using a strong circular motion, grind the dill seed and dried pepper with ¼ teaspoon of the salt until fragrant. Add the garlic and chopped chile peppers and mash well. Set aside.

In a large pot, combine 6 cups (1½ liters) of strained broth along with the sumac-flour mixture and whisk thoroughly to avoid clumping. Heat through, then stir in the meat along with the onions and chard. Add the dill, garlic, and chile mixture, chickpeas, coriander, and remaining salt. Bring to a boil, stirring continuously then reduce the heat to medium and cook for an additional 10 minutes, stirring as it thickens.

سماقية

Of all the dishes in this book, perhaps none is as quintessentially Gazan—especially Gaza City—as *sumagiyya*. It is a classic dish, traditionally made in large batches for Eid el Fitr at the close of Ramadan and distributed to friends, family, and neighbors, who reciprocate with *Ka'ik* (*Date Cookies*, page 314), salted fish (*fseekh*), or a *sumagiyya* of their own making. One's generosity is judged by the quantity and quality of the meat in the bowls given as gifts.

While this dish is usually made with an infusion of whole sumac berries, ground sumac will do in a pinch.

To finish, stir in the tahina. Heat through.

Pour into individual-sized bowls. Garnish with a sprinkling of ground sumac and finely chopped green chiles, if desired. Serve at room temperature with *Khubz Kmaj* (page 100) and fresh green chile peppers.

A large apartment block pockmarked with artillery fire towers incongruously over a dirt road and rubble-strewn lots. We climb the stairs to the apartment Um Imad (Khadra Abu Alees) shares with her daughter's family. A gust of air-conditioning greets us as we enter, lush drapes and elegant furnishings contrasting sharply with the building's stark exterior. Um Imad and her daughter bustle to make us feel welcome, the ingredients for *sumagiyya* already artfully arranged on the kitchen counter.

Um Imad's daughter and son-in-law are both administrators and professors at the Islamic University in Gaza City. They are scholars who earned their graduate degrees abroad and who now work hard to keep Gaza's universities operating at an international level, despite repeated bombardments and the near-impossibility of acquiring books or laboratory equipment. Um Imad lives with them, helping to keep house and look after their kids.

Her daughter, who wears niqab in public, prefers not to be photographed. Um Imad doesn't mind the camera and generously walks us through making *sumagiyya* while recounting anecdotes from her life: how she was given her first name (Khadra, meaning "green") in hopes of keeping her alive after the untimely and peculiar deaths of several siblings, a calamitous first marriage when she was very young, the difficulty of obtaining a divorce, the satisfaction of a happy second marriage. Her six children have scattered far and wide, emigrants in Europe and the Gulf.

Um Imad herself was born in Bir el Sabi' and fled to Gaza as a child in 1948. When the border opened after the 1967 war, she tells us, she and her family travelled to Bir el Sabi' to see what was left of their hometown. They found their old house just as they left it, though the city had been renamed Beersheba and nothing was left of the community they remembered.

She recalls, "An Israeli settler family was living there. They had been given the house by the government. They were nice enough to let us look around, but their children were sleeping so we didn't stay long."

Rumaniyya

Sour Lentil, Eggplant, and Pomegranate Bowl

Serves 6–7

¾ cup (150 grams) brown lentils, picked over and rinsed

3 tablespoons pomegranate molasses plus ¼ cup (60 milliliters) freshly squeezed lemon juice (or the juice of 3 white pomegranates, where available)

2 heaping tablespoons flour

2 teaspoons dried chile flakes

1½ tablespoons dill seed

1½ teaspoons salt

5 cloves garlic

1½ pounds (750 grams) unpeeled eggplant, cut into 1 inch (2 1/2 centimeters) pieces

½ teaspoon cumin

2 tablespoons red tahina (or 2 tablespoons regular tahina whisked well with 1 teaspoon toasted sesame oil)

1 onion, very finely chopped

½ cup olive oil

Red pomegranate seeds and dill (for garnish)

Submerge the lentils in 2 quarts (2 liters) of water in a large pot and bring to a boil over high heat. Simmer, partially covered, until the lentils are tender, about 25 minutes. Set aside. Do not strain.

Meanwhile, whisk the pomegranate molasses well with lemon juice. Combine the pomegranate liquid with the flour and stir until the consistency of the mixture is smooth and uniform.

In a mortar and pestle, crush the dill seeds and dried chile flakes using a strong circular motion along with ½ teaspoon of salt until fragrant. Add the garlic and mash well. Set aside.

Add the eggplant to the reserved lentils and lentil water and simmer over a medium flame, stirring occasionally until soft and deflated, about 15 minutes. If the water has been absorbed, compensate by adding just enough to almost cover the surface of the eggplants. The eggplants will release some liquid as they cook.

Stir in the crushed dill, chile flakes, and garlic, as well as the cumin and remaining salt. Slowly incorporate the pomegranate-flour mixture, stirring continuously for 5 to 7 minutes. If the stew becomes too thick to stir comfortably, add a little more water and boil it through.

Finally, add the tahina and heat it through, then pour into individual serving bowls.

رمانية

This unusual late-summer vegetarian dish, known as *habbit rumanna* by Palestinians from Yaffa and El Lydd, combines sour pomegranate juice—extracted from a unique variety of green pomegranate known as the Babylonian White Pomegranate—with lentils and eggplants. As white pomegranates are probably not available, this recipe substitutes their juice with diluted pomegranate molasses. A perfect dish for bidding goodbye to summer on the first cool day of fall.

Meanwhile, fry the chopped onion in olive oil over low heat until it is golden and crisp. Top each bowl with some of the fried onions and a few spoonfuls of the oil. Garnish with fresh red pomegranate seeds and fronds of dill.

Serve at room temperature with *Khubz Kmaj* (page 100) and olives.

Hamasees

Sour Greens and Lentils

Serves 4–5

½ cup (100 grams) brown lentils, picked over and rinsed
13 ounces (360 grams) common sorrel, finely chopped
4 cups (1 liter) water
2 teaspoons dill seeds
2 teaspoons red pepper flakes
5 cloves garlic
1 teaspoon salt
1 teaspoon ground cumin
1 onion, finely chopped
¼ cup (60 milliliters) olive oil

Boil the lentils in approximately 6 cups (1½ liters) of water, until tender—about 25 minutes. Strain, reserving the lentil water.

Combine the lentils, 4 cups (1 liter) of the reserved lentil water, and the greens in a pot and bring to a boil over medium heat. You may also use your broth of choice, if you prefer. Reduce the heat and simmer for about 15 minutes, then pulse in a food processor or blender until nearly smooth. Return to the pot.

In a mortar and pestle, grind the dill seeds and dried red pepper flakes with salt until they become fragrant, using a circular motion. Add the garlic and mash well.

Stir the garlic-pepper mixture, along with the cumin, into the stewed greens and bring to a boil. Lower the heat and simmer for about 3 minutes, until the stew begins to thicken. (If you are using chard instead of sorrel, add the lemon juice and zest now.) Pour into individual serving bowls.

In a separate pan, fry the chopped onions in olive oil over medium heat until they turn a deep golden brown, then pour both the onions and the oil over the *hamasees*.

Serve with *Khubz Kmaj* (page 100).

حماصيس

Often found growing between almond trees in southern Palestine, *hamasees* is also known as *humayda*, "the sour one." Foragers in North America or Europe may also know it as common sorrel, a delightfully tart perennial that can be found growing in the spring. If sorrel is unavailable, chard may be substituted. Compensate for what the latter lacks in sourness by adding ½ cup (118 milliliters) of lemon juice and 1 tablespoon of zest.

Ruz eb Maya

Chickpeas and Rice

Serves 2–3

1½ teaspoons salt
1 tablespoon dill seeds (optional)
1 teaspoon red pepper flakes
3 garlic cloves
1 onion, finely chopped
5 cups (1¼ liters) water or broth
1 cup (200 grams) dried chickpeas, soaked overnight in cold water or
    two 15-ounce cans (425 grams each), strained
1½ cups (375 milliliters) liquefied and strained fresh tomatoes or plain
    tomato sauce
½ cup (approximately 100 grams) rice
½ teaspoon black pepper

In a mortar and pestle, grind the dill seeds and red pepper flakes with
½ teaspoon of salt until they are fragrant. Add the garlic and mash well.
Set aside.

Next, fry the onion in 3 tablespoons of olive oil over medium heat until
well browned. Add the water or broth and the chickpeas. If you are using
canned chickpeas, reduce the amount of water or broth by half. Bring to
a boil. Cook until the chickpeas are tender (if using dried chickpeas, this
will take approximately one hour), then stir in the tomato sauce or liquefied tomatoes, rice, remaining salt, and black pepper. Partially cover
and simmer until the rice is tender, about 20 minutes. Finish by stirring
in the crushed garlic and dill seeds.

Variation: Labaya
*Omit the chickpeas and substitute chopped fresh tomatoes. This is a com-
mon meal made for small children among Gaza's poorer families.*

رز بالمية

This one of the many simple dishes
that emerged in the years following
the 1948 exodus, and as the literal translation of the name indicates
("rice with water"), it was a recipe born
of hardship. These dishes have the
virtue of turning the ingredients provided by UN emergency rations into
truly appealing and nutritious meals.

Kishik Beit Tima

Beit Tima Kishik Stew

Serves 5–6

1½ pounds boneless lamb, cut into ½ inch (1 centimeter) pieces
½ cup (95 grams) dried chickpeas, soaked overnight, or one 15 ounce (425 gram) can, strained and rinsed
3 rounds of *Kishik* (page 42) cakes, liquid *kishik* (page 42), or 1½ cups powdered *kishik* (available in Middle Eastern grocers)
⅓ cup (approximately 65 grams) short- or medium-grain rice
2 teaspoons dill seeds
1½ teaspoons salt
5 cloves garlic
2 teaspoons dried red pepper flakes (adjust to taste)
Olive oil or ghee

Prepare the lamb according to the instructions in the *Maraqa* recipe (page 24), adding the soaked chickpeas as the meat cooks, if you are using them. Once the broth is ready, remove and discard the whole spices and bring both the meat and the broth to a simmer in a clean pot.

If you are using dried *kishik* rounds, moisten them with a little water, then break them into pieces and pulse in a blender with 2½ cups (approximately 600 milliliters) of water until smooth. Strain to remove any remaining clumps and set aside. If using powdered *kishik*, mix with enough water to form a paste of medium consistency. If you are using a more liquid form of *kishik*, such as the recipe we provide on page 42, you may skip these steps.

Soak the rice in cold water for 10 minutes, then strain it. In a small pot, stir the rice over medium-high heat with 1 tablespoon of olive oil for about 30 seconds, then add ½ cup of boiling water and ½ teaspoon of the salt. Reduce the heat and cover for 20 minutes or until fully cooked.

Slowly stir the diluted *kishik* into the simmering broth. Mix until smooth. If you are using canned chickpeas, add them now. Add the cooked rice. Bring to a boil, stirring continuously as the mixture begins to thicken. Add more water or broth if necessary, depending on the consistency you prefer; traditionally, the stew should be quite thick.

In a mortar and pestle, crush the dill seeds and dried red pepper flakes with the remaining salt until they are fragrant. Stir the mixture into the stew. Add the garlic to same mortar and mash it to a paste. Fry the mashed garlic in 3 tablespoons of olive oil until it turns golden, deglazing the pan with a little stew broth, then stir the garlic into the stew.

Pour the stew into individual serving bowls and garnish with dried red pepper flakes. Serve at room temperature with *Khubz Kmaj* (page 100), *Filfil Mat'hoon* (page 28), and assorted pickles and olives.

كشك بيت طيما

This recipe for Beit Tima's famous *kishik* stew was given to us by Um Ibrahim, who enthused, "Ah! Kishik! It was one of our most favorite foods. Beautiful!"

Her grandchildren, she lamented, were not as excited about it: *Kishik* has one of those strong, pungent flavors you either love or hate. Um Ibrahim herself no longer felt up for cooking, so she sat in her sunny kitchen giving precise and exacting instructions to one of her several daughters-in-law, who showed us how the dish is prepared. Grandchildren and great-grandchildren poked their heads in to greet us, and a cat wound around her ankles while she held court in the kitchen.

Um Ibrahim

For some, the memory of village life before 1948 is inherited, by now more a legend than a memory. For others, like Um Ibrahim, it is as real and as vital as the present, perhaps more so. Her 89-year-old eyes gleam as she describes in detail the wild greens and handsome squashes of her home village, Beit Tima, where her father had been mayor, "mending relationships," before the villagers were driven out in 1948.

Beit Tima was famous for its fruit orchards and vegetables. Um Ibrahim recounts how they used to get fish by bartering with people from the village of El Jora, near the sea, and bought sweets during the spring festival in El Majdal. She takes pride in recalling how she, on her own, would plow six dunums of their land at a time, and how she knew every last one of the edible and medicinal plants growing there.

She describes the exodus at length, as though it had just occurred yesterday: Before fleeing to Gaza, the family sought safe haven in the neighboring town of El Majdal (now Ashkelon), west of Beit Tima. As the Zionist militias closed in, they decided to go back to the village to store their harvest of grain for safekeeping. When they got there, there was no one left. "We found many of our neighbors dead, shot between the eyes, limbs cut off. I fetched my gold from the chicken pen, where I had hidden it. We buried twenty people that day."

You can tell from how she talks about her long and eventful life that everything since they fled has been a shadow, a long wait. If she is to talk about food, she will talk about food before the exile. Since then, her family has lived in the Deir el Belah refugee camp, and the UN-provided rations—flour, beans, sugar, salt, powdered milk—are, according to her, scarcely worth calling food. While Palestinians have adapted to this reality, creating innovative dishes with what ingredients are available, for Um Ibrahim, as for many elders, food—*real* food—is always in the past tense.

"I am telling you about how we would cook and eat in the past, but here everything is unwholesome. It is bad food. In the past, we ate very heartily and were very healthy."

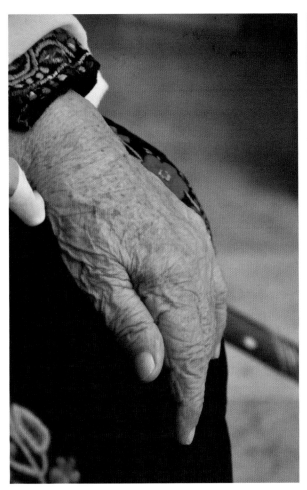

Bamia u Adas

Okra with Lentils

Serves 3–4

1 cup finely chopped onion
1 pound (approximately 450 grams) large okra, with each piece cut into
    four even pieces, or young, small okra, fresh or frozen
1 cup (200 grams) red lentils (or blanched fava beans or brown lentils)
1 teaspoon salt
¼ teaspoon black pepper
5 cups (1.2 liters) *Maraqa* (page 24), packaged broth, or water
4 cloves garlic
¼ teaspoon cumin
1 cup basil leaves (25 grams), coarsely chopped
Olive oil

Fry the onion in 3–4 tablespoons of olive oil on medium heat until golden. If you're using tough okra, add it now and sauté "until the okra overwhelms its mother" (this is a popular if somewhat obscure cooking phrase in Gaza, meaning "until it's wilted and soft"). If you're using tender okra, it seems you don't have to worry about its mother.

Add the lentils or blanched fava beans, salt and pepper, and liquid (water or broth). Mix well, then bring to a boil. Cover and reduce the heat. Simmer, partially covered.

When lentils are partially cooked but not completely soft, add the frozen okra (if you are using it). Continue simmering until the lentils are cooked through, stirring a few times. Adjust the amount of liquid if it appears too dry. The stew should have the consistency of porridge.

To finish, make a *taqliya*: Fry the garlic and cumin in 4 tablespoons of olive oil until it turns golden and fragrant. Add the chopped basil. Give it a quick stir to wilt it, then stir the entire *taqliya* into the pot along with any remaining oil. This crucial step, according to one of our informants, "makes the dish speak."

At this point, you may either serve the stew chunky or partially mix it with a whisk or immersion blender. Serve with lemon wedges, *Khubz Kmaj* (page 100), and *Filfil Mat'hoon* (page 28).

بامية وعدس

For Palestinians from the farming villages in the north of Gaza, this is a basic everyday dish; those from other regions hadn't even heard of it. This recipe was given to us by a woman from Hirbiya, just to the north of the present Gaza Strip. The village was attacked by war planes and its inhabitants driven from their homes in 1948, but the recipes live on.

The recipe makes use of the tough end-of-season okra not considered suitable for okra stew. Dr. Akram Saleh, whom we met at Gaza's Red Crescent Society Clinic, explained, "At the beginning of the season, okra was cooked in the normal way, but then, a hundred days into the season, we would start to eat okra with lentils."

In case your local market doesn't carry old, tough, late-season okra and you're not in a farming community with lots of late okra to consume, tender or even frozen baby okra works just fine.

Some cooks beat the finished stew with a wooden stirring tool called a *mufrak* until it is thick and smooth, and insist that it should be prepared with red lentils. Others say it should remain chunky and be made with brown lentils. Every single person who spoke to us about this dish did so with singular enthusiasm and passion, a tribute to this hearty, basic stew.

Nearly every family in the Gaza Strip has someone standing in line to fetch its food rations. Around the food distribution centers, donkey carts loiter around, for hire to haul home the heavy sacks marked with the names of donors: Japan, the European Union, USAID. Market tents spring up where many aid recipients sell part of their dry rations for cash to buy meat and vegetables.

In recent years, about 74 percent of the Gazan population has become food insecure or dependent on rations due to the destruction of Gaza's productive infrastructure and the closure of its borders. This means that more than a million people now rely on donor agencies for the bulk of their daily calories. The United Nations Relief and Works Agency (UNRWA) and the World Food Program (WFP) provide most of the staples: flour, sugar, salt, oil. What they provide is insufficient for health—lacking any fresh fruit, vegetables, or fresh meat—but is indispensable for survival.

Among the many consequences of this situation is a change in what people cook and eat. Rice, once a luxury, became extremely cheap for a time due to WFP distribution. Then, when the agency ceased to import it, it became prohibitively expensive again. Whereas Palestinian cooking once largely relied on healthful whole grains such as freekah, bulgur, and barley along with the healthy native olive oil, massive and long-term dependence on the white wheat flour and soy oil distributed by donor agencies has almost entirely eliminated these nutritious staples from the diet.

In January 2016, UNRWA announced that, after extensive consultation, it was changing its food baskets to improve nutrition among Gaza's abject poor, adding salt fish and more legumes. Several smaller NGOs are working to provide market vouchers or fresh vegetable baskets from local producers. All the same, poverty and relative plenty depend on the variable generosity of faraway donors.

Saliq u Adas

Chard and Lentil Stew

Serves 4–5

1 medium onion, chopped
13 ounces (360 grams) chard (one large bunch), trimmed of thick stems and finely chopped
1 cup (200 grams) red lentils, rinsed
6–8 cups (2 liters) water
1½ teaspoon dill seeds
¾ teaspoon salt
1 teaspoon dried red pepper flakes
5–7 garlic cloves
1 teaspoon ground cumin
Salt and pepper to taste
Olive oil

Fry the chopped onion in 3 tablespoons of olive oil on medium heat until golden brown. Add the chard and sauté it in batches until it is wilted. Stir in the lentils and water and cook until tender, about 40 minutes. In a mortar and pestle, grind the dill seed and red pepper flakes with salt, using a strong circular motion, until fragrant. Add the garlic and mash well. Stir this mixture directly into the stew and heat through. Remove from the heat and season with cumin and black pepper. Adjust the salt to taste. Garnish with lemon wedges.

سلق وعدس

Chard, now considered the new "supergreen," has been used extensively in southern Palestinian cuisine for centuries. This is a hearty and warming stew, perfect in autumn.

We met Dr. Akram Saleh by chance at the Red Crescent clinic in Gaza City where he works. He overheard us in the hallway talking about okra and leapt in to proffer his family's recipe, as well as a stunningly encyclopedic account of traditional farming practices. Originally from Jabaliya in the north of Gaza, Dr. Saleh is a passionate amateur historian and has collected extensive information about his family's lands since Ottoman times. Here is a small selection of what he told us:

> We had about 180 hectares [about 444 acres], spread between what is now Gaza and what is now the Israeli side, near the sea. We planted all kinds of fruit: peaches, apricots, apples, and pears. One hundred years ago, the famous citrus trees of Gaza did not exist; such trees require a lot of water. They were only introduced once people began to use well water for irrigation. Of course, now most of them have been uprooted by the Israelis.

> Besides fruit, people mostly grew wheat and barley—all rain-fed crops—and some okra, squash, tomatoes, and melons in the summer. Wheat was planted in October by a plowman specially designated for his good fortune. He said a prayer before planting, requesting that the wheat grow thick enough to feed both the people and the wild birds. By May the wheat was tall, and in June they harvested it. It was threshed and then ground between stones and stored in bins under the floors of the houses. The making of bread was such a revered art that there are poems about it.

> The vegetables—okra, eggplants, and tomatoes—were salted and sun-dried for winter use, or else they were pickled. Dairy products were also preserved…. Back then people lived only on what they grew in their fields and from the animals in their barns.

> But in these modern times—and I am not just talking about Gaza, but all over the world—the population has grown and crops are genetically altered to suffice for the needs of the growing population. In the past, tomatoes were left to grow on the ground, but now they are grown in greenhouses. A greenhouse of 1,000 meters must produce

100 tons of tomatoes just to cover expenses, because seeds and pesticides are very expensive.

Indeed, for all his interest in the land and in agricultural history, Dr. Saleh tells us that he and his brothers found themselves obliged to sell their family's land: taxes, the costs of irrigation, and the repeated destruction of crops made farming unviable. Now he just cultivates the stories.

Fogaiyya

Lemony Chard, Chickpea, and Rice Stew

Serves 5–6

1 lb (500 grams) lean stew beef or boneless lamb, cut into 1 inch (2½ centimeter) pieces

½ cup chickpeas (100 grams), soaked and precooked, or one 15 ounce can chickpeas, drained and rinsed

½ cup (100 grams) medium or short grain rice, rinsed

1 teaspoon salt, divided

13 ounces (360 grams) finely chopped chard, trimmed of thick stems

5 garlic cloves

2 tablespoon olive oil

½ cup (120 milliliters) freshly squeezed lemon juice

Prepare the meat according to the instructions in the *Maraqa* recipe (page 24), adding the soaked chickpeas along the way, if using. Strain out spices and set aside the broth, chickpeas, and meat.

Combine the chickpeas, the rice, and ½ teaspoon of the salt in a clean pot with 6 cups (1½ liters) of the broth and stew meat. Cook until the rice is tender, approximately 10 minutes. Add the chard, one handful at a time, stirring after each addition. Reduce heat to low and simmer until the stew thickens slightly, but is still somewhat soupy.

Mash the garlic in a mortar and pestle along with the remaining salt. In a separate pan, fry the garlic in olive oil until lightly golden. Stir this into the stew, deglazing the pan with a little of the liquid if necessary.

Finish by stirring the lemon juice into the *fogaiyya*. Pour the stew into individual bowls. Garnish with lemon slices and red pepper flakes. *Fogaiyya* can be eaten with a spoon or scooped up with *Khubz Kmaj* (page 100). It will thicken as it cools.

فقاعية

In the damp chill of Gaza's winters, rural people and their descendants crave the hearty, one-dish meals unique to the region, like *fogaiyya*. As meat is expensive, the *falaheen* often save the stock from stewing meat for festive dishes to use in everyday dishes like this one.

Ari' u Adas

Pumpkin and Lentil Stew

Serves 5–6

1 onion, chopped
6–7 cups (about 1½ kilograms) chopped pumpkin, butternut squash,
    kabocha squash, or other orange gourd, cut into bite-size pieces
Salt and black pepper to taste
1 cup (200 grams) red lentils, rinsed
6 cups (1.5 liters) broth, or water
¾ teaspoon cumin
½ teaspoon dried red pepper flakes
Juice of one lemon
5 cloves garlic
Olive oil

In a large pot, sauté the chopped onion on medium heat in 2 tablespoons of olive oil until it turns golden. Add the chopped squash and stir it to heat through. Season with salt and black pepper (about ½ teaspoon each). Add the lentils and broth or water and bring to a boil.

Lower the heat and simmer, partially covered, for about 35 minutes or until the lentils are falling apart and the squash is tender. Mix well with a wooden spoon or whisk, then stir in the cumin, dried red pepper flakes, and lemon juice. Adjust the salt and transfer to a serving dish.

Crush the garlic with the remaining salt in a mortar and pestle. In a separate pan, fry the garlic in 3 tablespoons of olive oil on medium heat until it turns lightly golden. Drizzle the garlic and oil onto the stew.

Garnish with a sprinkle of red pepper flakes. Serve with warm *Khubz Kmaj* (page 100), or top with toasted pieces of bread.

قرع وعدس

This is an old-time rural favorite that makes use of the pumpkin-like gourds that grow in the farming villages of the Gaza district. It should be thick enough to be scooped up with warm bread, though if you add a few more cups of liquid the same recipe also makes a splendid soup.

You will have to add more or less salt depending on the sweetness of the squash you use. Add it gradually, tasting as you go.

Adas wi Riqaq

Lentil Soup with Dumplings

Serves 4–5

For the dumplings
2 cups (240 grams) all-purpose flour
½ teaspoon salt
2 tablespoons ghee, softened butter, or olive oil
1 egg

For the stew
1 onion, chopped
6–8 cups (about 2 liters) broth or water
1 cup (200 grams) red lentils, rinsed
1½ teaspoons cumin
1½ teaspoons salt
½ teaspoon black pepper
5 cloves garlic
¼ teaspoon red pepper flakes
Olive oil, as needed

Mix the dumpling ingredients and knead well. Your dough should be elastic but not sticky; add a tiny amount of water if necessary to reach this consistency. Divide the dough into two portions. Cover it and set it aside to rest for 20 minutes while you proceed with the rest of the recipe.

Brown the chopped onion in 3 tablespoons of olive oil on medium heat. Add the broth or water, lentils, cumin, salt, and black pepper. Cook until the lentils are soft and falling apart, about 35 to 40 minutes. Puree the mixture until smooth in a blender and return to the pot.

Roll out each ball of dumpling dough to a log approximately ¼ inch (just under 1 centimeter) wide, sprinkling with a little flour to help the dough spread easily. Using a serrated knife, pastry cutter, or pizza wheel, cut across to form small dumplings. Sprinkle these with flour. Gently stir the dumplings into the lentil stew. They will cook very quickly, rising to float when they are done.

In a separate pan, make the *taqliya*: fry garlic and red pepper flakes in 4 tablespoons of olive oil until golden. Deglaze pan with some of the stew, then stir this back in.

Serve with lemon wedges and olives.

عدس ورقاق

Also known as *rushta* (a Persian name for pasta or noodles), this lentil stew was common in towns and villages in the northern Gaza district, such as Beit Jirja, Yaffa, and El Jora.

It is often served at funerals, we were told, in honor of the deceased.

Fattit Hummus

Hummus Casserole

Serves 8–10

¼ pound (120 grams) lean ground beef or lamb
1 small onion, chopped
¼ teaspoon salt
¼ teaspoon black pepper
¼ teaspoon ground cardamom
½ teaspoon ground allspice
⅛ teaspoon ground nutmeg
2–3 cups (100–200 grams) toasted *Khubz Kmaj* (page 100), torn into pieces
One quantity *Hummus Bil T'heena* (page 85), along with the reserved chickpea cooking liquid
½ cup (140 grams) yogurt
1 tablespoon parsley, finely chopped
2 tablespoon pine nuts
4 tablespoon olive oil
Ground red pepper and cumin, for garnish
A handful of cooked chickpeas, for garnish
1 quantity *Daggit Toma u Lamoon* (page 28)

Sauté the onion in the olive oil on medium heat until golden, then add the ground meat and cook until browned, approximately 8 to 10 minutes. Season with the spices. Set aside.

Briefly soak the toasted pieces of bread in the reserved chickpea cooking liquid for a few seconds. Spoon them out, then stir the soaked bread into the prepared *hummus*. Make a layer of this mixture on a serving platter, then spread the fried meat mixture over it, leaving a border around the edges.

Fry the pine nuts in olive oil on low heat until golden, stirring continuously for about one minute and taking care not to burn them: They brown very quickly! Drizzle them, along with their residual frying oil, over the layer of meat. Garnish the remaining dish along the borders with dollops of yogurt topped with a sprinkling of parsley, alternating with small mounds of the reserved whole chickpeas. Pour the hot garlic and lemon dressing in between the dollops. Finish by sprinkling red pepper and cumin in lines or any other pattern over the casserole.

Variation
For a more affordable vegetarian version, omit the layer of meat. Place dollops of yogurt directly on the hummus and bread mixture, then garnish as above.

This dish takes the standard *Hummus Bil T'heena* recipe (page 85) a step further, making a full meal out of it. It differs from the Lebanese dish of the same name in that the chickpeas are not left whole. Precooked chickpeas may be used instead of dried ones, though the resulting texture is never as good.

VEGETABLE STEWS

Most of the recipes in this chapter fall into the category of *tabeekh*: rich meat and vegetable stews served hot, usually over rice or else with Arabic bread. Meat imparts flavor but, depending on the economic situation of the family, is often used in very small quantities. This is home cooking *par excellence*. The basic techniques—a spiced meat broth, vegetables often pan-fried and then stewed, a *taqliya* of fried garlic or onion stirred in at the end—date back to medieval times and reliably produce a hearty, satisfying meal.

Khobeiza

Mallow Stew with Dumplings

Serves 3–4

½ teaspoon dill seed
1 teaspoon red pepper flakes
¾ teaspoon salt
3 cups (750 milliliters) *Maraqa* (page 24)
2 pounds (approximately 1 kilogram) *khobeiza* or other mild greens, chopped
1 cup (120 grams) flour
One egg
1 tablespoon fresh dill, finely chopped
1 medium onion, finely chopped
4 tablespoons olive oil
1 tablespoon fresh cilantro, chopped

In a mortar and pestle, grind the dill seeds, red pepper flakes, and ½ teaspoon of salt until fragrant. As Laila's grandmother used to say, "Grind it like you mean it." Set aside.

Bring the broth to a boil in a medium-sized pot. Add the ground spices, lower the heat, and simmer for 2 minutes. Stir in the greens, one handful at a time. Allow the greens to simmer until they soften. This will only take a few minutes.

Mix the flour with the egg, remaining salt, and fresh dill until a dense dough forms. You can pinch bits off this dough and drop them into the simmering greens, or roll out the dough (adding flour as needed) and cut it into small pieces, then add these to the stew. You may alternately use a sieve to grate the dough over the stew. The dumplings will firm up quickly and rise to the surface when they are done. Remove from the heat.

In a separate pan, fry the onions in olive oil over medium heat until they turn deeply golden. Add the chopped fresh cilantro to the onions and allow it to wilt, then pour (including the oil) into the *khobeiza*, deglazing the frying pan with a little of the stew. Serve hot with fresh hot green chiles and *Khubz Kmaj* (page 100).

Khobeiza, or common mallow, grows wild all over Palestine (and in many other countries, too). Any mildly flavored green (chard, beet leaves, and so on) may be substituted, though the effect will not be quite the same. For a quick preparation, 1/3 cup instant couscous or small pasta can be used instead of the dumplings, and store-bought broth instead of the *Maraqa*.

Tabeekh Sabanikh

Spinach Stew

Serves 4–5

1 pound boneless lamb cut into 1 inch (2½ centimeters) pieces
1 medium onion, chopped
2 pounds (1 kilogram) spinach, washed well and trimmed of stalks
½ cup (100 grams) dried chickpeas, soaked and precooked, or one
    15-ounce (425 gram) can, washed and drained
6–7 cloves garlic
1 teaspoon salt
Olive oil

Prepare the lamb according to the instructions in the *Maraqa* recipe (page 24), browning the meat before you boil it. Reserve meat and broth.

Coarsely chop the spinach. Brown the onion in 2 tablespoons of olive oil on medium heat until golden. Stir in the chopped spinach, one handful at a time, and sauté until just wilted.

Add 4 to 5 cups of the strained broth, the reserved meat, the chickpeas, and 1/2 teaspoon of salt to the spinach and bring to a boil. Cook on medium heat for about 10 to 15 minutes.

Meanwhile, crush the garlic in a mortar and pestle with the remaining salt. Once the stew has finished cooking, stir in the crushed raw garlic and mix well. Serve with lemon wedges and *Ruz Imfalfal* (page 206).

طبيخ سبانخ

When not used as a stuffing in savory pies, spinach is often chopped and stewed with chickpeas and lamb in this comforting wintertime stew. You can also substitute good-quality frozen chopped spinach out of season.

Um Rami

Her house next to Beach Camp, in the outskirts of Gaza City, is humid and spare; she has sold much of the furniture to make ends meet. But Um Rami (Nazmiya Mustafa) herself lights the place up. Bright-eyed and enthusiastic, she hustles us into her kitchen, where she is cooking *mulukhiyya*, a comforting stew made of corchorus leaves that is served in households from Egypt to Lebanon.

Both Um Rami's family and her husband's came from Beit Jirja, a village that used to lie just north of present-day Gaza. No trace of it remains. Her mother-in-law, she says, always talked about how they were forced to leave the village, fleeing to Gaza on foot and then living for years in tents and basic UN shelters before finally being able to buy a small house of their own next to the camp.

Um Rami's parents went to the Gulf looking for work not long after the *hijra* (the mass flight from historic Palestine in 1948); she herself was born in Saudi Arabia. She returned to Gaza to marry when she was eighteen and has been there ever since, except for one memorable visit to her father:

> I took him some *khobeiza* wrapped in newspaper. The first thing I did when I got there was cook this dish for him. He told me, "This is the best gift ever" because the poor thing hadn't eaten it for so long. It was so simple, just a weed, but he really appreciated it—it tasted like home.

Um Rami herself learned to cook all the Gazan dishes from her mother-in-law, whom she misses sorely. The assault against Gaza in 2009 was more than the elderly woman could take—she died months afterward from shock. Um Rami's husband followed suit shortly thereafter: "His health was good—he was just so tired, mentally, of everything."

Um Rami, now alone, fends for herself, her three children, and their two much-coddled cats ("I love cats. I don't think I could live without them.") as best she can. She is a cunning seamstress and takes in sewing from wealthy clients in Gaza City as well as from her neighbors in the camp. But money is tight, and the UNRWA rations she is entitled to as a refugee do not cover the family's basic needs for flour and oil. As for things that must be bought with cash:

> I used to buy several kilos of fresh fruit and vegetables a week, but now it's much less; they're so expensive…. In any case, we all just sort of lost our appetites after the last war. I cook the same things but in smaller proportions, and still there are leftovers.

She points to the bubbling pot of *mulukhiyya*—made with inexpensive chicken wings—and shrugs, her eyes still bright.

Mulukhiyya

Corchorus Stew

Serves 4–6

14 ounces (400 grams) frozen minced *mulukhiyya* or fresh *mulukhiyya* leaves

One whole 3 pound (1½ kilogram) chicken or one 3 pound (1½ kilogram) chicken or rabbit, cut into parts

10 garlic cloves

3–4 hot green chile peppers, finely chopped, seeds removed

2 teaspoons freshly ground coriander seeds

2 tablespoons olive oil or ghee

Salt

If using frozen *mulukhiyya*, place packets in a bowl of warm water until nearly defrosted.

Prepare the chicken or rabbit according to the instructions in the *Maraqa* recipe (page 24). If using a whole chicken, truss it before boiling. After boiling, lift the meat gently from the broth and set it aside in a baking pan. Reserve 6 cups (1.5 liters) of broth and set aside.

Meanwhile, mash the garlic, a few cloves at a time, with ½ teaspoon of salt in a mortar and pestle. Set aside.

Put the frozen *mulukhiyya* in a pot on medium heat. Gradually add the hot broth, 1 cup at a time, whisking well after each addition. (If using fresh *mulukhiyya*, do this in reverse: Add one ladleful of freshly minced leaves at a time to the boiling broth until fully incorporated.) Stir until the *mulukhiyya* is well incorporated and the soup has come to a boil. This will only take about 2 minutes. Add the finely minced chiles. Bring to a rolling boil and cook for approximately 4 to 5 minutes, removing any white or foamy scum that rises to the surface.

Brush the reserved chicken or rabbit with some lemon juice and olive oil and place it briefly under a broiler, just until it browns nicely.

In a separate frying pan, make the *taqliya*: Fry the crushed garlic in olive oil or ghee until it turns golden, then add the coriander and stir briefly until fragrant. Pour into the *mulukhiyya*, deglazing the frying pan with a little of the soup.

Adjust the salt and seasoning as necessary. Serve alongside the chicken or rabbit with *Ruz Imfalfal* (page 206), lemon wedges, whole chiles, *Khubz Kmaj* (page 100), and *Dagga* (page 50).

ملوخية

This soupy stew is a much-beloved comfort food all over the Levant as well as in Egypt and part of Cyprus, often to the perplexity of those who did not grow up with it. You either love it or you don't, and those who do love it have—over generations—gone to great lengths to smuggle fresh *mulukhiyya* leaves into the United States, leaving not a few customs officers scratching their heads.

Mulukhiyya is made with the mucilaginous leaves of the highly nutritious *Corchorus olitorius*, from which jute fiber is derived. Legend has it that *mulukhiyya* was a favorite among pre-Exodus Jews in Egypt, and it is sometimes referred to as "Jew's mallow" due to a reference to it in the Book of Job.

Frozen minced *mulukhiyya* can be found in almost all Middle Eastern markets, but if you are lucky enough to have access to fresh leaves, wash them well and mince them finely with a few hot green chiles, then proceed with the recipe. The key to a stellar *mulukhiyya* is in the color: It should be a bright, vivid green. Boil it too long and the leaves will turn black and acrid. Also, make sure to remove any scum that surfaces during the cooking process—this will result in a less gooey soup!

The broth for *mulukhiyya* can be made with any meat—chicken, beef, rabbit—in pieces or whole. To economize, many households in Gaza these days use chicken wings or necks. In general, the richer the broth, the better. Traditionally in Palestine, it is made using an entire chicken, which is stuffed and trussed, boiled to extract the broth, then brushed with lemon juice and olive oil and browned briefly in the oven. It is then served alongside the *mulukhiyya* and white rice. In Gaza, as a rule, it is also served with fresh hot green chile peppers and *Dagga* (page 50).

Tabeekh Zahra

Cauliflower Stew

Serves 4–5

1 pound (500 grams) stew beef or lamb, chopped into 1 inch (2½ centimeters) pieces
1 whole medium head of cauliflower, cut into florets
1 teaspoon cumin
5 very ripe tomatoes, in season, or 3–4 tablespoons tomato paste
½ cup (100 grams) dried chickpeas, presoaked and cooked, or one 15-ounce (425 gram) can, washed and drained
1 medium onion, chopped
5 cloves garlic
Salt
Olive oil

Prepare the meat according to the instructions in the *Maraqa* recipe (page 24), browning the meat before you boil it. Reserve the broth and meat.

In a large pan, fry the cauliflower florets in ½ cup (118 milliliters) of oil until they are golden brown on all sides. Season with the salt, pepper, and ½ teaspoon of the cumin. Alternately, you can drizzle the florets with a little oil and roast them in a 400°F (200°C) oven on a greased baking pan until they are golden and tender, for about 25 to 30 minutes. Season as above, then set aside.

If you are using fresh tomatoes, grate them or liquefy them in a blender, then whisk or strain them through a sieve to discard the excess pulp. In a large, clean pot, sauté the onion in 2 tablespoons of olive oil on medium heat until it caramelizes. Add the liquefied or grated tomatoes or the tomato paste. Stir until the color turns slightly orange, about 2 to 3 minutes.

If you are using fresh tomatoes, add 2 cups of the strained broth along with the reserved meat and the chickpeas. If using tomato paste, add 5 cups of the broth. Bring to a boil, then gently stir in the fried or roasted cauliflower and allow it to heat through.

Finish off with the *taqliya*: In a mortar and pestle, crush the garlic with ½ teaspoon salt. Fry it in 2 tablespoons of olive oil or ghee until slightly golden. Just before the garlic begins to brown, add the remaining ½ teaspoon of cumin. When it is fragrant, pour this mixture into the stew and stir, deglazing the frying pan with some of the stew.

Adjust the seasonings and serve hot, with lemon wedges, *Ruz Imfalfal* (page 206), and *Salata Khadra Mafrooma* (page 54).

Variation: Zahra Bil T'hina (Tahina Cauliflower Stew)
Follow the recipe as above, omitting the tomatoes or tomato paste. When the stew is finished, dilute Salsit T'heena *(page 30) in 2 cups of the broth, then stir this back into finished stew and bring it to a boil. Stir in 1 tablespoon of pomegranate molasses.*

طبيخ زهرة

A hearty and delicious way to prepare cauliflower, which is abundant in winter and—like many of its cruciferous cousins—keeps for a long time without spoiling.

Tabeekh Fool Akhdar

Green Fava Bean Stew

Serves 4–5

1 pound (500 grams) lean stew beef or boneless lamb, in 1 inch (2½
 centimeters) pieces
2 pounds (approximately 1 kilogram) tender green fava bean pods
1 teaspoon salt
5–6 cloves garlic
½ packed cup (10 grams) chopped fresh cilantro
Olive oil

Prepare the meat according to the instructions in the *Maraqa* recipe
(page 24), browning the meat before you boil it. Reserve broth and meat.

Trim the bean pods by pulling off the thick strings on either side of
the seams. If the pods have thicker, drier skins, use only the beans and
discard the pods. Chop tender pods into ½ inch (1¼ centimeters) pieces,
then sauté in about ¼ cup (60 milliliters) of olive oil on medium heat for
about 5 minutes, until slightly softened and charred.

Add the strained broth and reserved meat to the sautéed bean pods and
bring to a boil. Reduce the heat and cook for 15 to 20 minutes.

Meanwhile, make the *taqliya*: Crush the garlic along with the salt in a
mortar and pestle. Fry in 2 to 3 tablespoons of olive oil on medium heat
until golden, then add the cilantro and allow it to wilt. Add this to the
bean stew, deglazing the frying pan with a little broth, and stir. Serve
with *Ruz Imfalfal* (page 206), plain yogurt, and freshly cracked black
pepper.

طبيخ فول أخضر

Tender young fava beans may be
cooked—pods and all—in this simple
but sublime stew. In the eastern and
northern parts of Palestine, sour yogurt (full-cream yogurt left out overnight) is whisked in with the broth; in
Gaza, it is left as-is. This stew works
best with very tender pods with thin
skins.

Rural areas of Palestine make broad and original use of wild greens, herbs, and root vegetables in humble but satisfying stews like *hamasees*, *khobeiza*, or *rijliya*. Increasingly, though, as Palestinians become separated from one another and from their historic lands, the greens and herbs they have picked for centuries are becoming inaccessible: the best *zaatar*, for example, grows on the hills of the West Bank as well as elsewhere in historic Palestine (modern-day Israel), off-limits to the Palestinians of Gaza due to an Israeli-imposed travel ban. It is even off-limits to Palestinians of the West Bank and Israel: In 1977, Israeli law declared *zaatar*—that ultimate symbol of Palestinian identity—a "protected species," claiming the fast-growing perennial was on the verge of extinction. This law was extended to the West Bank by military order in 2007, where plants have been confiscated by Israeli forces at checkpoints. Foragers are subject to hefty fines.

Lamya Hussain, founder of the grassroots initiative Refutrees, writes in her doctoral dissertation, "By mitigating *baladi* or indigenous versions of *zaatar* while simultaneously producing export-grade versions, Israeli settler-colonialism is very clear in how it seeks to disconnect and disjoint Palestinians from their heritage, make profit where possible, and reinvent and normalize traditions and cultures to its advantage."

Similar laws ban the collection of *akub* or Gundelia thistles, popular in the Galilee, as documented by Israeli journalist Ronit Vered in her excellent 2008 *Haaretz* article "Forbidden Fruit": "To families that have picked these plants from ancient times and learned from their ancestors that land must be used carefully, with consideration for the yield of future years, this law is considered almost anti-Arab."

Fortunately, the edible weeds of Palestine are nearly as tenacious as its people: they crop up everywhere, under the most uncongenial circumstances, their bright flowers and tart flavors mocking all efforts to eradicate them.

Rijliya/Tabeekh Baqla

Purslane Stew

Serves 3–4

6 cloves garlic

1½ teaspoons salt

2 pounds (approximately 1 kilogram) purslane, trimmed of thick stems and chopped

1 large onion, chopped

3–4 tomatoes, finely chopped

½ cup dried chickpeas, soaked and precooked, or one 15-ounce (425 gram) can

½ packed cup (10 grams) fresh cilantro, chopped

½ teaspoon red pepper flakes

Olive oil

In a mortar and pestle, crush the garlic with ½ teaspoon of salt.

Chop the purslane, then set it aside to drain off the excess mucilage on a kitchen towel.

Sauté the chopped onion in 3 tablespoon olive oil until golden. Gradually add the purslane in small batches and cook it until just wilted. Stir in the crushed garlic, tomatoes, and chickpeas and simmer for 10 minutes. Stir in the cilantro, remaining salt, and red pepper flakes. Adjust to taste. Serve with *Khubz Kmaj* (page 100) and olives.

Variation

Prepare as directed above, but add Maraqa *(page 24) made with 1 pound (500 grams) of stew beef, as well as the meat itself.*

رجلية/طبيخ بقلة

Rijla, or *baqla*—purslane in English—is a small-leafed annual succulent found growing through sidewalks and in abandoned lots pretty much all over the world. Though it may go largely unnoticed, it is a favorite of the *falaheen* from the Gaza district. Many remember eating purslane during the Palestinian exodus: "We would find it growing between the bushes where we hid, and for a long while it was all we survived on," explains Um Ibrahim.

Considered a weed by most, purslane is one of the most highly nutritious wild greens available, rich in dietary minerals and vitamins and with more plant-based omega-3 fatty acids than any other leafy vegetable. It also tastes great.

When Israel completed its disengagement from Gaza in 2005, it dismantled all its settlements and military infrastructure within the territory but, much to the detriment of its residents, retained control over borders and commerce, airspace, maritime access, taxation, and population registry. It did, however, return the large swathes of rich agricultural land it had colonized inside the Strip (some 30 percent of the total surface area) to the Palestinians of Gaza.

These lands fell to the then-ruling Fatah party to administer. There was much fantastical talk of turning Gaza into a tourist haven and these lands into hotel complexes, but in the end, they were largely neglected due to a combination of Israeli raids, hermetic border closures, governmental inefficiency, and infighting between rival parties.

No longer. Renamed *al-Muharrarrat*, or the "Liberated Lands," these areas have been key in the Hamas-led government's ambitious ten-year plan to reinvent Gazan agriculture. The main aim of the plan, minister of agriculture Muhammad Agha explained in 2010, has been to conserve water and natural resources and work towards relative food security.

A range of pilot projects has been established, mostly in the fertile southwest area of the Strip where the Gush Qatif settlement bloc used to be. They often represent a return to old agricultural ways, before water-intensive cash crops were introduced. There are organic composting facilities, which make use of wastewater and vegetable plant remains; fish, chicken, and dairy farms; and rows upon rows of olive saplings, date palms, and fruit trees of every kind.

One of the pilot initiatives is a mushroom cultivation facility. It prepares mushroom-growing baskets for distribution to local women, who tend them and sell the product, providing income for their families and much-needed nutrition for consumers. Why mushrooms? The turnaround is quick and the space required is minimal; they can be cultivated in "agriculturally marginal" areas. They also need very little water, essential in a place where water salinity and overdrilling are major problems.

Some of the land is rented out at a nominal cost to charities, which then run agricultural projects of their own. Besides agricultural ventures, there are also a media-production village, a petting zoo, and an amusement park. In all, the projects employ hundreds of people. But they are not without critics; products from government farms sometimes drive market prices down, to the detriment of private farmers. Others argue that Hamas may be investing too much in such projects while raising taxes on people already struck by economic sanctions.

Aysh il Ghurab bil Dajaj

Oyster Mushrooms with Chicken

Serves 3–4

1 pound (450 grams) turkey or chicken breast
Juice of one lemon
1 tablespoon flour
16 ounces (500 grams) oyster mushrooms
1 medium onion, chopped
5 cloves garlic, crushed
½ teaspoon red pepper flakes
1 bunch (approximately 60 grams) parsley or dill, chopped
1 teaspoon salt
½ teaspoon black pepper
½ teaspoon allspice
¼ teaspoon cardamom
¼ teaspoon nutmeg
Olive oil

Cut the poultry into small pieces. Rub it with the lemon juice, flour, and ¼ teaspoon of salt. Rinse, strain, and pat it dry.

Meanwhile, clean the mushrooms carefully using a damp paper towel. In a skillet, heat 4 tablespoons of oil and sauté the mushrooms until they are slightly golden. The mushrooms may release moisture and then reabsorb it.

Add the chopped onions and garlic and sauté until they have browned. Lower the heat, then stir in the parsley, red pepper flakes, ¼ teaspoon of the allspice, ¼ teaspoon of salt, and ¼ teaspoon freshly cracked black pepper (or to taste). Set this aside.

Brown the poultry in 3 tablespoons of olive oil and season it with the remaining spices and salt. Stir in the mushroom mixture. Cook for 5 more minutes. Serve with *Ruz Imfalfal* (page 206) or *Khubz Kmaj* (page 100).

عيش الغراب بالدجاج

The following two recipes are not traditional, but have been introduced by NGOs and agricultural unions in order to teach families what to do with the oyster mushrooms now being cultivated as an agricultural supplement. Mushrooms were completely unknown in Gaza before these initiatives, but they are growing in popularity. The combination of tastes in these dishes is recognizably Gazan.

Aysh il Ghurab bil Salsa

Oyster Mushroom Stew

Serves 2–3

16 ounces (500 grams) oyster mushrooms
Juice of one lemon
4 cups (1 liter) water
¼ cup olive oil
1 medium onion, finely chopped
3 cloves garlic, crushed
1 green chile pepper, finely chopped
2 tablespoons tomato paste
3 tomatoes, finely chopped or grated or liquefied and strained
2 tablespoons chopped parsley or dill
Salt and black pepper to taste

Clean the mushrooms carefully using a damp paper towel, then slice or chop them coarsely.

Combine the water and lemon juice in a saucepan. Bring to a boil, then add the mushrooms and cook for 5 minutes. Strain, discarding the water.

Meanwhile, sauté the chopped onions and garlic in olive oil until they are deeply golden. Stir in the pepper, tomato paste, and chopped tomatoes. Reduce the heat. Simmer for 10 minutes, partially covered to prevent splattering. Add the mushrooms and season with salt and black pepper.

Bring this mixture to a boil, then stir in 1 tablespoon of the parsley and remove the pot from the heat.

Garnish with remaining chopped parsley and thinly sliced lemon wedges.

عيش الغراب بالصلصة

An incredibly quick and absolutely delicious dish.

Tabeekh Batata u Lamoon

Lemony Potato Stew

Serves 4–5

1 pound (approximately 500 grams) boneless stew beef, cut into 1 inch (2½ centimeters) pieces
3 pounds (approximately 1½ kilograms) potatoes, peeled and cut into 1 inch (2.5 centimeters) pieces
6–7 cloves garlic
½ cup (120 milliliters) fresh lemon juice
1 packed cup (approximately 25 grams) chopped parsley
Salt and pepper to taste
Olive oil

Prepare the meat according to the instructions in the *Maraqa* recipe (page 24), browning it in a little oil first before proceeding. Strain the broth and set it aside, reserving both broth and meat.

Pan-fry or oven-roast the potatoes in ¼ cup (60 milliliters) of olive oil on medium-high heat until golden. Transfer to a medium-sized pot, then add 4 to 5 cups of strained broth, along with the reserved meat.

Crush the garlic in a mortar and pestle with ½ teaspoon of salt, then fry it in 2 tablespoons of olive oil until it turns golden. Add this to the stew, deglazing the pan with some broth.

To thicken the stew, scoop about 1½ cup of potatoes out of the pot and mash them with a fork. Return the potatoes to the pot and mix well, then bring to a boil again.

Stir in the parsley and lemon juice and remove from the heat. Season with the remaining salt and pepper to taste.

Serve with *Ruz Imfalfal* (page 206), olives, and pickled lemons.

طبيخ بطاطا وليمون

This tart stew is also sometimes referred to as *imqalqasa*, because of the way the potatoes imitate the wild winter vegetable *qulqas*, or taro root, which can be prepared in the same manner, but makes a thicker stew.

Tabeekh Bamia

Okra Stew

Serves 5–6

3 pounds (about 1.4 kilogram) lamb shank (with bone) cut into 3–4 pieces each

2 pounds (900 grams) young fresh okra or frozen baby okra

6–7 cloves garlic

1 teaspoon salt

4 tablespoons tomato paste or 6–7 ripe tomatoes, grated or liquefied in a blender and strained of excess pulp

¼ cup fresh basil, coarsely chopped or torn

1 tablespoon rendered lamb tail fat, olive oil, or ghee

Juice of two lemons

Freshly cracked black pepper

2–3 hot green chiles

Prepare the lamb shanks according to the instructions in the *Maraqa* recipe (page 24), making sure to brown the shanks first before proceeding to make the broth.

Wash and dry the okra well, then trim the stem caps into a cone shape, making sure not to release any of the mucilage from inside the pods.

With a mortar and pestle, crush the garlic with ½ teaspoon salt. Set aside.

In a wide skillet or pot, sauté the okra in ¼ cup (60 milliliters) of olive oil for 5 to 7 minutes, until it is slightly charred on the outside. If you are using tomato paste, add it to the okra and cook a few minutes to heat through and develop flavor. Add about 6 cups (1½ liters) of strained broth, plus the reserved lamb meat and remaining salt. If you are using strained liquefied tomatoes instead of tomato paste, reduce the amount of broth by half.

Simmer on medium heat for about 15 minutes on medium heat, or until the okra is tender to the bite.

In a separate pan, fry the crushed garlic in 1 to 2 tablespoons of lamb fat, ghee, or olive oil until it turns golden, then add the basil and stir for just a few seconds until it is barely wilted. Add this garlic-basil *taqliya* to the stew, deglazing the pan with some broth. Finish by adding the juice of two lemons to the stew.

In Gaza, *bamia* is traditionally eaten with *Khubz Kmaj* (page 100), but it may also be served with rice. Accompany with hot green peppers, *Dagga* (page 50), and freshly cracked black pepper.

طبيخ بامية

For this dish, tender young okra pods are best, since the okra is cooked whole, never chopped. Most Middle Eastern grocers carry frozen baby okra. Traditionally, a small piece of *li-yyeh*, the highly prized tail fat of the Asian lamb, is added to give this stew its unique flavor. If it is unavailable, use a teaspoon of ghee in the *taqliya* instead. Using a bony cut of meat will result in a richer broth, but feel free to substitute boneless lamb instead.

Tabeekh Looz Akhdar

Green Almond Stew

Serves 4–5

3 pounds (about 1.4 kilogram) lamb shank (with bone) cut into 3–4 pieces each, or 1 pound (450 grams) boneless lamb pieces

2 pounds (900 grams) tender green almonds (check ethnic grocers in spring), cut into thirds

6 cloves garlic

1 teaspoon salt

1 tablespoon rendered lamb tail fat, olive oil, or ghee

1 packed cup basil, coarsely chopped

Juice of one lemon

Freshly cracked black pepper

2–3 hot green chile peppers

Prepare the lamb shanks or lamb cubes according to the instructions in the *Maraqa* recipe (page 24), making sure to brown them in some oil before proceeding to add the water and make the broth.

In a wide skillet or pot, sauté the almonds in ¼ cup (60 milliliters) olive oil for 5 to 7 minutes, until they are slightly charred. Add about 6 cups (1½ liters) of strained broth, plus the reserved lamb meat and ½ tsp of the salt.

Cook for about 15 minutes on medium heat.

In a mortar and pestle, crush the garlic with the remaining salt. In a separate pan, fry the garlic in 1–2 tablespoon lamb fat, ghee, or olive oil until golden, then add the basil and stir for just a few seconds until it is wilted. Add this garlic-basil *taqliya* to the stew, deglazing the pan with some broth. Finish by adding the lemon juice to the stew.

Serve with *Khubz Kmaj* (page 100), *Ruz Imfalfal* (page 206), and salad, along with hot green chile peppers and freshly cracked black pepper.

طبيخ لوز أخضر

Asma Abu Daff gave this recipe to Laila, describing it as a classic but little-known springtime dish to be made when okra is not in season. It's not clear what green almonds have to do with okra, but Abu Daff says that's the idea.

This stew may also be made with a yogurt base: simply reduce the quantity of broth by two-thirds and compensate by whisking in strained yogurt that has been left out over-night to sour slightly, along with two tablespoons of flour.

Back when most Palestinians were farmers, meat was an expensive luxury, as it has now become again in Gaza. As several of the older Palestinians we met told us, people ordinarily ate meat only for festive occasions—holidays and birth celebrations—when the wealthy slaughtered sheep and distributed thirds to neighbors and to the needy.

Eating meat daily was almost unthinkable. Instead, the prized tail fat was rendered, preserved with salt, and stored in clay jugs. This fat, called *liyyeh*, was then used sparingly throughout the year for making *taqliya*, the fried garlic or onion so often used to finish stews.

This imparted the flavor of lamb to the dish even when there was no meat to be had. *Samneh baladiya*, or rendered goat-milk butter, was also sometimes employed for the same purpose. These fats are now seldom used, but their taste is remembered with nostalgia.

Tabeekh Ri'abi

Calabash Stew

Serves 5-6

1 pound (approximately 500 grams) beef or lamb, cut into 1 inch (2½ centimeter) pieces
6–7 cloves garlic
1 teaspoon salt
1 medium onion, chopped
2 pounds (1 kilogram) calabash squash, chopped into 1 inch (2 1/2 centimeter) pieces
4 tablespoons tomato paste or 6–7 liquefied ripe tomatoes, strained of excess pulp
2 tablespoons dried mint
Olive oil or ghee

Prepare the meat according to the instructions in the *Maraqa* recipe (page 24), browning the meat first. Reserve both broth and meat.

Crush the garlic in a mortar and pestle with ½ teaspoon salt and set aside.

Sauté the onion in 2 tablespoons of olive oil, then add the squash, stewed meat, remaining salt, tomato paste, and approximately 6 cups (1½ liters) of reserved broth. If you are using liquefied tomatoes, reduce the quantity of broth by half. Cook for 10 to 15 minutes on medium heat, or until the squash is tender but not falling apart.

In a separate pan, fry the crushed garlic in 2 tablespoons of olive oil or ghee until it turns golden. Add the garlic and remaining oil to the stew, deglazing the pan with some broth.

Rub the dried mint between your fingers to extract the flavor, then stir it into the finished stew. Serve with *Ruz Imfalfal* (page 206), olives, and pickled lemons.

طبيخ رقابي

This buttery, nutty squash—called "the necky one" in Arabic—was reportedly a favorite of the prophet Muhammad (PBUH) and is also mentioned in both the Quran and the Bible. Its vine is thought to have provided the prophet Jonah with shade and to have healed his wounds after the whale incident.

Tabeekh Bazayla

Pea and Carrot Stew

Serves 5–6

1 pound (approximately 500 grams) beef or lamb, cut into 1 inch (2½ centimeter) pieces

6–7 cloves garlic

1 teaspoon salt

1 medium onion, chopped

2 pounds (900 grams) shelled or frozen peas

3 medium-sized carrots, peeled and diced

4 tablespoons tomato paste or 6–7 liquefied ripe tomatoes, strained of excess pulp

Olive oil or ghee

Prepare the meat according to the instructions in the *Maraqa* recipe (page 24), browning the meat first. Reserve both broth and meat.

Crush the garlic in a mortar and pestle with ½ teaspoon salt and set aside.

Sauté the onion in 2 tablespoons of olive oil, then add the stewed meat, peas, carrots, remaining salt, tomato paste, and approximately 6 cups (1½ liters) of reserved broth. If using liquefied tomatoes, reduce the quantity of broth by half. Cook for 10 to 15 minutes on medium heat, or until the carrots are tender.

In a separate pan, fry the crushed garlic in 2 tablespoons of olive oil or ghee until it turns golden. Add the garlic and remaining oil to the stew, deglazing the pan with some broth.

Serve with *Ruz Imfalfal* (page 206), olives, and freshly cracked black pepper.

Variations: Tabeekh Fasuliya (Green Bean Stew)
Substitute green beans for the peas and carrots. Chop them into 2 or 3 pieces, and cook as above.

طبيخ بازلاء

This is a Palestinian family favorite, and is particularly delightful with fresh spring peas.

Tabeekh Bitinjan

Eggplant Chickpea Stew

Serves 5–6

1 pound (500 grams) boneless stew beef or lamb, cut into 1 inch (2½ centimeters) pieces
2 pounds (1 kilogram) eggplants, cut into 2-inch (5 centimeters) cubes
1 onion, chopped
5 tablespoons olive oil
½ cup (100 grams) dried chickpeas, soaked overnight, or one 15-ounce (425 gram) can
4 tablespoons tomato paste or 6–7 liquefied ripe tomatoes
6 cloves garlic
1 teaspoon salt
Fresh basil or parsley, to garnish

Prepare the meat according to the instructions in the *Maraqa* recipe (page 24), making sure to brown it before making the broth. If you are using dried chickpeas, add them to the meat as it cooks.

Meanwhile, prepare the eggplants: Spread them over a kitchen towel and sprinkle both sides with ½ teaspoon of the salt. Alternately, you can soak them for 20 minutes in salted water. Rinse them off and pat them dry, then fry in very hot vegetable oil until they are brown. Set aside on a plate lined with paper towels to drain the excess oil. You may also drizzle the eggplants with olive oil, then oven-roast them at 400°F (200°C) or grill them on an indoor grill or panini press (this is the method we prefer) until they are golden and slightly charred.

In a clean pot, bring to a boil 5 cups (about 1⅓ liters) of strained broth, along with the reserved meat, chickpeas, and tomato paste or liquefied tomatoes. If you are using liquefied fresh tomatoes, reduce the quantity of broth by half. Lower the heat and gently stir in the fried, roasted, or grilled eggplant.

While the stew simmers, make the *taqliya*: Mash the garlic with the remaining salt in a mortar and pestle. In a separate pan, fry the garlic in 2 tablespoons of olive oil or ghee until it turns lightly golden, about a minute. Add the garlic to the pot, deglazing the pan with a little of the stew.

Garnish with chopped parsley or snipped basil and serve with *Khubz Kmaj* (page 100) or *Ruz Imfalfal* (page 206), and green chiles or *Dagga* (page 50).

طبيخ باذنجان

This stew is traditionally made with fried eggplants, but oven-roasting them proves just as good. You can roast the eggplants in advance and refrigerate them if time is an issue.

Mohammed Ahmed El Soltan

Mohammed Ahmed El Soltan is from Jabaliya, in the northern Gaza Strip. He is a jovial man with the leathery hands of a farmer, who interrupts his own story every few seconds to point out the different crops and wild herbs growing in the fields of the agricultural training center where we meet him.

Dear reader, we have a dilemma here. How can we express in words the *joie de vivre*, the cheerful optimism and impossible good humor with which one after another person recounts tales of destruction, dispossession, and survival?

Perhaps reading these profiles feels like an insistent lament. It is, but much more than that, it is a matter-of-fact summary of their situation by people who—in their voices and gestures and ways—are much more occupied with the business of living than with mourning their losses.

Mohammed says:

I had 10 dunums of land near El Rayyes mountain, all planted with lemons, olives, and oranges, with a four-story house and a vegetable garden. There were also 550 beehives there. I also had another 32 dunums near the border planted with almonds, but those vandals and their bulldozers ruined them all, and I can't get to that land to replant.

Now it is all destroyed, and I had to ask the government for help supporting my family while we replant. But of course the trees will need at least five or six years to begin to produce fruit, and meanwhile we have nothing.

Way back, my father had a donkey with a plow, and he taught me to use it. Later on we had tractors. We cleaned the lands and irrigated and removed the weeds. It was beautiful. You would take guests there; it was like visiting the sea. You would present them with pears and almonds, and they would admire the land.

Back then we exported fruit to Europe and we lived very well. But after Hamas took over we couldn't export anything because the borders were closed and the sea was blocked. Now we can't even afford to buy a chicken for our children to eat. The only thing that helps us is the food aid we get.

Now we are just waiting and praying that God will keep us safe from the Israelis and that there might be an agreement between the Israelis and us so that our trees get a chance to grow.

Tabeekh Ari' Hilew

Sweet and Sour Pumpkin Stew

Serves 5–6

1 pound (500 grams) stew beef, cut into 1 inch (2½ centimeters) pieces

2 pounds (1 kilogram) pumpkin, butternut squash, or other orange-fleshed gourd, cut into 1 inch (2½ centimeters) pieces

¼ cup (30 grams) golden raisins

¼ cup (30) grams dried sour plums or 2 tablespoons pomegranate molasses

8 prunes (if using pomegranate molasses)

¼ teaspoon ground black pepper

¼ teaspoon ground cinnamon

½ cup (100 grams) dried chickpeas, soaked overnight, or one 15-ounce (425 grams) can

Olive oil

Salt

Prepare the meat according to the instructions in the *Maraqa* recipe (page 24), browning the meat before boiling it. If you are using dried chickpeas, add them to the boiling broth. If you are using canned chickpeas, add them at the end, just before serving, and heat through.

Deep fry the squash in hot oil or oven-roast it, drizzled with olive oil, in a 400°F (200°C) oven for about 35 minutes, until golden.

Once the meat is tender, strain it from the broth, discarding the spices. Pour the broth into a clean pot along with the stewed meat, fried or roasted squash, raisins, sour plums or prunes, pomegranate molasses (if using), cinnamon, and pepper.

Simmer the stew over a very low flame for 20 minutes, add salt to taste, and serve with *Ruz Imfalfal* (page 206).

طبيخ قرع حلو

In her never-ending quest for undocumented traditional recipes, Laila obtained this one for a sweet pumpkin stew, popular among Gaza City's older families, from her cousin in 2013. It highlights the sweet and sour fruit-and-meat flavors so characteristic of Persian-influenced medieval Islamic cooking—a real gem.

If dried sour plums (not to be confused with the salty dried Asian ones) are unavailable in your area, substitute 2 tablespoons of pomegranate molasses and prunes.

Zibdiyit Khudar

Lenten Vegetable Stew

Serves 5–6

زبدية خضار

1 large eggplant
½ cup olive oil
½ teaspoon red pepper flakes or 2 whole sun-dried red chile peppers, crushed
1 teaspoon dill seeds
5 cloves garlic, crushed
2 onions, chopped
2 medium carrots, chopped
1 small handful green beans, trimmed and cut in half
1 red or yellow bell pepper, seeds removed and chopped
1 Middle Eastern *koosa* squash or other summer squash, chopped
3–4 firm tomatoes, chopped
1 cup (200 grams) precooked chickpeas, rinsed well
2 cups (400 grams) liquefied fresh tomatoes or canned plain tomato sauce
1 teaspoon ground cumin
½ teaspoon ground black pepper
2 large potatoes, thinly sliced
Olive oil
Salt and pepper

Gaza has a small Christian population. During Lent, they enjoy this vegetarian stew, traditionally prepared in handmade, unglazed clay bowls and slow-cooked in a large communal stone oven. The following mixture of vegetables works nicely, though almost any vegetables may be substituted; use what you have on hand. The important thing is the long slow-cooking, over real coals if at all possible.

Preheat your oven to 400°F (200°C) degrees.

Peel the eggplant in alternating vertical strips, then chop them into 1 inch cubes. Sprinkle the cubes with salt and place them in a colander for about 20 minutes, or until beads of moisture appear on the surface. (Alternately, you can soak them for 20 minutes in salt water.) Pat them dry, then fry them in olive oil or coat them well with oil and oven-roast until golden, and set aside.

Reduce the heat to 350°F (176°C).

Crush the dried red pepper and dill seeds with ½ teaspoon of salt in a mortar and pestle until fragrant. Add the garlic and mash well.

Sauté the onion in the remaining olive oil (add a little more if necessary) until it is nearly golden, then add the garlic, dill, and red pepper mixture and continue to sauté another few minutes.

In a large *zibdiya* or other unglazed clay pot, combine the fried eggplant with the onion and garlic mixture, then add the carrots, pepper, squash, beans, finely chopped tomatoes, and precooked chickpeas. Mix the cumin and black pepper with the liquefied tomatoes or tomato sauce and salt to taste, then pour this over the vegetable mixture. Layer thin slices of potato over this and sprinkle it with salt and pepper.

Seal the pot tightly with aluminum foil. For a more traditional prepara-tion, seal the pot with basic unleavened dough (use the recipe for *Khubz Saj* on page 102), and bake for two hours. Remove the foil or dough, driz-zle olive oil over the surface of the potatoes, and switch your oven to broil. Allow the potatoes to brown for 5 minutes. Serve with *Khubz Kmaj* (page 100) or *Ruz Imfalfal* (page 206).

RICE DISHES AND STUFFED VEGETABLES

Rice dishes run the spectrum from simple everyday fare to splendid gala meals. In this chapter we present some of the classic Palestinian rice dishes, like *maqlooba*, as well as a sampling of the dazzling array of stuffed vegetable dishes beloved all over the region.

Ruz Imfalfal

Basic White Rice

Serves 5–6

2 cups (approximately 390 grams) medium-grain rice
1½ teaspoons salt
Olive or vegetable oil, as needed
3½ cups (approximately 840 milliliters) water
Cold water for soaking

In a bowl, wash the rice well, adding fresh water until it no longer runs cloudy (probably 3 or 4 times), then soak it in clean, cold water for 10 to 15 minutes. Strain well.

Heat 4 tablespoons of oil in a medium saucepan. Add the rice and the salt and stir on medium-high heat for 2 minutes or until well coated and slightly translucent.

Add the water and boil vigorously for 5 minutes. Reduce the heat to medium-low. Cover completely and cook for an additional 15 minutes or until grains from the middle of the pot are tender to the bite. Remove the pot from the heat and let it rest, covered, for 5 to 10 more minutes. Transfer to a serving platter and fluff with a fork.

Serve with stews (*tabeekh*) of all varieties.

Variations

• *Add 1 tablespoon nigella seeds to the olive oil and sauté along with the rice. Proceed as directed above.*

• *Brown a generous handful of uncooked vermicelli in 2 tablespoons of oil or butter, then add the rice and proceed as above.*

رز مفلفل

In Gaza, the most widely available rice is the Egyptian medium- or short-grain rice provided through emergency rations. In recent years, Palestinian expatriates returning home from the Gulf states have introduced their families to basmati rice, though this is a luxury few can afford in large quantities.

Mjadarra

Lentils and Rice

Serves 6–7

2 cups (400 grams) brown lentils, rinsed
3 medium onions, julienned
½ cup (120 milliliters) olive oil
5 garlic cloves, crushed
1½ cups (300 grams) long-grain rice, such as basmati
2 teaspoons salt
1 teaspoon cumin
1½ teaspoons *qidra* spices (page 34)

Wash the rice (or bulgur) several times and rinse it until the water runs clear, then soak it for about 10 minutes.

In a medium saucepan, bring approximately 8 cups (2 liters) of water to a boil. Add the lentils, along with ½ teaspoon of the salt and ½ teaspoon of the cumin. Reduce the heat and cook, partially covered, for approximately 25 minutes or until the lentils are tender (not mushy) but still holding their shape. Strain the lentils, reserving any leftover lentil water.

Meanwhile, warm the oil in a large skillet. Add the onions and fry on medium heat, stirring occasionally until they are deeply golden and crisp, taking care not to burn them.

Set aside half of the fried onions. Add the crushed garlic to the remaining fried onions and cook for an additional 2 to 3 minutes.

Strain the soaked rice, then add it to the onions and garlic in the pan, along with the remaining salt and spices. Stir in the lentils and 3½ cups (820 milliliters) of the reserved lentil water. Add more water as necessary to compensate if the reserved lentil water is not enough.

Bring the entire pan to a boil, then reduce the heat and cover. Cook for approximately 20 minutes, or until the rice is soft to the bite. Set aside, covered, for 10 to 15 minutes, then transfer to a serving dish and top with the remaining fried onions.

Mjadarra is traditionally served with plain yogurt and *Salata Khadra Mafrooma* (page 54).

مجدرة

This Levantine favorite is no less popular in Gaza, where it is made at least once a week as a break from meat. Especially now, when most families can no longer afford the luxury of animal protein on a daily basis, *mjadarra* is a household staple. In rural Palestine, it is often made with bulgur instead of rice and known as "red *mjadarra*."

Rabee'iya/Fooliya

Green Favas and Rice

Serves 5–6

2 cups (420 grams) basmati or other long-grain rice
1 pound (450 grams) ground beef or lamb
1 medium onion, chopped
1 teaspoon cumin
1 teaspoon *qidra* spices (page 34)
2 teaspoons salt
½ teaspoon black pepper
1 pound (500 grams) fresh tender fava pods or green fava beans
2 bunches cilantro, chopped
3½ cups (830 milliliters) water
Olive oil

Wash and rinse the rice three times until the water runs clear, then set it aside to soak in a bowl of cold water for 10 minutes. Strain.

Meanwhile, in a large skillet, warm 3 to 4 tablespoons of olive oil. Sauté the meat, onions, and spices until they are browned. Set aside.

If you are using tender fava pods, remove the stringy stems, then cut the pods into pieces roughly 1 inch (2½ centimeters) long. If tender pods are unavailable, remove the shells and use only the beans. Frozen green fava beans, available from many ethnic grocers, will do just fine.

In a separate pan, sauté the fava beans in 2 tablespoons of olive oil for a few minutes until they turn bright green. Add the cooked meat, then stir in the strained rice and water.

Bring to a boil, then reduce the heat and cover the pan. Cook until the rice is tender, approximately 20 minutes. Remove the lid, then stir in the chopped cilantro. Serve with plain yogurt or, if you are in a particularly self-indulgent mood, *Tabkeekh Laban Bil Mozat* (page 239).

ربيعية/فولية

This springtime favorite, known as "spring's dish," was given to us by an enthusiastic collector of Gazan recipes in America, Asma Abu Daff, who advises that it is usually eaten with plain yogurt, "but if someone really likes to treat themselves well, then they have it with a side of lamb shanks cooked in yogurt stew." If you switch stew beef for the ground beef, the result is called *maqloobit fool* or *maqlooba* with fava beans, prepared as *maqlooba* would be, but with fava beans.

As a general rule of thumb (so to speak), if your fava-bean pods are smaller in diameter than your finger, you can cook and eat the whole pod, cutting it into lengths. Thicker pods are velvety and tough: In this case, shell the beans from the pods. Unless the beans themselves are very large and hard, don't bother to slip each individual bean out of its skin or you'll be at it all day.

Many urban families in Gaza rely on professionals to prepare food for them, particularly for parties or special events. Some do this to save time, others to save on cooking fuel. This is where Um Hamada and the women of *Jamiyit Juthour al-Zeitoun*, the Olive Roots Cooperative, step in.

Tired of the helplessness many Gazan homemakers feel in an economic situation of nearly universal male under- and unemployment, Um Hamada and her neighbors in Gaza City's historic Zeitoun neighborhood decided to put their cooking skills to work in the organization's kitchen cooperative to support their families.

The women take orders for festive foods and—in a tiny but astonishingly efficient kitchen—prepare great vats of *mahshi*, towering mounds of *maqlooba*, and all manner of pastries and sweets for every kind of special event. All of the women learned slightly different versions of the dishes from their families, so debates over recipes rage in the kitchen without slowing the six or seven pairs of hands that deftly chop, slice, measure, and stir in harmony.

In addition to the cooking space, the organization offers the women workshops on topics ranging from literacy to basic entrepreneurship. More than anything, though, it serves as a safe and uplifting alternative space for them. Here in this sweltering little room, surrounded by piles of platters and pots, they find companionship and some modest measure of control over their destinies.

Maqlooba

Upside-Down Casserole

Serves a large and hungry crowd, about 8 servings

2 pounds (approximately 1 kilogram) lean lamb, cut into chunks, or
  one whole chicken, skin removed and cut into 8 pieces

1 large onion, julienned

8 cloves garlic, peeled

2 medium potatoes, peeled and thinly sliced

2 large tomatoes, sliced

1 sweet red pepper, cut into strips

3 carrots, peeled and sliced

2 pounds (1 kilogram) eggplant or 1 head of cauliflower

4 tablespoons olive oil

½ cup (100 grams) dried chickpeas, presoaked, or one 15-ounce (425
  gram) can of chickpeas

2 cups (370 grams) extra-long-grain rice, washed well

3 teaspoons salt

1½ tablespoons *qidra* spices (page 34)

½ teaspoon cinnamon

¼ cup pine nuts or almonds

2 tablespoons finely minced parsley

This all-star of Palestinian dishes, literally called "upside-down," makes a spectacular presentation: a dome of rice jeweled with bright vegetables. Traditionally made with lamb, *maqlooba* is also wonderful with chicken or beef. We find that oven-roasting rather than frying the vegetables makes the dish more flavorful and less greasy; decide for yourself which you prefer.

Prepare the meat according to the instructions in the *Maraqa* recipe (page 24). If you are using beef or lamb, there is no need to brown it first. Chicken, however, should be lightly browned in a little oil before adding the water for the broth. If you are using dried chickpeas, skim the scum that rises to the surface of the broth as you boil it, and then add the chickpeas along with the spices and onion. Set the meat aside.

While the broth is simmering, prepare the eggplant as follows. Peel in alternating strips: Peel off one strip of skin, then leave a strip on, then peel another, such that the eggplant has longitudinal zebra stripes. Then slice the eggplants uniformly, in 1 inch (2½ centimeter) pieces. If you are using smaller eggplants, you may slice them vertically. Sprinkle the slices with salt and set them aside in a colander until beads of moisture appear on the surface, about 20 minutes. Alternately, you can soak them for 20 minutes in salty water. Rinse them off and pat them dry.

Fry the eggplant slices in very hot vegetable oil until brown and set on paper towels to soak excess oil, or slather them with olive oil on both sides, then oven-roast at 400°F (200°C) until golden, flipping them halfway through the cooking process. You can also use an indoor grill or panini press (this is the method we prefer).

If you are using cauliflower, wash the head well, then separate the florets, drizzle them generously with olive oil, and roast them in the hot oven until they are well browned. This will take about 25 to 30 minutes.

Meanwhile, wash and rinse the rice several times until water runs clear, then soak the in a bowl of cold water for 15 minutes.

Next, fry the onions and garlic in 2 to 3 tablespoons of the olive oil on medium heat until deeply golden. Strain the soaked rice and transfer it to a bowl. Add the onions and garlic along with the salt, cinnamon, and *qidra* spices. Set aside.

Grease the bottom and sides of a large nonstick pot with olive oil. Arrange the potato slices in a circular, overlapping pattern, followed by the tomato slices, red pepper, carrots, meat (reserved from making the broth), roasted eggplant or cauliflower, and chickpeas, all in successive layers.

Pack the spiced rice into the pot on top of the vegetables using the palm of your hand. Ladle the reserved broth over the rice until just covered, using approximately 1½ cups (355 milliliters) of broth for every cup (185 grams) of rice. Bring this to a boil, then reduce the heat to low and cover the pot tightly. If you have a plate that fits inside the pot, you may want to place it on top of the rice, then cover the pot tightly; this helps press the rice down and keep it compact while it cooks.

After 30 to 35 minutes, taste the rice: If it is still too hard, add a bit more broth, a few spoonfuls at a time, and leave it on low heat until the rice is tender. You can also try placing a wet kitchen towel on top of the rice toward the end of the cooking process, then cover.

Remove the pot from the heat and let it rest, covered, for 30 minutes. In the meantime, pan-fry the pine nuts or almonds and set them aside.

Uncover the rice and place a large round tray, serving side down, on top of the pot. Hold on carefully and swiftly and—in one continuous motion—flip both the pot and tray upside down. Take care not to burn yourself! At this point, if it appears a lot of extra liquid has seeped out of the pot, strain it out while keeping the pot firmly secured against the tray.

Finally, tap on the pot with a wooden spoon (a task ordinarily assigned to children), then gently lift the pot off, allowing the *maqlooba* to slide out as out of a mold. It's okay if it falls apart. Adorn the *maqlooba* with fried nuts and chopped parsley.

Serve immediately with *Salata Khadra Mafruma* (page 54) and plain yogurt.

Mahshi

Stuffed Summer Vegetables

Serves 10–12

6 pounds (about 3 kilogram) assorted vegetables for stuffing:
koosa squash (also known as grey zucchini or magda squash),
    bell peppers, baby eggplants, firm tomatoes, or Middle Eastern
    cucumbers
2 cups (390 grams) medium-grain rice or grade #3 bulgur
½ pound (250 grams) lean ground beef
1 onion, very finely chopped
½ cup (120 milliliters) olive oil
2 tomatoes, very finely diced
1 packed cup (25 grams) parsley, finely chopped
2½ teaspoons ground allspice
1 teaspoon ground cardamom
1 teaspoon black pepper
½ teaspoon ground nutmeg
3½ teaspoons salt
2–3 tomatoes (cut to size for plugging vegetables)
2 teaspoon dried mint
5 cloves garlic, crushed
2 hot green chiles, chopped
9 ounces (260 milliliters) tomato paste, diluted in 6 cups (1½ liters)
    boiling water

Wash and rinse the rice or bulgur several times. Soak it in 1 cup (235 milliliters) cold water for 15 minutes or until nearly absorbed. Do not strain.

Core the vegetables using a special squash corer (*man'arit koosa*) which can be easily obtained from a Middle Eastern market, or the tip of a long vegetable peeler, taking care not to pierce the skin. Core in slow, circular motions, as you twist your wrist. With each subsequent entry into the squash, remove a little more of the pulp on the inside walls and bottom of the squash, until you have a nearly empty cavity. Several gentle rotations in and out along the inside edges of the squash should do the trick. With eggplants, you will benefit from kneading them a few times back and forth under the palm of your hands before coring. Place the cored vegetables in a vat of salted water. Submerge the vegetables, making sure water has entered the insides, then shake them out and strain. This will help them retain their shape while cooking. Before stuffing, rinse and pat them dry.

In a large bowl, combine the meat with the damp rice and its soaking water, the olive oil, chopped onions, parsley, tomatoes, allspice, cardamom, black pepper, and nutmeg, along with 3 teaspoons of the salt. Mix well. If the stuffing appears crumbly and dry, add a couple of tablespoons of water to moisten it. With your hands, carefully fill each

محشي

This is a dish best made in company. Coring vegetables can be onerous if done alone but is downright festive when many hands are at work together.

Some prefer to substitute medium-grain bulgur for the rice in this classic dish. A mix of the two grains can also be used.

Choose the smallest available squashes and very taut eggplants. Do not be tempted to substitute dark-green zucchini for the pale-skinned *koosa*: they tend to get too soft when boiled.

hollowed-out vegetable with this rice mix, leaving a little space (about 1 inch or 2½ centimeters) on the top for the rice to expand as it cooks. Plug the opening of each vegetable with a piece of tomato cut to size.

Gently set the stuffed vegetables in the bottom of a large pot, laying them neatly and snugly on their sides.

For the broth: In a mortar and pestle, crush the garlic with the remaining salt. In a small saucepan, bring the water, mixed with the tomato paste, to a boil. To this, add the chopped chile peppers and crushed garlic. Add mint only if you are not using eggplants. Pour this sauce over the vegetables. There should be enough liquid to completely submerge the vegetables. If there isn't, add a bit more water. Close the pot tightly. Bring to a boil, then simmer, partially covered, for 30 minutes on medium-low heat.

Check the rice for doneness after 20 minutes.

Turn off the heat and let the vegetables rest in the pot for at least 20 minutes. Gently remove the vegetables from the sauce and arrange them on a serving platter. Serve the sauce alongside them.

Variation
Stuffed koosa *can be prepared together with stuffed grape leaves (page 216). Omit the mint and hot peppers from the broth and invert the pot onto a platter when fully cooked and rested.*

The El-Samouni name is a tragically famous one in Gaza: In one of the most internationally recognized and widely criticized incidents of the war on Gaza in 2008–09, the entire extended El-Samouni family was ordered into one house, which was then demolished. Forty-nine members of the family—mostly women and children—were killed.

Lulu wears her surname like an onerous medal; in the Zeitoun Cooperative's kitchen, eyes are lowered in a meaningful pause after she is introduced. But the respect she commands is not only because of her family's tragedy. She has a gravity of her own.

Zeitoun is a poor urban neighborhood that has been struck especially hard by the collapse of industrial employment; here there is no agricultural land to fall back on for subsistence. Lulu's brother is one of those who lost his work and, like so many others in Gaza, succumbed to acute diabetes, leaving his wife and seven children in abject poverty. To keep the family afloat, Lulu began making and packaging sun-dried *maftool* to sell on the local market. With a ban on the export of most goods from Gaza, selling it abroad or marketing it via fair-trade organizations is not an option.

Lulu is unmarried and has no children, but her precarious little enterprise now supports a crowd of her siblings' offspring. When we spoke to her, her dream was to be able to print labels for her product to market it at local stores, but the up-front cost of printing was more than she could come up with.

Warak Inab

Stuffed Grape Leaves

Serves 8–10

One 2 pound (850 grams) jar of grape leaves
2½ cups (490 grams) short- or medium-grain rice or a combination of
  rice and #3 bulgur
1 pound (450 grams) extra-lean ground beef
½ medium onion, very finely chopped
½ packed cup (12 grams) finely chopped parsley
1 tomato, very finely diced
¼ cup (60 milliliters) olive oil
2¾ teaspoons ground allspice
1 teaspoon ground cardamom
1 teaspoon black pepper
2½ teaspoons salt
¾ teaspoon ground nutmeg
2 tomatoes, thickly sliced
6 tablespoons tomato paste, diluted in 5–6 cups (1½ liters) hot water

Wash and rinse the rice or bulgur several times, then set aside to soak
in 1 cup (235 milliliters) cold water for 15 minutes or until most of the
water has been absorbed. Do not strain.

Combine the meat with the soaked rice and its soaking water, chopped
onions, parsley, finely diced tomato, oil, allspice, cardamom, nutmeg,
black pepper, and salt in a large bowl. Mix well.

Rinse the grape leaves well. Gently unfold them and spread them out
on your work surface. Trim the stems and cut the larger leaves in half
lengthwise, starting from the stem and going down the center seam.
Place about 1 teaspoon of the rice stuffing at the edge of the leaf closest
to the stem. (If you are using a cut leaf, turn so the cut edge is facing you,
then place the stuffing near that edge.) Shape the stuffing into a small log
at least ½ inch away from the frilly edges of the leaf. Roll the leaf once
over the stuffing, then fold in the edges and roll again. Continue in this
manner (rolling tightly, folding in, rolling tightly) until the leaf is fully
rolled. Secure each roll by squeezing it gently with your hand. Reserve
any torn or imperfect leaves.

Arrange an overlapping layer of sliced tomatoes in the bottom of a large
pot. On top of this, arrange the stuffed grape leaves in a circular pattern
like the spokes of a wheel, adding layers as the pot fills. When all the
rolls are arranged, cover them with a layer of torn leaves.

In a large saucepan, bring the diluted tomato paste to a boil, adding
more water if it appears to be too thick. Pour it over the grape leaves,
then cover them with a heatproof flat plate (preferably a heavy one) to
weigh them down. The tomato sauce should cover the grape leaves. If
not, add water to compensate.

ورق عنب

Women joke that this dish takes hours to make and minutes to consume, but everyone loves it so much that somehow it is worthwhile anyway.

Throughout Palestine, tender grape leaves are picked in the spring and sold at public markets. Nothing tastes quite like these fresh leaves. If you can't get fresh ones, the best substitutes are Orlando brand jarred grape leaves. Several varieties of vacuum-sealed Turkish leaves have recently become available in US markets as well. If the leaves tear easily, you know they are of poorer quality.

Cook on medium-high heat for 10 minutes. Reduce the heat to low and simmer gently, partially covered, for 40 minutes or until the water is absorbed. Test some rice from a sample grape leaf to see if it is cooked through. If the sauce has reduced and the rice is still not cooked through, add more water or chicken stock, ½ cup at a time, and cook until the rice is cooked through.

Remove from heat and let the pot rest for at least 15 minutes, covered. Carefully invert it onto serving platter (place a platter on top of the pot, then flip it all over in a quick motion). The grape leaves will form a compact and elegant mound.

Serve with yogurt or a salad of yogurt and cucumbers.

Variation

Instead of lining the bottom of the pot with tomatoes, use 1 pound (450 grams) of thinly sliced boneless steaks, pierced several times with a fork, pounded slightly with a kitchen mallet, and rubbed with a grated onion and ½ teaspoon each of allspice, salt, black pepper, and cardamom. This makes for a particularly lovely presentation once inverted and adds a delicious layer of flavor to the grape leaves.

Sheikh el Mahshi

Stuffed Baby Eggplants

Serves 4–6

8–10 small eggplants, about 4 inches (10 centimeters) long
1 pound (450 grams) lean ground beef or lamb
1 medium onion, finely chopped
1 green chile pepper, finely chopped
1 teaspoon salt, more as needed
½ teaspoon black pepper
¼ teaspoon ground nutmeg
¼ teaspoon ground allspice
5 very ripe tomatoes
2 tablespoons pine nuts
Water
Olive oil

Preheat your oven to 350°F (180°C).

Peel the eggplants in alternating strips: Peel off one strip of skin, then leave a strip on, then peel another, such that the eggplant has longitudinal zebra stripes. Soak them in a cold bath of salty water for 20 minutes. Pat dry.

Sauté the finely chopped onion in 2 tablespoons of olive oil until translucent. Add the chile pepper, ground meat, salt, pepper, nutmeg, and allspice. Grate or blend 2 tomatoes and add them to the meat. Allow them to cook down over medium heat until nearly but not quite dry. In a separate pan, lightly fry the pine nuts in 1 tablespoon of olive oil, taking care not to burn them, then stir them into the meat and set it aside.

Grate or liquefy the remaining 3 tomatoes in a blender (or substitute a few tablespoons of tomato paste diluted in 2 cups or 473 milliliters of water). Set aside.

Pan-fry the eggplants in olive oil until they are browned on all sides. Allow to cool on a plate lined with paper towels. Once they are cool enough to handle, cut a lengthwise slit in each eggplant and stuff it with a few tablespoons of the meat mixture, depending on the size of the eggplant.

Arrange the stuffed eggplants in a baking tray and cover them with the grated or liquefied tomatoes. Add ¼ teaspoon of salt and enough water to submerge about ⅓ of the eggplant.

Bake for 45 minutes or until the eggplants are soft throughout (this will depend on their size). If they appear to be drying out, cover them with aluminum foil or adjust the liquid quantity.

Garnish with a sprinkling of chopped parsley and serve hot, with *Ruz Imfalfal* (page 206) and salad.

Its name meaning the "sovereign of stuffed things," this classic dish is ideally made with eggplants that are very small, taut, and shiny. Larger eggplants will work, but the result is less delicate.

Though it was historically frowned upon for its strong flavor, an eggplant properly prepared is indeed the queen of vegetables, inspiring the tenth-century Syrian poet Kushajim to write, memorably, "My doctor makes ignorant fun of me for loving eggplant, but I will not give it up. Its flavor is like the saliva exchanged by lovers in kissing."

The eggplant should be fried very hot so it doesn't absorb too much oil, and should be given enough time in the oven to become quite soft.

Variations

• ***Maghshi****: Substitute small Middle Eastern squash for the eggplant. Instead of cutting a slit down the middle, however, core the squash as you would with* koosa mahshi *(page 212), then pan-fry them, strain off the excess oil, and proceed with the recipe as above.*

• ***Mahshi Batata (Stuffed Potatoes):*** *Peel, then blanch and hollow out, a few small baking potatoes. Pan-fry them whole and proceed as above. This is a good use for leftover stuffing if you run out of eggplants.*

Malfoof

Garlicky Stuffed Cabbage Rolls

Serves 8–10

ملفوف

1 compact head green Asian-variety cabbage (approximately 4–5 pounds/2 kilograms)
6–8 cups (approximately 2 liters) water or broth, as needed
20 cloves garlic (yes, 20 cloves)
2½ cups (490 grams) medium-grain rice, washed well
½ pound (225 grams) lean ground beef
3 green chiles, thinly sliced
3 teaspoons ground cumin
2 teaspoons allspice
½ teaspoon cardamom
½ teaspoon black pepper
¼ teaspoon nutmeg
Juice of 3–4 lemons
1 tablespoon dried mint leaves
½ cup (120 milliliters) olive oil
Salt

Large, sweet cabbages are grown in patches all along Gaza's main coastal road—an area once slated to become the seaport—and sold at roadside stalls. They are exquisite stuffed, rolled, and simmered in a garlicky broth.

Look for cabbage with tightly packed, moist-looking leaves: The finer and more tender the leaves, the better. In the United States, Asian cabbage varieties work best. If you have extra stuffing, roll a few lettuce leaves to finish it off.

Wash and rinse the rice several times, then soak it in 2 cups of cold water (470 milliliters) and set aside.

Trim the cabbage of any rough exterior leaves that are not compactly attached to the main head, then submerge the head in water or broth with 1 teaspoon each of cumin and salt, and boil it whole for 10 to 15 minutes or until the leaves are tender. Carefully remove it from the water using tongs or wooden spoons. Leave the water simmering on the stovetop. You might also try microwaving the entire head of cabbage to moisten and loosen the leaves.

Cool the cabbage by running it under cold water, then separate the individual leaves, starting from the outside. If you can no longer peel away leaves without breaking them, return the cabbage to the pot of water and boil it for a few more minutes. Repeat until all the larger leaves are separated and you reach the heart of the cabbage. Reserve this: It is known as *jajit il malfoof*—the chicken of the cabbage—and can be stuffed along with rest of the leaves. It was Laila's favorite as a child!

Prepare the stuffing: In a mortar and pestle, crush 10 of the garlic cloves, a few cloves at a time, with ½ teaspoon of salt, until well mashed. Strain the rice, then combine it with the olive oil, ground meat, 1 teaspoon of cumin, mashed garlic, cardamom, allspice, black pepper, 2½ teaspoons of salt, and nutmeg.

Spread each cabbage leaf flat. Cut the large leaves in half vertically, removing any hard veins with a knife. Reserve the veins and broken bits of cabbage.

Stuff the rolls: Place approximately 1 tablespoon of stuffing inside each flattened cabbage leaf and spread it into a thin log. Roll the cabbage leaf closed over the stuffing. There is no need to tuck the ends of the cabbage leaf inside—it will seal itself. The rolls needn't be uniform or even tightly rolled: Cabbage leaves hold their shape surprisingly well during cooking. Squeeze each roll gently to strain off excess moisture. Finally, put several spoonfuls of stuffing inside the cabbage heart and squeeze it closed (no need to roll it).

Roughly slice the remaining garlic cloves. Line the base of the pot with the reserved hard cabbage bits, then arrange the stuffed cabbage leaves over them, scattering chopped chiles and sliced garlic between each layer.

Pour the water in which the cabbage was initially boiled over the stuffed leaves, just enough to cover them. Boil it for 5 minutes, then reduce the heat to medium-low and cover the leaves with a heavy heat-proof plate to weigh them down. Simmer for approximately 40 minutes or until the rice is cooked through. Combine the lemon juice and dried mint, then pour them over the cabbage rolls. Remove the pan from the heat and let it rest, covered, for 15 minutes.

Carefully drain any excess liquid from the pot, then invert the stuffed rolls onto a round platter as you would *maqlooba*.

Serve with yogurt or a salad of cucumbers, yogurt, and mint.

economic reasons or, in the case of Abu Ameen, for "peace of mind."

We meet Abu Ameen in his home in Edgewater, Maryland, a serene little bayside town, his adopted home of thirty-some years. We have come to document his purported prowess in preparing all manner of Gazan meals, with hacks that include using a power drill to core the stiff, stubborn red carrot.

But Abu Ameen refuses to budge, citing social impropriety. At 84 years old, it seems he just doesn't feel like cooking today. But talking? Well, that he can do plenty of.

He dives right in, detailing the various substitutes one could use for red carrots, his signature dish. "Fat, firm orange or even white carrots will do," he insists, adding the following caveat: "But don't ever be tempted to shred or layer the carrots and stuffing like a casserole—that's just going too far! It's like a friend of mine whose wife couldn't cook and so she decided it would be easier to deconstruct *malfoof,* cabbage rolls, and cook them in a baking pan. Abominable! A travesty!" He shakes his head in disbelief.

Where one draws this murky line and how one determines whether and when it has been breached is not entirely clear, but in Abu Ameen's mind, there's no question: You simply can't make a cabbage lasagna and call it *malfoof*.

Abu Ameen's father, Nazmi, was a headmaster who taught at various schools throughout historic Palestine, eventually settling in Gaza City to ensure an education for his children. Like his father before him, Abu Ameen chose to migrate, this time westward, in the early eighties to join his two brothers and live a more "orderly and calm life."

He shares the story of his travel to America from Palestine, one that still has him in stitches decades later:

> It was the day that forty Jewish extremists tried to break into the Al-Aqsa Mosque in 1979. I was getting ready to travel and the Israelis had imposed a curfew in Gaza. We had picked olives and needed to take them to the press, but due to the curfew, we couldn't. Instead, we cracked the olives, then placed them in a large basin and extracted the oil the old-fashioned way—by adding hot water to the olives and waiting for the oil to rise to the surface, *zait tfah*. It's something my mom

This book documents life within Gaza. But what of all those Palestinians, including many from the Gaza district, who live on the outside? In *Seeking Palestine,* Raja Shehadeh writes, "Palestine evokes a particular obligation of belonging in its far-flung 'inhabitants,' for whom insistent memory becomes a mode of habitation." There are at least 12 million Palestinians living in diaspora, more than are living within the land itself. Half of these live in the Arab world, whether in permanent refugee camps or as long-term stateless residents in other countries. They have lived through various waves of exile, impelled by ethnic cleansings or discriminatory rules and regulations meant to rid the land of its native inhabitants by way of "indirect transfer." Then there are those who chose to migrate voluntarily, for

Unlike many other Palestinians abroad whose residency rights were revoked or denied by Israel, Abu Ameen was able to visit Gaza regularly until the near-hermetic border closure of recent years rendered the journey impossible.

What does he miss the most?

"Friends. But most of mine have moved on from this life.... It's not so much about missing *things*—it's about adapting and it's about memories."

For Abu Ameen, as for so many immigrants, cooking became the means of retaining and passing those memories on to the next generation. For Palestinians, this legacy takes on heightened significance and a perceived sense of urgency: a last straw to clutch onto before all that was known is erased forever. Abu Ameen considers it a blessing and a reminder.

Outside in his little yard, he picks a leaf of common sorrel growing in the patchy spring grass. "Look! *Hamasees!*" Home is always elsewhere, and right under our feet.

picked up during her time living in Nablus. I took several bottles with me on the plane. Little did I know the bottles weren't properly sealed, and during the plane ride, due to cabin air pressure, the bottles opened and slowed dripped out from the overhead compartment onto the head of the bald guy seated in front of me. I pretended not to know what was going on, and when the worst was over, I went to search for the olives, only to find that the stewards had disposed of them in in the trash. A calamity! I can't forget those olives and oil and all the hard work we put into cracking them to this day! *Allah yirhamhum!*

MEAT, POULTRY, AND DISHES FOR SPECIAL OCCASIONS

While this book principally focuses on Gaza's rich and varied everyday home cooking, there are times that call for festive and often lavish meat-based dishes. This chapter brings together these classic meals for special occasions, as well as an array of street and restaurant foods such as roast chicken and kebabs.

Kebab Mashwi

Grilled Kufta Kebab

Serves 4–6

2 pounds (1 kilogram) ground beef, with some fat for taste, or 1½ pounds (750 grams) ground beef with ½ pound (250 grams) ground veal

1½ teaspoons ground cardamom

2½ teaspoons ground allspice

2 teaspoons salt

1 teaspoon black pepper

1 ounce (30 grams) lamb tail fat (optional)

1 packed cup (25 grams) parsley, chopped

2–3 hot green chile peppers

4–5 cloves garlic

1 medium onion, quartered

Place the ground meat in a large bowl. Add the spices. Run the lamb fat, parsley, chiles, garlic, and onion together through a meat grinder or pulse them gently, adding one ingredient at a time, in a food processor, beginning with the lamb fat and ending with the onions. Combine with the ground meat.

With slightly damp hands, mold a small quantity of the meat mixture around skewers, forming elongated, thin kebabs. If you are using wooden skewers, soak them in water first.

To grill: Prepare the coals, forming one large mound and one shorter one, and wait until the fire dies down and the coals are grey. Sear the kebab skewers on high heat for about 2 minutes, then transfer away from the direct heat of the coals.

Fan the flames occasionally to keep them hot. The kebabs should only cook for 6 to 8 minutes or they will dry out. You may also wish to grill separate skewers of small onions and tomatoes to serve alongside the kebabs.

Serve the kebabs with assorted pickles, *Hummus Bil T'heena* (page 85), *Imtabbal Bitinjan* (page 84), minced green salad, and *Khubz Kmaj* (page 100).

كباب مشوي

Few things are more enticing than the smell of kebab grilling over hot coals, luring passersby into sidewalk restaurants for a quick meal. This recipe is from Salih Atiya al-Shawa, one of Gaza City's most well-known *kebabjis*. Al-Shawa says clients sometimes request that a little premium lamb tail fat be ground into the mixture, making the meat juicier, or else extra cardamom or garlic. For a small extra price, of course! If you can, try grinding the ingredients yourself at home or ask your butcher to do it for you. Use flavorful cuts of beef.

Jaj Mashwi Bil Furun

Oven-Roasted Chicken

Serves 4–6

One 3 pound (1½ kilogram) chicken
1 tablespoon ground sumac
1½ teaspoons salt
½ teaspoon cardamom
2 teaspoons red pepper flakes
1 onion, grated
1 very ripe tomato, crushed
1 teaspoon tomato paste
¼ cup (60 milliliters) fresh lemon juice
¼ cup (60 milliliters) olive oil
2 tomatoes, quartered
1 potato, cut into 1 inch slices
6 cloves garlic, whole
1 large onion, quartered
2 carrots, cut into 1 inch pieces
1 summer squash, sliced

Wash the chicken well, as instructed on page 26 in the section "Common Sense," and set it aside in a colander to drain off the bloody juices.

Rub the sumac, salt, cardamom, and pepper flakes under and over the skin of the chicken, making sure to reach inside to the thighs. Combine the onion, tomato, tomato paste, lemon juice, and olive oil and mix well. Rub this mixture all over as you did with the spices, and inside the body cavity. Set the chicken aside for at least 2 hours.

Preheat your oven to 400°F (200°C).

Set the chicken in a roasting pan with the whole garlic cloves and vegetables, then place it in the preheated oven. The roasting time will depend on the size of the chicken, but it should take about 1 hour. The chicken is done when piercing between the body and the thigh releases clear (not pink or cloudy) juice.

دجاج مشوي بالفرن

Whether left whole or cut into parts, spicy roast chicken is a perennial favorite in Gaza. This is an adaptation of a recipe given to us by Lulu from the Olive Roots Cooperative in Zeitun.

Jaj Mashwi El Fahem

Charcoal-Grilled Chicken

Serves 4–5

One 3 pound (1½ kilogram) chicken
1½ teaspoons salt
2 green chile peppers, chopped
5 cloves garlic
1 teaspoon black pepper
3 tablespoons sumac
2 tablespoons vinegar
1 tablespoon ground red pepper (cayenne or similar)
¼ cup (59 milliliters) olive oil

Wash the chicken well, as instructed in "Common Sense" (page 26). Set the chicken aside in a colander to let the bloody juices drain.

Butterfly the chicken: Start by using a pair of kitchen shears or a sharp butcher's knife and cut out the back. Spread the chicken out and press it flat.

In a mortar and pestle, crush the garlic and chile peppers along with ½ teaspoon of salt. Mix this together with the pepper, sumac, vinegar, ground red pepper, olive oil, and remaining salt. Slather the chicken with this marinade, place it in a large bowl, and refrigerate it, covered, for several hours or overnight.

Lay the chicken out flat in a grill cage and lock it. (If you don't have a grill cage, it's worth the investment, though you can also make this on a simple grill.) Meanwhile, prepare the coals: Pile them into a mound on one side of the grill. When the coals are red and coated in grey ash, you are ready to begin.

First, place the cage on the cooler side of the grill, away from the mound of coals, skin side up. Close the grill cover and cook the chicken for about 50 minutes. Test the doneness of the chicken by piercing the thigh with a skewer: If the juice that runs out is pink, it needs more time.

Once it is cooked through, transfer the chicken cage to the part of the grill directly over the mound of coals and flip so it is skin side down. Sear the chicken over direct heat until the skin is charred and crispy.

Serve with *Khubz Saj* (page 100), assorted pickles, *Hummus Bil T'heena* (page 85), and *Imtabbal Bitinjan* (page 84).

دجاج مشوي على الفحم

We had of lot of requests from nostalgic visitors to Gaza for this particularly delicious grilled, butterflied whole chicken, often served by small restaurants in the business districts of the city. It can also be made with chicken parts with excellent results.

Sayniyit Jaj Bil Batata Wil Bandora

صينية دجاج بالبطاطا والبندورة

Baked Chicken with Potatoes and Tomatoes

Serves 5–6

A simple but sublime preparation for baked chicken, the perfect comfort food.

One 3 pound (1½ kilogram) chicken, skinned and cut into parts
1 teaspoon salt, plus more for cleaning the chicken
½ teaspoon black pepper
1½ teaspoons allspice
½ teaspoon ground cardamom
2 medium potatoes, peeled and sliced
1 medium onion, sliced
2 tomatoes, thickly sliced
10 whole garlic cloves
2–3 green chile peppers, cut into thin strips
Olive oil
½ cup (120 milliliters) water, tomato sauce, or liquefied strained
    tomatoes

Preheat your oven to 375°F (190°C).

Clean the chicken well, bathing it in a bowl of cold water mixed with a fistful of flour. Rub the chicken pieces with a spent lemon rind or some vinegar and a little coarse salt, removing any veins and extra fat. Rinse the chicken and set it aside in a colander for about 10 minutes to let the bloody juices drain.

Next, rub the chicken pieces with the salt, pepper, and remaining spices, along with ½ cup (120 milliliters) of olive oil. Drizzle a little of the oil on the bottom of a baking pan, then layer the potatoes and onions on top. Transfer the chicken pieces to the pan, arranging them on top of the potatoes, followed by the tomatoes and the peppers. Scatter the garlic cloves all over.

Add ½ cup of water and the tomato sauce, or tomato water, to the pan. Cover the pan with aluminum foil and bake for approximately 40 minutes. Uncover the pan and set the oven to broil, then return it to the oven for about 5 minutes to brown. Serve with *Hummus Bil T'heena* (page 85), *Khubz Kmaj* (page 100), salad, and an assortment of pickles.

Jaj Bil Filfil Wil Lamoon

Baked Chicken with Chiles and Lemon

Serves 5–6

One 3 pound (1½ kilogram) chicken, cut into parts
1 medium onion, julienned
1 teaspoon salt
½ teaspoon black pepper
3 green chile peppers, sliced
5 garlic cloves, crushed
Juice of two lemons
3 baking potatoes, evenly sliced
Parsley and lemon slices, for garnish

Preheat your oven to 375°F (190°C).

In a large bowl, wash your chicken with water and a fistful of flour, then rub it with a spent lemon rind or a little vinegar and some coarse salt. Rinse it clean and set it aside in a strainer for 10 minutes to let the bloody juices drain.

Season the chicken with salt and pepper. In a large skillet, warm a few glugs of olive oil (about ⅓ cup, or 80 milliliters) and pan-fry the chicken pieces, a few at a time so as not to overcrowd the pan, along with the onion until they are browned all over. Add approximately 2 cups (240 milliliters) of water to the pan. Turn the heat down to low and simmer it for about 15 minutes, skimming any scum or grease that rises to the surface.

Meanwhile, fry or oven-roast your potato slices (simply slather in olive oil and bake) and season them with salt. Set aside.

Transfer the chicken and its broth to a baking pan, along with the chile peppers, crushed garlic, and lemon juice. Arrange the potato slices all around.

Bake, covered, for about 30 to 40 minutes. Remove the chicken from the oven and transfer it to a serving dish. Garnish with chopped parsley and lemon slices.

دجاج بالفلفل والليمون

This recipe came our way in the course of an energetic and chaotic conversation on the subject of baked chicken with the women at the Olive Roots Cooperative in Zeitun. There were as many recipes as there were cooks. And they're all fantastic!

Kufta al Ghaz

Stovetop Kufta

Serves 4–6

2 pounds (1 kilogram) lean beef
1 packed cup (25 grams) parsley
1 medium onion, chopped
½ teaspoon black pepper
1 teaspoon ground allspice
½ teaspoon ground red pepper
1½ teaspoons salt
4–5 ripe tomatoes, grated or liquefied
2–3 potatoes, peeled and thinly sliced
Olive oil

Run the meat, parsley, onions, black pepper, red pepper, and allspice together through a food grinder, or pulse the parsley and onion in a food processor one at a time, then mix them well with preground meat and spices. Form this mixture into small oblong patties.

In a wide pot, pan-fry the patties in a little olive oil, about ⅓ cup (80 milliliters), until they are slightly browned on all sides. Drain off and discard the excess fat and return the kufta to the pan. Pour the liquefied tomatoes on top.

Neatly spread an overlapping layer of sliced potatoes over the tomato. Season this with salt and pepper. Bring to a low boil and cover, lowering the heat. Allow this to simmer for about 30 minutes or until the potatoes are fully cooked.

Serve with *Khubz Kmaj* (page 100), assorted pickles, and *Ruz Imfalfal* (page 206).

كفتة عالغاز

Um Sultan, a magnificent cook and farmer, was appalled that we were going to cite her on such a simple recipe. *Kufta* is considered a lazy cook's food, something almost effortless for an everyday meal. But it is no less delicious for all that, and with fresh tomatoes and potatoes from Um Sultan's farm, it was divine. While urban Gazans tend to use an elaborate range of spices, rural tastes rely on farm-grown ingredients.

eastern border, but their farm there was destroyed by an Israeli incursion in 2003. She told us:

> First they uprooted all the olive trees around our house. Then the livestock, the pigeons, the clay oven.... They destroyed it all. I was scared for my children; they were little then. So we fled and rented this place. It's expensive, but I have more peace of mind this way. We don't even try to go to our land now; it's in the buffer zone and they're always out there with their tanks and shells....

This was not the first time the family had been forced to flee. Before 1948, they had owned farms near Yaffa. They fled to Gaza and lived in tents in the Khan Younis refugee camp until the mid-1950s, when they managed to buy land and return to the farming life:

> Our grandfather was still alive then, so he taught my uncle and father [to farm]. I learned from them. Then we began going to farming cooperatives and unions, taking courses... how to manage the land, how to plan, when to harvest. It's not like we were born with this knowledge. And then we taught it to our children.

Few of the many refugees originally from rural areas in Gaza have been able to obtain land and return to farming. Um Sultan is justifiably proud of her family's accomplishment, and as she cooks she introduces each ingredient with a grin: "Fresh from our farm!"

When Laila went back to visit Um Sultan's family in 2013 (while showing chef Anthony Bourdain around Gaza), she found the farm still prospering and employing several neighbors, but now divided into individual lots for each of the daughters of the family. Like many villages in southern Gaza, Bani Suhayla is historically a matriarchal society, with land and property passed from mothers to daughters. Despite multiple displacements and losses, Um Sultan forges ahead, brash and big-hearted, transforming her small foothold in Gaza into a legacy for her daughters.

We arrived at the farm of Um Sultan (Nabila El-Shami) in the eastern village of Bani Suhayla just as she and her exuberant extended family had finished harvesting a field of hot red chile peppers. The sacks of peppers were carried off to a nearby factory to be turned into *filfil mat'hoon*, and the family reclined in the shade to rest a bit. Ruddy and energetic, Um Sultan showed us around the meticulously organized and very productive farm, with orchards, vegetable fields, and animal pens all tidily packed into a few rented acres. The family owns land near the

236

Kufta bi Saniya

Pan-Baked Kufta

Serves 6–7

2 pounds (1 kilogram) extra-lean ground beef
1 packed cup (25 grams) parsley
6 cloves peeled garlic
2 green chile peppers
1 medium onion
2½ teaspoons ground allspice
1 teaspoon black pepper
½ teaspoon ground nutmeg
1 teaspoon ground cardamom
2 teaspoons salt
¼ cup (25 grams) bread crumbs
2 potatoes, thinly sliced
1 onion, evenly sliced
2 tomatoes, thickly sliced
3–4 very ripe tomatoes, liquefied in a blender and whisked through a sieve *or* 5 tablespoons tomato paste diluted in 2 cups (480 milliliters) water

Preheat your oven to 400°F (200°C).

Wash the parsley well and remove any thick stems. Run the beef, parsley, onion, garlic, and chile peppers through a meat grinder, or pulse them in a food processor. (If using this method, use preground beef, then pulse the remaining ingredients one at a time, beginning with the parsley and proceeding to the garlic, peppers, and onions). Transfer to a bowl. Stir in the spices and then the bread crumbs and mix well, adding a little more if mixture appears too loose.

Spread the meat mixture out evenly onto a 12-inch (30 centimeter) round oiled pan or a 9 x 13 inch (22 x 33 centimeter) casserole dish, completely covering the bottom. (Alternatively, the mixture may be shaped into 2 to 3 inch—5 to 6 centimeter—oblong ovals). Using the tips of your fingers, make a spiral indentation on the surface of the meat for the fat to rise into.

Bake for about 10 minutes. Remove the pan from the oven and drain off any excess fat that has accumulated, then top the meat mixture with neatly arranged overlapping layers of sliced potatoes, onions, and tomatoes.

Douse with liquefied tomatoes or tomato sauce, and cover the pan with aluminum foil. Return it to the oven and bake for an additional 40 minutes or until the potatoes are tender.

Serve with *Khubz Kmaj* (page 100) or *Ruz Imfalfal* (page 206) and salad.

كفتة بالصينية

A more elaborately spiced Gaza City *kufta*, made in the oven. Fresh tomatoes are used in this dish in summer; canned tomato sauce or paste are substituted in the off-season.

Tabkeeh Laban Bil Mozat

Lamb Shank Yogurt Stew

Serves 5–6

3 pounds (1½ kilograms) lamb shanks, cut into 3 parts each
64 ounces (1¾ liters) full cream yogurt at room temperature) full cream plain or strained yogurt, left out at room temperature
2 tablespoon flour
Olive Oil

Prepare the lamb shanks according to the instructions in the *Maraqa* recipe (page 24).

Whisk the yogurt through a fine mesh strainer into a large pot. Sift the flour into the yogurt. Turn the stove to medium heat and cook the yogurt for about 7 minutes, whisking continuously to keep it from separating.

Once it has come to a gentle boil, gradually add about 2 cups (500 milliliters) of the reserved lamb broth to thin it out and impart flavor. Continue cooking for an additional 5 minutes or so. Add the reserved meat chunks and serve with *Rabee'iya* (page 208).

طبيخ لبن بالموزات

Yogurt-based stews are more common in northern and eastern parts of Palestine and the greater Levant, but they are also made in Gaza, especially in spring. The stew goes by many names depending on region, including *laban umo* and *shakreeya*. Ideally, the yogurt should be left out overnight to sour slightly. Do not use yogurt with thickeners such as carrageenan or gelatin, or it will separate upon cooking.

On Schnitzel

Most little restaurants and fast-food joints in Gaza feature schnitzel on their menus. This may come as something of a surprise to the visitor: schnitzel? Yes, your classic pan-fried *weinerschnitzel* is a favorite in Gaza, one of many tastes acquired over the years through contact with Israelis. Now, with Gaza totally isolated, it is easy to forget that for decades thousands of Palestinians in Gaza went every day to work in Israel, that Israeli and Gazan entrepreneurs had partnerships, that both commerce and social relations existed (though on vastly unequal footing). Adult Gazans remember this, and many speak admiringly of aspects of Israeli society or maintain contact with Israeli business partners, employers, and friends.

For the enormous population of young people who were not old enough to work or travel before Israel sealed the borders in 2000, though, this is impossible. Though their lives are completely conditioned by Israel's political decisions, they have never laid eyes on a single Israeli except for the soldiers who come in on tanks or bulldozers, wreaking destruction and destroying livelihoods. The generation of young Israelis to which those soldiers belong has likewise never met a single Gazan Palestinian in any other context. While interpersonal relations alone will not bring an end to this decades-long colonial occupation, they are still vital for instilling a sense of the other's humanity.

239

Fatta Bil Aranib/Jaj

Buttery Rice and Griddle Bread with Rabbit or Chicken

Serves 6–7

1 whole rabbit or chicken

For the stuffing
1 onion, finely chopped
⅓ cup (65 grams) short- or medium-grain rice
⅓ cup (65 grams) bulgur
¾ teaspoon salt
¼ teaspoon black pepper
½ teaspoon ground cardamom
⅛ teaspoon ground nutmeg
1 teaspoon *qidra* spices (page 34)
1 rabbit or chicken liver, chopped
½ cup (35 grams) toasted almonds
½ cup (10 grams) chopped parsley
Olive oil

For the broth
1 medium onion, chopped
1 teaspoon peppercorns
1 teaspoon cardamom pods
1 teaspoon allspice berries
1 very small piece of cracked nutmeg
1 cinnamon stick
2 bay leaves
2–3 pearls of mastic

For the rice
1½ cup (300 grams) rice, washed well and soaked in cold water
⅛ teaspoon ground allspice
¼ teaspoon ground cinnamon
2 tablespoons chopped parsley
2 tablespoons almonds, toasted and chopped

For the bread base
Several sheets of *Khubz Saj* (page 102)
3–4 tablespoons butter or ghee, melted

Wash the meat carefully in a bath of cold water, a little flour, salt, and lemon juice or vinegar. Set aside to let the bloody juices drain.

Prepare the stuffing: Rub the salt into the onions with your hands and sauté them in 2 tablespoons of olive oil until translucent. Add all the other stuffing ingredients except the parsley and nuts. Add ½ cup (120 milliliters) water and cook on medium heat, stirring occasionally, until

فتة بالارانب/دجاج

Often made for guests, *fatta* is heir to a long Arab tradition of serving roasted meat with broth-soaked bread, said to be the favorite food of the Prophet Muhammad (PBUH). This is Gaza's much-loved version, although the chicken or rabbit *fatta* served in modern Gaza would have been an embarrassment in more prosperous days. Several of the older women we interviewed described how, in the past, a guest's arrival warranted the slaughter of a sheep, which would be roasted whole and presented on a bed of rice and bread. Given current shortages, being served a whole chicken or rabbit constitutes an equivalent honor.

Fatta is comprised of several layers: We have divided the ingredients by layer to avoid confusion. The final result is a bed of torn griddle bread lightly soaked in broth, then covered with a layer of buttery rice and topped with stuffed meat. It is customary to eat *fatta* with one's right hand, while seated on the ground: the broth-soaked bread is used to scoop up the rice.

the rice is al dente. When the rice is cool enough to handle, mix in the parsley and nuts. Stuff this mixture into the cavity of the chicken or rabbit. Leave a little space for the rice to expand. Sew the cavity shut with a needle and thread or weave several toothpicks through.

Next, brown the whole stuffed rabbit or chicken in a large pot in 3 to 4 tablespoons of oil. Add the chopped onion and sauté it together with the meat. Add enough water to fully submerge the meat. Bring to a boil and then reduce the heat, removing any froth or scum that rises to the surface. Add the whole spices (tied in a piece of gauze or disposable teabag, for easy disposal later) and the mastic. Simmer until the meat is cooked but not falling apart, about 30 minutes. Remove the chicken or rabbit carefully and set it aside. Strain the broth and reserve it.

Cook the rice: Strain the soaking water out of the rice, then sauté for about 1 minute in 2 tablespoons of oil until the rice turns slightly translucent. Add the 3 cups (720 milliliters) of reserved broth. Bring the broth to a boil, then lower the heat and simmer, covered, for about 20 minutes or until the rice is tender to the bite.

Prepare the base of *saj* bread: Dip each round of bread into the reserved broth, then tear all of the bread into short strips and layer them on a tray. Grease your hand with some ghee or butter and spread it across the warm, broth-soaked bread. Top the greased bread with the cooked rice, then sprinkle it with the allspice, cinnamon, chopped parsley, and browned nuts.

On top of this bed, in the center, place the stuffed chicken or rabbit. Serve alongside small bowls of *Daggit Toma u Lamoon* (page 28) and separate bowls of the remaining broth. Guests can then spoon these over their food as they eat. You may also serve *fatta* with bowls of plain yogurt.

Fatema Qaadan

Fatema Qaadan greets us clad in a bright orange dress that matches her henna-dyed hair, one gold tooth in her radiant smile. A widow, she lives with her teenage daughter in a single room inherited from her late husband. It is a painfully hot summer day with a strong sandy wind, and to boot, it is Ramadan, the holiest month of the Muslim calendar, in which the observant fast from dawn till sunset. No matter: in this tiny space, using a single detached gas burner, she prepares a splendid *Iftar* meal for us of *fatta bil aranib* from one of the rabbits she raises in the sandy lot abutting her room.

Because her family is small, Fatema doesn't qualify for most of the aid distribution packages that have become the primary means of subsistence for the overwhelming majority of Palestinians here. Tired of feeling helpless, she applied to participate in a new rabbit-rearing initiative she heard about at the local community center. To the envy of her neighbors, she was awarded one of the few available grants, providing her with a breeding pair of rabbits, materials for a hutch, and a few sacks of feed. She now boasts a flourishing family of young rabbits.

Originally from the village of Beit Jirja, just outside of modern-day Ashkelon, Fatema's family had orchards and livestock in plenty. When Beit Jirja was attacked in 1948, her parents fled with thousands of others, leaving their gold and property behind. They found refuge in the Beach Camp in Gaza City, only to flee again in 1970 when Israeli troops under the command of Ariel Sharon (who was then defense minister) besieged the camp for months, razing their entire neighborhood and killing one of Fatema's brothers.

Her family made their new home in nearby Beit Lahiya, where she married but was widowed one year after her daughter was born. Fatema recalls:

I asked my mother to make me a *thobe* [a traditional Palestinian embroidered dress] for my wedding. She would sit up on the roof, sewing the dress while crying, thinking of her son, Hasan. She embroidered the pieces, red on white cloth, then gave them to me and said, "I did my part, now it's up to you sew it together." So I did, and it's my pride and joy. This dress means everything to me.

She holds the dress up to her breast as though she were a new bride.

Fir Mahshi

Stuffed Quail

Serves 5

2 pounds (about 1 kilogram) of small quail (defrosted, if using frozen ones)

For the stuffing
1 onion, finely chopped
Reserved quail organs, rinsed and chopped
1 teaspoon salt
¾ teaspoon turmeric
½ teaspoon allspice
½ teaspoon cardamom
¼ teaspoon black pepper
¼ teaspoon nutmeg
1 cup (200 grams) medium-grain rice, rinsed well
Olive oil

For the broth
1 onion, coarsely chopped
1 teaspoon cardamom pods
1 teaspoon allspice berries
1 teaspoon peppercorns
1 bay leaf
1 cinnamon stick
1 very small piece of cracked nutmeg
2–3 pearls of mastic
Salt to taste
Juice of half a lemon

Wash the quail well, rubbing them inside and out with a spent lemon rind and some salt, then bathe them in a bowl of cold water with a fistful of flour mixed in. Rinse them, then set them aside to let the bloody juices drain for about 15 minutes.

Prepare the stuffing: Rub the salt into the onions and sauté them in about ¼ cup (60 milliliters) of olive oil on medium heat until they turn lightly golden. Add the chopped organs. Cook these for about 3 minutes, stirring occasionally. Stir in the spices and rice, sautéing for about 2 minutes, until the rice is well coated and slightly translucent. When it is cool enough to handle, divide the rice mixture into equal portions and stuff it into the cavity of each quail. Leave a little space for the rice to expand. Sew the cavity shut with a needle and thread or several toothpicks.

Gently stack the quail in a large pot, then add enough water to submerge them. Bring this to a boil over medium-high heat, skimming any froth that rises to the surface. Add the chopped onion, along with the assorted whole spices (tied together in a piece of gauze or a disposable teabag)

فر محشي

Many residents of Khan Younis in the southern Gaza Strip will cite this as one of their most beloved delicacies. Our thanks to a gentleman who approached us after a talk we gave in Somerville, Massachusetts, and drew our attention to this historic favorite, which we had not included in the first edition of this book.

Quail-trapping season is in the fall, when the birds migrate from Europe to their wintering grounds in Africa. Many Gazans fondly remember camping out on the beach in the summer: they would rig nets along the shore in the evening and then wait until dawn, when the nets would be crowded with weary birds just landing from their flight across the Mediterranean. It is a practice that is said to date back to pharaonic times (a flock of quail succor the Israelites in the book of Exodus) but, due to massive and unregulated over-trapping around the Mediterranean, the migrating flocks have been drastically reduced. Quail are now rarely seen in Gaza at all.

You can find frozen (farm-raised, not wild) quail in many Middle Eastern markets or halal grocers. Stuffed quail may be served on its own, accompanied by one of the many autumn stews we feature in this book, or on top of a bed of buttery rice and griddle bread, like *fatta* (page 240).

and salt, then lower the heat and simmer, partially covered, for approximately 40 minutes or until the rice is cooked through.

Turn off the heat and set the pot aside until the quail are cool to the touch, then gently remove each quail with a slotted spoon and transfer to a baking pan. Brush the surface of each quail with a little olive oil and lemon juice. Broil on high heat for about 5 minutes, until the skins are golden brown and crispy.

Transfer to a serving platter and enjoy atop a bed of buttery rice and griddle bread, as in *fatta* (page 20) or alongside an assortment of small dishes.

Qidra

Spiced Rice with Lamb, Chickpeas, and Garlic

Serves 7–8

2–3 pounds (1 to 1½ kilograms) boneless lamb or goat, trimmed of fat and cut into 2 inch (5 centimeter) pieces

2½ (450 grams) cups extra-long-grain rice

¼ cup (60 milliliters) olive oil

2½ tablespoons *qidra* spices (page 34)

1 teaspoon turmeric

1 tablespoon cardamom pods

2 teaspoons salt

½ teaspoon black pepper

½ teaspoon ground cardamom

¼ teaspoon ground cumin

2 whole heads of garlic, cloves unpeeled

½ cup (100 grams) dried chickpeas, soaked, or one 15 ounce (425 gram) can of chickpeas

4 tablespoons ghee

Prepare the meat according to the instructions in the *Maraqa* recipe (page 24). In this case, it is unnecessary to brown the meat. Strain, reserving both the broth and meat.

Soak the rice in cold water for 15 minutes, then strain it well.

In a clay pot or Dutch oven, sauté the rice in olive oil until it is well coated, about 2 minutes. Add 4 cups (about 1 liter) of strained broth along with the meat, salt, whole unpeeled garlic cloves, chickpeas, cardamom pods and all spices. Mix well and bring to a boil. Cook on medium-high heat for 5 minutes, then reduce the heat to low and cover the pot tightly.

The dish can be finished on the stovetop or in a preheated oven. If using an oven, preheat to 325°F (160°C). Tightly seal the pot with aluminum foil and bake it for about 45 minutes. Increase the oven temperature to 400°F (200°C) and bake for an additional 15 minutes or until the rice is cooked through and the broth has been absorbed. Check rice occasionally: If it seems to be drying out, add a little more broth, ¼ cup at a time. If you are finishing it on the stovetop, the rice will need approximately 25 to 30 minutes on a low flame, with the lid tightly closed.

Remove the pot from the heat and let the rice rest in the covered pot for 20 minutes. Meanwhile, melt the butter or ghee. Uncover the finished *qidra* and pour the melted butter or ghee over it. Carefully transfer to a serving platter or serve out of the clay pot. Serve with plain yogurt, *Filfil Mat'hoon* (page 28), and olives.

قدرة

Qidra is a richly spiced, festive rice dish named for the hand-turned clay urn in which it is cooked. In southern Palestine it is prepared for major occasions such as weddings, birth ceremonies (*aqiqa*), and funerals. Traditionally it was cooked over slow-burning coals outdoors. In the city, the clay pots are taken to a community oven to be cooked, though few such ovens still remain. To serve, the urn is dramatically cracked open and the fragrant, buttery rice pours out.

Assuming there is no community stone oven where you live, a tightly sealed clay pot or a Dutch oven works well for making *qidra*.

While lamb is traditional, chicken or beef may be used instead.

At the end of a sandy alley near the Palestinian Sports Stadium and right behind the Holy Mary School lives the last man in Gaza City who still makes qidra as it is supposed to be made: in great handmade unglazed clay pots, tightly sealed and slowly cooked in a blazing stone oven. While Jamal does prepare the rice himself for some clients, mostly his is an oven service: the client provides and mixes the rice, spices, and meat, then Jamal takes care of the cooking.

He learned the art of the *qidra* oven from his father and grandfather and hopes to pass the oven on to his son. The oven was built in the early 1960s, all of stone, with intense butane heat. Jamal dexterously rotates the pots in the oven with a long hooked pole so they cook evenly. Each pot has the client's name written on it with chalk.

Most of his clients are restauranteurs, but he also makes *qidra* for weddings, parties, and events. On Fridays there is a rush and the oven is full.

One of his clients comes by to pick up *qidra* for his restaurant. He opens each pot, smells it to make sure it is perfect, and pours a bowl of fragrant *samna bala-di* (clarified sheep's-milk butter) into each one before heaving the three hot urns into the trunk of his car.

Behind the oven building is an airy garden surrounded by fig and lemon trees, a big date palm, and climbing jasmine. An enormous dog—extremely uncommon in Gaza—lounges in the shade, and on the broad verandah are several birdcages with bright canaries jumping and singing. Two of Jamal's daughters lean over the rail to say hello, pigtails bobbing.

Under the fruit trees are hundreds of clay pots of various sizes, ordered directly from a local potter. This scene, this gracious garden, this family: they feel as indigenous to this place as the red clay, and as fragile as the vessels into which the clay is shaped.

Maftool

Palestinian Couscous

Um Khalid's Traditional Maftool

Makes 2½ pounds (1 kilogram)

2 pounds (about 1 kilogram) white flour
½ pound (250 grams) whole wheat flour
Olive oil, as needed
Water, as needed
Salt, as needed

Mix the flour and a pinch of salt on a large tray. Add cold water bit by bit, massaging the flour with your hands until a rough, dry dough is formed.

Place a sieve (a *kurbala* is dedicated to this specific purpose, but any wide based sieve should do) over a clean dry tray and put a handful of dough into the sieve. With an open palm, make a circular motion over the dough, pressing it against the sieve, so tiny pieces fall onto the tray below. At first this is somewhat difficult, but with practice it becomes easier. The resulting fine grain is the *maftool*. After each handful of dough has been pushed through the sieve, stir a few drops of olive oil into the *maftool* gently with your hand, making sure the grains don't stick to each other, then pour it onto an open surface covered with a dish towel to dry a little. Repeat with the next handful of dough.

When all the *maftool* has been made, it is ready to either be sun-dried for later use or steamed for consumption (see "How to Steam *Maftool*" on page 250).

مفتول

Maftool is a special source of local pride in the Gaza district. Much like Moroccan couscous (which is Berber North African in origin), it consists of tiny pearls of wheat steamed and served with a stew called *yakhni*. In the north, they make a slightly different version with larger, more circular grains called *moghrabiya* ("of Moroccan origin").

The *maftool* itself can be made in quantity and sun-dried for later use or steamed immediately.

Here are two ways to make *maftool*, one more traditional, the other a modern labor-saving method taught to us by the ever-efficient Um Sultan. Both give excellent results. Don't feel intimidated or let the apparent complexity of hand-rolling *maftool* dissuade you from trying the recipes!

If you are short on time, substitute store-bought instant Moroccan couscous (the whole-wheat varieties available in specialty grocers more closely resemble the Palestinian version) or, better yet, purchase handmade *maftool* sold by various Palestinian women's cooperatives, such as Hadeel and Zaytoun in the United Kingdom or Canaan Fairtrade in the U.S. and elsewhere. Add the seasonings described in the recipes below when cooking.

Maftool is sometimes made with fine semolina, which is considerably more expensive in Gaza, and sometimes with a mixture of whole and white wheat flours. Feel free to use either.

Um Sultan's Quicker Maftool

Makes 2 pounds (approximately 1 kilogram)

2 pounds medium grind (#2) white bulgur
White whole-wheat flour, as needed
Salt, as needed
Olive oil, as needed

Soak the bulgur for an hour in cold water until swollen, then squeeze out any remaining water.

On a large tray, place a few handfuls of soaked bulgur. Sprinkle one generous handful of flour on top of it. Roll your hands gently over the bulgur with open palms in a circular motion for several minutes, until all the flour is clinging to the bulgur and no longer visible, and the bulgur has formed more or less regular, even little balls. This is the *maftool*.

Add a little salt and rub it in, then transfer the *maftool* to a fine sieve and shake out any remaining flour. Pass the *maftool* into a coarser sieve and shake it back and forth, as if winnowing. The *maftool* will slip through, leaving only a few oddly shaped clumps trapped in the sieve. If, like Um Sultan, you have some chickens, feed these clumps to them.

Pour a little olive oil over the winnowed maftool and with the same circular, open-palmed motion, work it into the grains until it is absorbed. Repeat this process until you've used up all the bulgur. Once the maftool is finished, mix it gently with your hands, again with palms open, for a few minutes. It is now ready to steam or sun-dry.

How to Steam Maftool

1 pound (500 grams) maftool (fresh or dried)
Olive oil, as needed
Salt, as needed
2 tablespoons dill seed
2 teaspoons red pepper flakes or 1 cup dill greens, chopped
1 small onion or 3 shallots, finely chopped
1 teaspoon cumin
2 lemons, quartered

In a two-part steamer or *couscousiere*, fill the bottom part with water and the lemon pieces. Bring to a boil. Meanwhile, smear the top part with oil and fill it with half the *maftool*. If the steamer's holes are large, you may want to cover them with a strip of cheesecloth or other pure cotton cloth before adding the *maftool*. Allow this half of the *maftool* to steam uncovered for about half an hour.

Meanwhile, in a mortar and pestle, grind the dill seeds with ½ teaspoon of salt until fragrant. Add the onion and red pepper flakes and pound until they are coarsely mashed. Stir in the cumin and 4 tablespoons of olive oil. This dressing is called *aroosit il maftool*—"the bride of the *maftool*" for the enticing and discreet way it perfumes the grains. In

Rafah, finely chopped dill greens are also added; in Gaza City, red pepper flakes are preferred. Spread a layer of the *aroosit il maftool* on top of the *maftool* in the steamer.

Cover the *aroosit il maftool* with the remaining *maftool,* and continue steaming. After 15 minutes, remove it from the heat and gently stir it with a wooden spoon to fluff the *maftool,* so each grain is separate.

Yakhni

Stew for *Maftool*

Serves 5

3 pounds (about 1½ kilograms) chicken or turkey, cut into parts, bone-in
1 small onion, chopped
2 large onions, julienned
5 medium tomatoes, cut into vertical wedges
½ cup (100 grams) dried chickpeas, soaked overnight, or one 15 ounce (425 gram) can
6 cups (about 1¼ kilograms) butternut squash or carrots, cut into 1 inch (2 1/2 centimeter) pieces
¼ cup (35 grams) dried sour plums or 1 teaspoon pomegranate molasses
2 teaspoons *qidra* spices (page 34)
1 teaspoon ground cumin
½ teaspoon turmeric
½ teaspoon black pepper
2 teaspoons salt
Olive oil, as needed
1 quantity steamed *maftool* (see recipe on page 249)

Wash the chicken pieces well, as instructed on page 26 in the section "Common Sense," in a bath of cold water, vinegar, a little flour, and salt, and massage with spent lemon rinds. Rinse them well and set aside to let the bloody juices drain.

Warm some oil in a wide skillet and add the chicken or turkey pieces. Cook until it is golden brown on all sides. Add the onion, salt, and pepper and fry until the onion is translucent. Lower the flame and add water (about 7 cups, or just under 2 liters, enough to fully submerge the meat). Bring to a boil and remove any froth that rises to the top. Add the *qidra* spices, cumin, sour plums (or a teaspoon of pomegranate molasses), turmeric, and soaked chickpeas (if you are using dried chickpeas). Lower the heat and simmer, partially covered, for an hour. Strain and reserve the broth, and set the meat and chickpeas aside.

In a separate pot, sauté the julienned onions in 2 tablespoons of olive oil until they become slightly limp. Add the squash or carrots and tomatoes and stir for 2 minutes. Add 5 to 6 cups of the reserved broth, then cover the pot and allow it to simmer for 30 minutes or until the squash is tender. If you are using canned chickpeas, add them in the last few minutes of cooking, to heat through.

To serve, spread a bed of steamed *maftool* on a serving platter. Top this with the *yakhni*, using a slotted spoon to scoop it out of the pot, and ladle a little of the broth over this. Arrange the turkey or chicken pieces on top of the vegetables.

Serve with small bowls of extra broth and pinch-bowls of cumin, which each person may add to taste.

يخني

Abu Sultan, Um Sultan's husband, used a freshly slaughtered turkey from their farm to make this *yakhni*, under the careful instruction and supervision of his wife—from whom, he says, he learned to prepare "just about everything."

Yakhni is one of those culinary terms which reveals a whole history of relationship and exchange. From Southeast Asia to the Balkans, the term is used to refer to different dishes—always some kind of meat-based stew—in each local context. In Gaza, *yakhni* is always served with *maftool*.

Ibtisam Zimmo, from Gaza City, rest her soul, a dear family friend of Laila's, told us that dried *arasiya* (native sour plums) used to be added to the broth to lend a note of sourness.

Um Khalid

Off a dusty road on the outskirts of Rafah, Um Khalid (Nabila Qishta) welcomes us into a newly built concrete-block house with fantastic yellow loofah flowers starting to climb up the façade. Devastation and rubble surround the well-tended dooryard; the skeletons of two completely destroyed buildings loom over it. A tractor rolls by, carrying fodder to some sheep penned among the debris next door. Um Khalid explains:

> My family has owned this land for a long time, but after my father died, my brothers decided it wasn't worth the effort to continue farming it since so much of what they earned had to go toward taxes and irrigation. We couldn't pay, and the family scattered: some to work

in Saudi Arabia, others to the Emirates. The rest stayed in Khan Younis.

> I got married and lived near the border here in Rafah. But then our house got demolished; it was January 20, 2004, at 7:20 PM, I'll never forget it. When we left the house, we had nothing at all. Thank God we were all okay. It was a big house. The first time the bulldozers came was early in the morning, and all the neighbors came to our house, escaping from the demolition of their own houses. They started to tear down our house with all of us inside, but they stopped halfway through. A month later they came back and demolished it completely.

In those days, we didn't make time-consuming foods like this (*maftool*). We had to buy take-out; there was no place to cook. Luckily we could afford it—not everyone could. For a long time, we were staying with friends and family members, then we rented one place and then another.... Finally, we built this house.

In those days, a lot of internationals came through here, and some stayed with us—people involved in solidarity campaigns. Sometimes they still write.... We miss those people, they were lovely. And they really enjoyed our food! But now they can't get through the borders.

It is not just the solidarity volunteers who cannot cross the border anymore. With the Rafah border just a few hundred meters away, one feels its closure with special intensity. Everyone is stuck, on one side or the other. Um Khalid's eldest son, an engineer, moved back to the family home after losing his job, joining the swelling ranks of unemployed young men desperate to get out of Gaza to seek employment. He calls us every so often asking for any lead, any work, we might know of. Her daughter Fida, a writer, teacher, and activist, is on the other side: she went to the United States to promote her widely acclaimed film about Gaza, *Where Should the Birds Fly,* and has since been unable to return to Gaza to see her family. She is now pursuing a master's degree in film studies in California.

Musaqa'a

Eggplant, Tomato, and Beef Timbale

Serves 5–6

1½ pounds (approximately 750 grams) eggplant

1 medium onion, chopped

½ pound (approximately 250 grams) finely minced beef (preferably sirloin tips) or boneless lamb

¾ teaspoon salt, more for sprinkling on eggplant

¼ teaspoon black pepper

½ teaspoon cardamom

1 teaspoon allspice

⅛ teaspoon nutmeg

1 onion, julienned

8 garlic cloves, split into halves

1 green or red bell pepper, sliced into 1 inch (2½ centimeter) vertical strips

2–3 hot green chile peppers, thinly sliced into vertical strips

2 large tomatoes, sliced

Salt and black pepper to taste

¼ cup (60 milliliters) hot water or tomato sauce

Olive oil

Preheat your oven to 375°F (190°C).

Partially peel the eggplant in alternating fashion (one strip peeled, the next unpeeled, and so on), then cut these into slices 1 inch (2½ centimeter) thick. If you are using thinner eggplants, peel and slice them lengthwise.

Sprinkle the eggplants generously with salt and place them in a colander for 30 minutes in a sunny location until beads of moisture appear on the surface, or else soak them in a saltwater bath (¼ cup salt (75 grams) to 4 quarts (4 liters) water) for 20 minutes.

Drain the eggplant well, pat it dry with paper towels, then fry the pieces in hot vegetable oil until they turn golden. If you prefer to avoid frying, you can oven-roast them: Toss the eggplant pieces with olive oil, then arrange them on an oiled baking pan or cookie sheet and roast them in a 400°F (200°C) oven until they are browned on the bottom. Then broil them for 5 to 10 minutes. An indoor grill or panini press also works extremely well.

Meanwhile, in a skillet, sauté the chopped onion for a few minutes until it turns translucent, then add the meat and brown it well. Season it with the salt, black pepper, cardamom, allspice, and nutmeg. Add the liquid (water or broth) and simmer for 10 minutes.

In a separate skillet, warm 2 to 3 tablespoons of olive oil, then sauté the julienned onion and the garlic until they turn deeply golden. Add the peppers and cook until they are slightly charred.

مسقعة

While many in the West are familiar with the heavier Greek version of this dish, *moussaka*, few are aware that it is originally an Arab dish, still popular in Palestine. While talking about the origins of things is a dangerous business, especially in former Ottoman lands, in this case the etymology seems pretty clear: *musaqa'a* comes from the Arabic for "chilled" or "cooled." As its name indicates, the dish is served cold, a perfect slice of summer.

In Gaza, the most typical recipe uses finely chopped beef or lamb stewed with spices and then layered between the eggplants and tomatoes, though for a quicker version you can also use fried ground meat. You can also omit the meat altogether and double the quantities of vegetables for a lovely vegetarian dish.

In a shallow casserole dish, arrange layers of eggplant slices, followed by layers of meat, tomato slices, pepper, and onion. Season with salt and freshly cracked black pepper. Pour in the hot water or tomato sauce. Cover with foil and bake for about 40 minutes. Remove from oven to cool.

Musaqa'a should be served cool or at room temperature, with *Khubz Kmaj* (page 100) or *Ruz Imfalfal* (page 206).

Ijrishit Bir el Sabi'

Bir el Sabi' Lamb and Wheat Stew

Serves 6–8

2 pounds (1 kilogram) lamb chunks, bone-in
2 cups (400 grams) soft spring wheat berries or grade 4 (extra coarse) bulgur
2 onions, finely chopped
2 rounds *Khubz Saj* (page 102) or other thin bread
3 or more tablespoons ghee or butter, melted
½ cup (35 grams) sliced almonds, fried
Chopped parsley, for garnish

If you are using wheat berries, coarsely crush them in a heavy mortar and pestle or pulse them a few times in a food processor or high-powered blender.

Prepare the lamb according to the instructions in the *Maraqa* recipe (page 24). Skim the broth, then add the wheat or bulgur and salt along with the whole spices. Simmer on low heat until the wheat is cooked through and the meat is fork-tender, approximately 90 minutes. The wheat will have absorbed much of the water. Strain, reserving the broth, meat, and wheat.

Meanwhile, submerge the rounds of *saj* bread quickly into some of the reserved broth, then tear them into small strips and spread these evenly in a high-rimmed serving platter or tray. Smear the bread with melted ghee or butter, using your hand or a brush.

Spread the wheat and meat mixture on top of the torn bread, along with a few ladles of the reserved broth. Serve the remaining broth in bowls alongside the *ijrisha*.

Garnish with nuts and chopped parsley.

جريشة بئر السبع

Ijrisha is the name generally used for bulgur pilaf, but in the desert oasis town of Bir el Sabi', it was also the name of a celebrated dish made for weddings and other special occasions, taught to us by Um Hazim Al-Ajrami. In Gaza, refugees from Bir el Sabi' still make it to celebrate their important events. As with other wheat berry–based dishes, don't be alarmed if the kernels don't actually appear to get crushed: the point is to release some of the natural starches. If this appears too daunting, you can substitute the largest size of bulgur instead.

Fattit Ajir

Roasted Baby Watermelon and Vegetables *Fatta*

Serves 6

One 3–5 pound unripe baby watermelon (1½ kilograms), calabash squash, or ash gourd of equal weight
1 large or 3 small eggplants, about 1 pound (500 grams)
3 Middle Eastern *koosa* (also known as grey squash)
2 teaspoons salt
5 hot green chile peppers, chopped
1 bunch green onions (scallions), chopped
1 medium-sized white onion, finely chopped
1 pound (approximately 500 grams) very ripe tomatoes, chopped
1 pound (approximately 500 grams) cucumbers, peeled and finely chopped
2 lemons, peeled, segmented, and chopped
1 bunch fresh dill (about 25 grams), chopped
1 bunch parsley (about 25 grams), chopped
1 cup (240 milliliters) tahina
Freshly squeezed juice of two lemons
½ cup (120 milliliters) high-quality extra-virgin olive oil
1 *qursa* or other thick flatbread (such as naan), toasted and torn into pieces

Wrap the watermelon or gourd in foil, then roast it over a gas range, on a grill, or directly over an open fire or hot coals until it is soft to the touch and charred on all sides. It may be easier to pierce the watermelon with a thick skewer or stick while it is roasting. If you are doubling the recipe, skewer the melons or gourds with a thick wire. Repeat this procedure with the eggplants and squash, skipping the foil. Set all of the vegetables aside to cool.

Using a mortar and pestle, crush the hot peppers with the salt until they are well mashed. Add the tomatoes and pound until uniform and thick. The tomatoes can also be mashed by hand or pulsed in a food processor a few times.

Peel the cooled melon, squash, and eggplants and discard the charred skin. Chop them roughly, then mix the chopped pulp of these vegetables with the chile-tomato mixture, using your hands, in a large bowl until well combined. Add the scallions, cucumbers, onion, lemon segments, dill, and parsley and mix well.

In a separate bowl, combine the tahina and the lemon juice, thinning it with a little extra juice if necessary. Stir this, along with the olive oil, into the vegetable mash.

Add the torn pieces of toasted bread (enough so that the bread makes up roughly half of the dish) and knead the entire mixture well by hand

This unusual dish is a specialty of the southern Gaza Strip and neighboring Sinai. *Fattit ajir* is a family affair (specifically a men's affair) that can take more than half the day to prepare, as Laila discovered when visiting the Sheikh family, descendants of refugees from Bir el Sabi' now living in Bani Suhayla. The dish is enjoyed out in the open in late spring or early summer, when baby watermelons are in season. The recipe calls for skewering young, unripe watermelons on a wire and fire-roasting them until charred, then mashing the pulp together with an array of vegetables, olive oil, and torn pieces of thick, unleavened fire-baked bread. The final dish is served in a large tray on the ground, and family members gather around to eat together using their hands.

If you cannot find unripe watermelon, use a small out-of-season melon or one that has white or pale green patches on its side. Use this part of the melon with its rind, wrapping it in foil. Otherwise, calabash squash or winter melon may be substituted.

The bread traditionally used is made from unleavened dough shaped into a thick disk, or *qursa*, which is then wrapped in newspapers or foil and buried in low-burning embers in the ground. Any thick, unleavened, and well-toasted flatbread can be substituted, though making your own *qursa* is relatively simple (we provide the recipe). Here, we have scaled down the recipe to serve just six, though traditionally *fattit ajir* would be made for a whole clan until the bread has absorbed the liquids from the salad. Transfer and arrange on a large round platter, then drizzle it generously with olive oil.

Serve with small quartered white onions, olives, and assorted pickled vegetables.

For the qursa
3 cups (380 grams) flour
⅔ cup warm water (160 milliliters), more as needed
½ teaspoon salt
3 tablespoons warmed olive oil, plus more for drizzling

Knead together all ingredients until the dough is elastic and no longer sticky, for about 5 minutes. Form the dough into a ball, then flatten using the palm of your hand into a single 1-inch-thick disk. Drizzle both sides with olive oil. Bake on a grill rack, preferably on a wood-fired grill; alternately, cook in a frying pan on a stovetop or in the oven until well browned. A traditional *qursa* is placed directly on the grey embers of an open fire and covered in sand, which is then scraped off, along with any charred bits, before using.

The Economy of Uncertainty

While a large majority of Gazans are stricken with systematic unemployment and acute poverty, shops are still stocked with consumer goods, and there are still restaurants and cafés operating, some of them quite elegant. With the borders closed, industry ruined, and exports impossible, who is buying these goods at inflated prices? Where is the money coming from? The Gazan economy is so bizarre that it is worth taking a moment to trace the cash flows.

The United Nations Relief and Works Agency (UNRWA), which provides all services to the Palestinian refugee population, is one of the principal employers in Gaza, paying decent salaries to 11,000 people. These individuals in turn support many unemployed family members. The United States is the main UNRWA donor, followed by various European countries and Japan. No one in Gaza fails to note the irony of such a massive U.S. expenditure to feed and educate the same people it also pays (by way of aid to Israel) to bomb and imprison: "They feed us with one hand and strangle us with the other" is the common refrain.

The next main employer is the government, although one of the peculiarities of Gaza is that it is not entirely clear just who that is, and whoever it is can only barely be called a "government," since the powers accorded to Palestinian self-rule by the Oslo Accords are so limited. That said, between 2007 and 2014, the Hamas party ruled in Gaza, with its corresponding body of civil servants, ministry workers, police, and so on. During that same period, the Fatah Party–led Palestinian Authority (based in Ramallah, in the West Bank) did not acknowledge the Hamas government's legitimacy and maintained its own parallel government—with all the corresponding employees.

In 2014, a Consensus Government was forged under the leadership of Ramallah-based prime minister Rami Hamdallah in an effort to bridge the growing rift between the two territories, although this unity government's actual presence and role in Gaza now is unclear. Suffice it to say that at least one and possibly two governments are paying salaries with funds drawn principally from international donors: the United States and Europe in the case of the Palestinian Authority, Qatar in the case of Hamas. Support from Iran, while still trickling in, has been reduced dramatically since 2011, when Palestinian factions refused to take sides in the ongoing war in Syria.

Lastly, as a sort of shadow structure to make up for the absence of any kind of economy *besides* aid

and governance, there are all the many internationally funded nongovernmental organizations (NGOs) operating in Gaza to assist the hundreds of thousands of impoverished Gazans who are not refugees and therefore are not entitled to UNRWA services. These NGOs employ thousands of Gazans, as well as some international workers (at much higher salaries).

These systems—all of which compete for competencies that would normally belong to the state—are the principal means by which currency enters Gaza. Some additional money enters through remittances from Palestinians living abroad who send money transfers to their families in Gaza. Then this cash circulates: employees and their families shop for goods and services, sustaining a whole commercial and service sector as well as local market agriculture.

Many other places in the world have also seen their productive sectors destroyed and now survive only on government employment, remittances, and aid, but we don't hear about them so often in the news; they don't have highly publicized flotillas attempting to change their situation. Gazans themselves are quick to recognize this. Much of the formerly colonized world has been de-developed; what is peculiar about Gaza is how clearly, rapidly, and violently the process has occurred. Processes like what has happened in Gaza have happened elsewhere, from Dakar to Detroit, but seldom in such an explicitly intentional and violent manner.

What adds insult to injury is the fact that all of this is so very profitable for its perpetrators: Economists estimate that every dollar of aid that enters Gaza ends up in Israeli pockets, with a 120 percent increase in value. Gazan fruit trees are destroyed; then Israeli fruit is sent in and sold at inflated prices, with Gaza serving as a very profitable dumping ground for Israeli agricultural products. Houses are demolished, then aid organizations are obliged to buy reconstruction material from Israeli enterprises. This goes for most agricultural and all manufactured products. Since the borders are closed and Gazan manufacturing has been systematically destroyed by direct bombardment and by a ban on the import of materials and machinery, Gaza depends entirely on Israel to send in consumer products, which it does to the enormous benefit of its own export market. So all the millions of dollars being poured into Gaza by the international community to keep Gazans alive and relatively complacent serve as an indirect subsidy for Israel.

SEAFOOD

If it weren't for the shimmering blue horizon of the Mediterranean, Gaza might feel like a dungeon. The long coastline of sandy beaches is an outlet for Gazan's *joie de vivre*, teeming with families picnicking, children flying kites, and brightly painted boats plying the waters. This intimate relationship with the sea makes for magnificent seafood. While most of the population of coastal pre-1948 Palestine is now confined to the landlocked West Bank or in diaspora far from the Mediterranean coast, Gaza remains as one of the last repositories of the Palestinian fishing and seafood tradition. These fresh and spicy preparations are consistent crowd-pleasers.

Shorabit Fawakih al Bahar

Seafood Soup

Serves 4–6

شوربة فاكهة البحر

A rich, flavorful mixed-seafood soup from old Yaffa. To minimize waste, many home cooks use just the stalks of the parsley for making the broth, and the leaves for adorning the soup.

For the broth

½ pound (approximately 250 grams) fish bones and heads for broth, or 8 cups (2 liters) packaged fish broth

1 onion, quartered

7 cardamom pods

2 bay leaves

2 teaspoons salt

One bunch cut parsley stalks, tied with kitchen twine

For the soup

1 pound (approximately 450 grams) mixed seafood: shell-on shrimp, crab claws, small clams or sea snails, cleaned small calamari rings (in whatever proportions are available)

Flour, salt, and lemon juice, for washing the seafood

1 teaspoon cumin powder

1 teaspoon salt

½ cup (approximately 120 milliliters) olive oil

1 onion, julienned

2 hot green chile peppers, finely chopped

2 heaping tablespoons flour

¼ teaspoon freshly cracked black pepper

¼ teaspoon ground allspice

Juice of one lemon

½ cup (approximately 12 grams) chopped parsley leaves

Wash the fish bones carefully with a little flour, 1 teaspoon salt, and lemon juice, then set them in a strainer for approximately 10 minutes.

To make a simple fish broth, bring the water to a boil together with the fish bones and heads. Skim off any scum that rises to the surface, then reduce the heat and add the quartered onion, bay leaves, cardamom pods, remaining salt, and parsley stalks. Cook for about 40 minutes or until the water has reduced in quantity by a cup or so, then strain it. Discard the bones and set aside the broth.

Meanwhile, wash the seafood carefully in a bowl of cold water with a little flour, salt, and lemon juice, then set it in a strainer for approximately 10 minutes. Sprinkle it with ½ teaspoon of the cumin and 1 teaspoon of salt. Sauté the seafood very briefly in 1 tablespoon of the olive oil over medium-high heat, just until the shrimp become opaque. This will take approximately 3 minutes. Transfer the seafood to a separate platter.

In the same pan, add about half of the remaining olive oil and sauté the julienned onion on medium heat until it turns dark golden. Add the chopped hot peppers and cook for another minute, then set aside.

In a clean soup pot, heat the remaining oil over medium heat and add the flour, stirring continuously until it becomes fragrant and toffee-colored. Add one cup of fish broth and whisk thoroughly and quickly until the flour is fully dissolved, then add the remaining fish broth. Bring to a boil. Add the onion and chile mixture along with the remaining cumin, ground pepper and allspice.

Bring to a new boil. Finally, stir in the mixed seafood and heat through. Finish by stirring in the fresh lemon juice, chopped parsley, and additional salt to taste.

Variation
The famous Gazan seafood restaurateur Abu Hasira adds garlic, freshly snipped basil leaves, and a little minced ginger after sautéing the onion. In this case, omit the chile peppers.

Shorabit Salfooh

Stingray Soup

Serves 4–6

For the broth

½ pound (approximately 250 grams) fish bones and heads for broth, or 8 cups (2 liters) packaged fish broth
7 cardamom pods
2 bay leaves
1 onion, quartered
2 teaspoons salt
One bunch parsley stalks, tied with kitchen twine

For the soup

Olive oil
1½ pounds (approximately 750 grams) guitarfish steaks (cut from the tail or the meaty central portion), or other fish as suggested above
1½ teaspoons salt
2 teaspoons ground cumin
2 medium onions, julienned
2 heaping tablespoons flour
1 teaspoon cumin seeds, toasted until fragrant
½ teaspoon allspice
Black pepper, to taste
⅓ cup (approximately 80 milliliters) fresh lemon juice
Parsley or dill, for garnish

Wash the fish bones carefully in a bowl with a little flour, water, 1 teaspoon of salt, and lemon juice, then set them in a strainer for approximately 10 minutes. With the fish bones and other broth ingredients, prepare a basic fish broth as described in the previous recipe. If you are using packaged fish broth, skip this step. Set the broth aside.

Debone fish and chop into large chunks, or else use meaty fillets. If you are using skate, leave the bones in and debone as you eat.

Wash the fish in a bath of salt, flour, and water, then set it in a strainer for 10 minutes. Season it with salt and 1 teaspoon of the cumin, then fry it in hot vegetable oil until it is golden. Set the fish on a paper-towel-lined plate to cool.

In a frying pan, sauté the julienned onions in ¼ cup (60 milliliters) of olive oil on medium heat until they turn deeply golden.

In a separate pot, warm about 4 tablespoons of oil on medium heat and add the flour, stirring continuously until brown and fragrant. Stir in the broth, a little at a time, whisking thoroughly after each addition. Bring to a boil, then add the caramelized onions, fish chunks, remaining ground cumin and cumin seeds, black pepper, and allspice.

Cook on medium heat for 10 minutes, partially covered, then remove from the heat. Finish the soup with lemon juice and garnish with chopped parsley or dill.

شوربة سلفوح

A lemony delicacy beloved of Yaffa winters. Like the renowned rice dish *Sayadiyya* (page 280), it is typically made with the buttery, sweet tail meat of the guitarfish or *salfooh*, a type of ray with an elongated body and a flattened head. Substitute any other meaty, sweet flatfish, such as skate. In a pinch, fish like haddock, grouper, ocean perch, or orange roughy would work. If you are using an entire guitarfish or skate, bread and fry the wings separately, seasoning with cumin and lemon juice, and serve as an appetizer.

Tatbilit Samak

Fish Marinade

Makes enough to marinate about 1 pound (approximately 500 grams) of fish

5 cloves garlic
½ teaspoon salt
2 green chile peppers, chopped
¼ cup (60 milliliters) freshly squeezed lemon juice
Peel of 4 lemons, cut into slivers
1 tablespoon cumin powder
¾ teaspoon black pepper

In a mortar and pestle, mash the garlic with the salt. Add the chiles and crush well. Stir in the remaining ingredients and mix well. Massage this marinade into and on top of the fish to be cooked and refrigerate it for 15 to 30 minutes before grilling, frying, or baking.

تتبيلة سمك

This is a perfect marinade for simple grilled or fried fish. It is also used as a first step in several of the more elaborate recipes in this chapter.

Samak Mahshi

Herb-Stuffed Fish

Serves 3–4

3½ pounds (about 1½ kilograms) small white-fleshed fish, such as
   red mullet or perch, for frying or 3½ pounds (about 1½ kilograms)
   medium-sized fish, such as gilt-head bream, red snapper, rockfish, or
   sea bass, for grilling
2 quantities *Tatbilit Samak* (page 269)

Stuffing
10 cloves fresh garlic
Two hot green chile peppers
Two hot red chile peppers
1 cup (approximately 50 grams) chopped fresh dill
3 teaspoons ground coriander seeds (preferably freshly toasted before
   grinding)
⅓ cup (80 milliliters) olive oil
2 teaspoon salt
Flour
Oil for frying

For the garnish
Chopped parsley
Tomato
Bell pepper
Lemon

سمك محشي

This is an especially attractive dish taught to us by Um Ramadan. The same method and ingredients can be used with a larger fish, grilling rather than frying it. If you are using a charcoal grill, coat the stuffed fish with wheat bran instead of flour to prevent sticking. The fish may also be grilled under a broiler in an oven with excellent results.

Wash the fish well in a bowl of cold water, along with a fistful of flour and a spent lemon rind and its juice, and scrub it inside and out with some coarse salt, removing any blood or gills that might remain. Rinse well, set aside in a strainer for about 10 minutes until the fishy juices have drained out, then pat dry.

Massage the *tatbilit samak* marinade into fish—inside and out—and set it aside for 15 minutes.

Prepare the stuffing: Finely chop the garlic and chiles. Mix them well with the dill and coriander, rubbing them together with your fingers to release the flavors. Stuff the cavity of each fish with as much of this mix as can reasonably fit inside—probably 2 to 3 teaspoons—and close the fish with a toothpick.

Dredge each fish in flour, then fry in hot oil until golden for approximately 4 minutes on each side. Place the fried fish on paper towels until you finish frying them all.

Transfer the fish to a serving platter, then garnish with parsley and slices of lemon and bell pepper. Serve with *Salsit T'heena* (page 30) and *Dagga* (page 50). If grilling, see tips in the note above.

"I always watched my mother cook," says Um Ramadan as she looks out the window at Gaza City's evening traffic, "but I didn't really learn to cook until I married and my mother-in-law taught me." Her husband's family, like her own, were fishing people from the bustling port city of Yaffa. They were exiled when her husband was just a child.

Her mother-in-law must have done a fine job, because Um Ramadan is a truly brilliant cook. Soft-spoken and unflappable, she effortlessly prepares a dozen things at once. After her eldest son left to join the Fatah Party in the West Bank in 2007, with her husband unemployed, the burden fell on her to support the family. She began to cook for busy urban professionals and wealthy city dwellers, making meals that rival those of Gaza's famous seaside restaurants. "Perhaps in another life, I could have been a chef," she imagines, somewhat dreamily. With a weighted smile and an understated tone, she recounts her family's history—interspersed with an encyclopedia of recipes.

Like those of so many Palestinians, her family story is one of continual displacement and multiple exile. Um Ramadan's parents fled Yaffa for Gaza in 1948. At that time, Gaza was administered by the short-lived All-Palestine Government; Um Ramadan's father worked as a mechanic for their vehicles. When Egyptian troops were deployed in Gaza during the Suez crisis, he got a job with them, repairing cars and tanks.

The family moved wherever the Egyptian Army needed them, settling for a few years in El Arish, in the Sinai. "I got to study there," says Um Ramadan. "I still have my school certificates. I was a very good student."

But her studies were interrupted when her father was moved into Gaza again just before the 1967 Six-Day War. Egypt was defeated and Israel began persecuting Palestinians who had worked for the Egyptian army. Her father fled to Egypt while the rest of the family stayed in Gaza. He was never able to return,

except for one risky and memorable clandestine visit. He died in a car accident on his way to Gaza just after the Camp David Accords, which would have allowed the family to reunite.

Um Ramadan shrugs. "The stories of the Palestinians are endless."

Kuftit Sardina

Sardine Croquettes

Serves 3–4

For the kufta

1 pound (approximately 500 grams) fresh sardine filets or 2 pounds (1 kilogram) whole sardines
1 medium-sized onion
3 cloves garlic
¼ packed cup (5 grams) cilantro
¼ packed cup (5 grams) green dill
⅓ packed cup (7 grams) parsley
½ teaspoon ground cumin
⅛ teaspoon ground nutmeg
½ teaspoon salt
¼ teaspoon black pepper
⅓ cup (30 grams) breadcrumbs

For the sauce

1 medium-sized onion
2 cloves garlic, chopped finely
½ green chile, chopped finely
1 cup (240 milliliters) *Salsit T'heena* (page 30)
¼ teaspoon ground nutmeg
Salt to taste
3 tablespoons olive oil

Vegetable oil, for frying

For the garnish
Finely chopped parsley
½ lemon, sliced

First, clean each fish very carefully: Remove the guts and slice the fish so that it lies open on its back. Carefully remove the head by cracking it backwards. Pull it back and remove the spine and the tail along with it. This will take care of the major bones. The smaller ones can be left in. Wash well in a bath of cold water, a little flour, lemon juice, and salt. Rinse well and set aside in a strainer to let the fishy juices drain.

In a meat grinder or food processor, grind the fish, then the onions, garlic, parsley, dill, and cilantro, until a smooth paste is achieved. Mix in the spices.

Begin the sauce: Finely chop the onion and brown it in a pan with the olive oil. Add the garlic and chile and cook just a minute more.

Mix the browned onions into the prepared tahina sauce and add another cup of water (as needed) until the sauce has a loose, liquid consistency. Add the nutmeg and salt to taste. Set aside.

كفتة سردين

These *kufta* are light and delicious and make an irresistible appetizer by themselves, or a complete meal bathed in tahina sauce and served with rice. If fresh sardines are not available where you live, substitute mackerel or herring. For a milder taste, any firm white fish fillets will do.

To the reserved fish paste, add the bread crumbs bit by bit until the consistency is dense enough to shape it into little logs about 2 inches (5 centimeters) in length and 1 inch (2 centimeters) in width. Pan-fry these *kufta* in very hot oil until they are browned on all sides. Drain them on paper towels, then transfer them to a serving dish.

In a saucepan over medium heat, bring the tahina mixture to a boil, stirring continuously. Immediately pour the sauce over the *kufta*. Decorate with the sliced lemons and chopped parsley. Serve with white rice.

Sardina ma' Daggit Bandora

Sardines with Spicy Tomato Sauce

Serves 3–4

2 pounds (approximately 1 kilogram) fresh sardines, gutted and
    trimmed of scales and fins, heads intact
2 quantities *Tatbilit Samak* (page 269)
2 medium onions, chopped
3 green chile peppers, chopped
¼ cup (60 milliliters) olive oil
3 medium tomatoes, finely chopped
1 teaspoon cumin
1½ teaspoons freshly ground coriander seeds
2 teaspoons salt
¾ teaspoon black pepper
Vegetable oil, for frying

Wash the fish well in cold water, some lemon juice, 1 teaspoon salt, and
a few spoonfuls of flour, massaging it carefully. Rinse well, then set them
aside in a strainer for 10 to 15 minutes. Pat dry.

Marinate the fish using the recipe for *tatbilit samak* on page 269.

While the fish is marinating, prepare the *daggit bandora*: Warm the olive oil in a skillet over medium heat, then sauté the onions and chiles
until they turn golden, about 5 minutes. Add the chopped tomatoes,
spices, and remaining salt. Simmer on low heat, partially covered, for
about 10 minutes, adding a few tablespoons of water if the sauce is drying up.

To fry: Coat the fish with flour and fry them in hot oil until they turn
golden. Set aside on a paper-towel-lined tray until you have finished frying all of the fish. Serve hot with the *daggit bandora* and lemon wedges.

To bake: Arrange the sardines in a baking pan and smother them with
daggit bandora. Cover with aluminum foil and bake in a 400°F (200°C)
oven for approximately 20 minutes or until the fish are flaky but not dry.

Serve with *Ruz Imfalfal* (page 206) or *Khubz Kmaj* (page 100) and an
assortment of pickles.

سردين مع دقة بندورة

Daggit bandora is a tomato dressing
used in various sardine recipes to offset the strong, oily taste of the fish.
Here we include versions for baked
and fried sardines.

Tagin Samak

Poached Fish and Tahina Stew

Serves 3-4

1 pound (approximately 500 grams) firm fish filets, such as grouper,
 red snapper, or sea bass
1 bay leaf
5 whole cardamom pods, cracked
1 small onion, quartered
¼ cup (60 milliliters) tahina
¼ cup (60 milliliters) lemon juice
1 medium onion, julienned
5 garlic cloves, crushed
2–3 green chile peppers, chopped
1 teaspoon salt
1 teaspoon cumin
¼ teaspoon allspice
Chopped parsley, for garnish
Olive oil

Bring a skillet filled with water to a slow boil. Add the bay leaf, carda-mom pods, and quartered onion. Simmer for 5 minutes. Gently place the fish fillets in the liquid and poach them for about 2 to 3 minutes. Re-move the skillet from the heat and set aside. Once the fish is cool, gently strain it, reserving the poaching liquid.

Combine the tahina and lemon juice, whisking well until they have emulsified. You can also use a blender. Thin this with a few tablespoons of water. Set aside.

In a separate skillet, warm 3 tablespoons of olive oil, and fry the onions, chiles, and garlic on medium heat until they are lightly golden. Add the fish, gently breaking it apart, along with about 4 cups (1 liter) of the reserved poaching liquid and the salt, cumin, and allspice. Bring to a gentle boil. Slowly stir in the tahina sauce. Cook for 1 to 2 minutes, then pour into individual bowls. Garnish with chopped parsley.

Serve with *Khubz Kmaj* (page 100).

طاجن سمك

Laila recorded this recipe at Hatem Bakr's seaside fish shack in the Beach Refugee Camp in 2013, accom-panied by Anthony Bourdain and his crew. All were blown away by it. It is very similar to the previous recipe, but more like a soup or stew.

Gaza was once famous for its fish. Just nine nautical miles off Gaza's shores, there is a deep channel used by great schools of fish in their migration between the Nile Delta and the Aegean Sea, a natural resource plied for centuries by Palestinian fishing boats. Until recently, Gazan catches often exceeded 1,650 pounds (750 kilograms) of fish a day; exports to Israel, the West Bank, and Jordan brought in millions of dollars. Fishing supported more than 30,000 people, many of them families with a long fishing tradition, whether from Gaza or the northern ports of Yaffa, Hamama, and El Majdal.

With the Oslo Accords, all that began to change. Under the guise of detailing Palestinian autonomy, the Interim Agreement established a fishing zone of twenty nautical miles where no such limits had existed. Over time, fishermen saw these restrictions grow ever tighter, reducing first to twelve miles, then ten, then six. Now the Israeli Navy limits Palestinian fishing boats to anywhere between three and five nautical miles from the coast, depending on the month and the mood, creating a situation that the Office for the Coordination of Humanitarian Affairs, the lead UN humanitarian body, has referred to as "fishing without water."

Violations are punishable by violent harassment, boat seizure, arrest, and gunfire. This has drastically reduced available catches, forcing today's fishermen—as they themselves are tragically aware—to cull from shoreline waters the undersize and juvenile fish that would guarantee future prosperity. With Gaza's commercial crossings all but sealed to exports, any fish caught are strictly for local consumption.

Inland fish farms are attempting to compensate for the lack of sea fish by producing quantities of inexpensive tilapia. Gradually Gazans are learning to accept this insipid new protein source ("It tastes like mud!" several told us) but, given a choice, they prefer the fresh Mediterranean species they've been eating for centuries: red mullet and sea bream, sardines and sea bass, as well as an exuberant diversity of crabs, shrimp, and other shellfish.

Sayadiyya

Fisherman's Delight

Serves 6

2 pounds (1 kilogram) firm-fleshed white fish steaks, bone-in
Tatbilit Samak (page 269)
2 large onions, julienned
3 cups (720 milliliters) water, more as needed
1½ teaspoon ground cumin
1 teaspoon salt
1 tablespoon *qidra* spices (page 34)
¾ teaspoon ground cinnamon
2 cups (400 grams) rice, washed well and soaked in cold water for 10 minutes
2 medium tomatoes, uniformly sliced
Oil, for frying

Wash the fish well in a bowl of cold water with lemon juice, 1 teaspoon of salt, and a little flour. Set it aside in a strainer for 10 minutes, then pat it dry.

Rub the marinade over the fish and set aside for 20 minutes. Lightly dredge the marinated fish in flour, then fry it in plenty of hot vegetable oil until it turns golden on both sides. This will only take a few minutes. Strain and reserve the oil.

Fry the julienned onions in a clean pan with ¼ cup of the reserved fish-frying oil on medium heat until golden. Remove half the onions and set them aside, then continue to fry the other half until crisp and deeply browned, taking care not to burn them. Add the 3 cups of water to the well-browned onions and boil for about 3 minutes, then strain them, reserving the water and the onions.

Drain the soaked rice well. In a bowl, combine the rice with the cumin, salt, *qidra* spices (page 34), cinnamon, and lightly sautéed onions.

Cover the bottom of a wide pot with tomato slices. Over these, place a layer of the fried fish, followed by the rice mixture. Gently pour the reserved onion water over the rice. Cook on medium heat for 15 to 20 minutes or until rice sampled from the middle is done. Allow it to rest for 15 minutes, covered, then invert onto a serving platter.

Garnish with chopped parsley and the reserved well-browned onions. Serve with *Salatit T'heena* (page 30) and olives.

صيادية

This is one of those dishes Gaza is famous for. Older Palestinians in the West Bank and in Israel who remember when one could simply go to Gaza for the day wax nostalgic about the little beachside restaurants serving *sayadiyya* by the sea.

Sea bass or the meatiest part of the guitarfish (a type of ray) are traditionally used for this dish, though any firm white fish such as grouper will do. What follows is Um Ramadan's classic recipe from old Yaffa.

To converse with Iyad and Ziyad Al-Attar is to find oneself unexpectedly playing the straight man in a comedy routine. The patter is fast, the tone is absurd, and political irreverence is meted out to all parties in equal measure. But they're not on stage or screen; their thing is fish. According to them, they are Gaza's premiere freshwater fish-farm entrepreneurs, responsible for introducing fish farming to Gaza and now cranking out 300 tons a year of tilapia and mullet.

They learned the trade in Israel in the 1990s and managed to save up enough to open their own fish farm in Gaza in 2004. When Gaza's borders were closed to imports in 2008, business got brisk and the brothers opened several more fish farms. For the moment, they only raise freshwater fish, though in collaboration with colleagues in Israel and Egypt (by way of the Internet and telephone) they are working toward the elusive goal of hatching sea bream in captivity.

As ever in Gaza, setbacks are met with ingenuity. No electricity to run the pumps that aerate the ponds? Just invite all the neighborhood kids over to splash around for an hour. Can't get commercially produced fish food through the borders? Mix flour rations with bone meal and roll it out just like *maftool*: Presto! Fish pellets!

At one-fifth the cost of sea fish, tilapia is a great alternative in a tight economy. But Iyad and Ziyad say they make few retail sales; those who can afford to choose prefer sea fish. Almost all the fingerlings they produce are sold to other urban fish farms or bought by major donor organizations and distributed to needy families as an essential protein supplement.

Since donor organizations are the biggest buyers in Gaza, this makes for a lucrative business. Fish farms have captured the interest of the private sector as well as the government; hatcheries are proliferating, and the newly introduced aquaculture classes at Gaza's universities are filling up. In many urban gardens, the nutrient-rich fish water is used to fertilize crops naturally, and some Gazans are developing hydroponic farming systems to make even more efficient use of this precious resource.

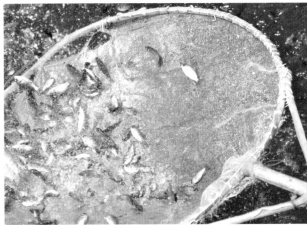

Sayadiyyit Abu Hasira

Abu Hasira's Fish and Rice

Serves 6

2 pounds (1 kilogram) firm white fish steaks, such as sea bass or grouper
Tatbilit Samak (page 269)
1 large onion, julienned
½ whole nutmeg, crushed into several small pieces
10 cardamom pods
5 cloves garlic, thinly sliced
¾ teaspoon ground cinnamon
2 teaspoons tomato paste
2½ teaspoons salt
3 cups (720 milliliters) water
2 cups (400 grams) rice, washed well and soaked in cold water for 20 minutes
Olive oil, as needed

Wash the fish well in a bowl of cold water with lemon juice, flour, and 1 teaspoon of the salt. Pat dry.

Prepare the fish marinade and rub it over the fish pieces. Set aside for 15 to 20 minutes.

Meanwhile, sauté the onion on medium heat in about ¼ cup (60 milliliters) of olive oil until deeply golden brown. Add the garlic, crushed nutmeg, cardamom pods, cinnamon, and tomato paste. Stir briefly, then add the 3 cups (720 milliliters) of water and remaining 2 teaspoons of salt and boil for 10 minutes. Lower the heat, then gently add the fish and poach it until fish is just cooked, about 6 minutes. Set aside.

Strain the soaked rice. In a separate large pot, sauté the rice on medium-high heat in ¼ cup (60 milliliters) of olive oil until it is toasted and golden, stirring continuously for about 15 minutes. Take care not to burn the rice; it will begin to brown suddenly. Gently transfer the poached fish on top of the rice, then pour in the broth mixture and cover the pot. Bring this to a gentle boil, then reduce the heat to low and cook for about 15 minutes, or until the rice is tender. This may take slightly more or less time.

Set the pot aside to rest for 15 minutes, then invert it onto a platter (as with *maqlooba*, hold a round tray on top of the pot and, in one swift motion, flip the whole thing).

Sprinkle with ground cumin and chopped parsley. Serve with lemon wedges and *Salatit T'heena* (page 30).

صيادية أبو حصيرة

In Gaza, the Abu Hasira name is synonymous with seafood. They come from a long line of fishermen and own several of the city's most famous fish restaurants. After much coaxing, Asad Abu Hasira shared his family's cherished *sayadiyya* recipe with us.

Landing Place, Jaffa. (3) Jaffa, la Rade.

Yaffa, "bride of the sea," a port city with an unbroken history of 4,000 years, was historically one of Palestine's main commercial, political, and intellectual centers. Before 1948, it was a seat of industry and banking, and most of the books and newspapers printed in Palestine came off its presses. The sophisticated city counted its cuisine among its many riches, specializing in elaborate preparations of local seafood and citrus.

When Yaffa was ransacked by Zionist militias in 1948, much of its population fled by sea to Gaza, making up a large part of the mass of refugees crowded into the Strip.

One of the remarkable things about contemporary Gazan culture is how rigorously the Strip's population, which is made up of refugees from all over historic Palestine, continues to marry into families from their own hometowns and villages, perpetuating very local cultures into the third and fourth generation of exile. So it is that delicate Yaffan cooking is alive and well in Gaza and is quite distinct from indigenous Gazan cuisine or the more rustic cooking from the rural interior of Palestine.

In the different exile communities crowded into Gaza, we find ghost cuisines: The cities and villages that gave rise to them have been demolished and the world has largely forgotten their names, but in Gaza we can still taste them. Their cooking styles are passed along, generation after generation, a thread of memory in the deft gestures of hands, the precision of palate.

Hbari Maqli

Gaza-Style Hot Fried Calamari

Serves 2–3

1 pound (approximately 500 grams) clean squid bodies
Filfil Mat'hoon (page 28)
½ teaspoon allspice
¾ teaspoon salt
½ teaspoon fresh black pepper
Breadcrumbs, as needed
Fresh chopped dill, for garnish
Lemon wedges, for serving
Oil for frying

Slice the clean squid bodies into rings about ¼ inch (½ centimeter) wide. Wash them carefully, then pat dry.

In a bowl, mix the *filfil mat'hoon* with allspice, salt, and black pepper. Add the squid and mix gently. Set it aside to marinate for 15 minutes.

Remove the squid rings from the pepper mix, shaking off any larger clots of pepper that may stick to them, but leaving them well coated.

Toss the pepper-coated squid in bread crumbs. Fry them in plenty of very hot oil until they are golden brown. Drain them on a paper towel and serve garnished with fresh chopped dill and lemon wedges.

حبار مقلي

This is, hands down, the best fried calamari we've ever had. Everyone we've made it for agrees.

Hbari Mahshi Abu Hasira

Abu Hasira's Rice-and-Shrimp-Stuffed Squid

Serves 5–6

1 pound (approximately 500 grams) small squid, cleaned (if squid is not cleaned, buy 2 pounds or 1 kilogram: half the weight will be discarded)

For the stuffing
4 ounces (125 grams) small peeled shrimp
½ cup (100 grams) short-grain rice
1 medium-sized onion, chopped
¼ teaspoon ground cloves
¼ teaspoon turmeric
½ teaspoon salt
¼ teaspoon ground pepper
Olive oil

For the sauce
1 medium-sized onion, chopped
5–7 ripe tomatoes or 3 tablespoons tomato paste
5 cloves garlic
½ teaspoon salt
1 green chile pepper
¼ packed cup (5 grams) fresh basil, chopped
Olive oil

Preheat oven to 300°F (150°C).

Clean and prepare the squid as indicated in the recipe on page 289. Cut the tentacles just above the eyes and chop finely. Place these chopped squid tentacles in a dry pan over high heat. They will release a great deal of water: Drain this off. Return them to the heat and cook until the pan is dry, stirring so they do not stick, and set aside. Repeat this process with the shrimp, finely chopping them.

Sauté the onion in 3 tablespoons of olive oil on medium heat, until it is translucent. Add half the rice, along with the cloves, turmeric, salt, and pepper, and stir until the rice is toasted, about 5 minutes. Add the other half of the rice along with the tentacles, the shrimp, and ¾ cups (180 milliliters) water. Bring to a boil, then lower the heat for about five minutes. Remove from the heat when the rice has absorbed almost all the water but is still quite hard. Fluff it with a fork and allow it to cool.

Meanwhile, prepare the sauce. Sauté the chopped onion in 3 tablespoons of olive oil on medium heat until translucent, adding ¼ teaspoon of salt. Grate or blend the tomatoes (you may also substitute crushed tomatoes, tomato sauce, or 3 tablespoons of tomato paste diluted in 2 cups or ½ liter of hot water) and add to the onions.

This stuffed-squid recipe is an adaptation of the one served at Abu Hasira's famous Gaza seafood restaurant, right next to the old fishing port. The final result is meltingly tender, a very elegant meal.

288

With a mortar and pestle, crush the garlic and the green chiles with the remaining salt and add this mixture to the pan. Heat this through, then stir in the fresh basil and simmer for about 10 minutes, or until the tomatoes have thickened slightly. Add a little more water if necessary to keep the mixture a thick liquid. Test for salt and set aside.

Stuff each squid cavity two-thirds full of the cooled rice mixture, stroking it to distribute the rice evenly inside. Close the squid with a toothpick and arrange them in a casserole. Pour the tomato sauce over the stuffed calamari and bake for 1 hour.

Hbari ma' Daggit il Samak

Herb and Pepper Stuffed Squid

Serves 2–3

1 pound (approximately 500 grams) small, clean squid bodies (if squid is not cleaned, buy 2 pounds or 1 kilogram: half the weight will be discarded)
6 cloves garlic
1 teaspoon salt
4 green chile peppers, chopped
2 teaspoons ground cumin
2 teaspoons ground black pepper
1 cup (25 grams) finely chopped parsley
1 cup (25 grams) finely chopped green dill
1 cup (25 grams) finely chopped cilantro
¼ cup (60 milliliters) olive oil
½ cup (45 grams) breadcrumbs (more as needed)
Oil for frying

If the squid are not already cleaned, carefully remove the heads and intestines and pull out the small transparent quill in each. Peel the colored skin off the outside of the body (soak it first in cold water for a few minutes, then rub it with a little salt) and cut away the rear fins. Wash the bodies, which are now like little empty white tubes closed at one end, in a cold-water bath, changing the water several times until it rinses clean.

Mash the garlic in a mortar and pestle with the salt, then add and crush the chopped chiles. In a bowl, combine this mixture with the spices, finely chopped herbs, and olive oil. Stuff each squid about ⅔ full of this mixture, making sure it is spread out throughout the cavity, then close the squid with a toothpick or sew shut with needle and thread.

Heat the oil for frying. Roll the squid in bread crumbs and fry them until slightly browned, turning them over several times. Remove the toothpicks and serve hot, garnished with lemon slices and chopped parsley.

حبار مع دقة السمك

Hbari literally means "inky" and is the name generally used for both squid and octopus in Gaza City and old Yaffa, whence this dish comes. There are many traditional ways to prepare stuffed squid; we provide two of our favorites.

Hbari u Ruz

Calamari and Toasted Rice

Serves 5–6

حبار ورز

1½ pounds (about 750 grams) small fresh squid (if squid is not cleaned, buy 3 pounds or 1½ kilograms: half the weight will be discarded)
2 medium onions, julienned
1½ teaspoon salt
2 teaspoons cumin
1½ teaspoons *Filfil Mat'hoon* (page 28)
6 tablespoons fresh lemon juice
2 cups medium- or short-grain rice, rinsed
4 pearls of mastic, where available
Olive oil
Lemon slices and chopped parsley, for garnish

If the squid are not already cleaned, prepare as instructed on page 289. Slice the bodies into thin rings or—if the squid are large ones—into matchstick pieces.

In a dry frying pan over high heat, pan-fry the squid until it has released all its liquid. Pour this liquid off and heat it until the pan is dry again. Set aside.

In a clean pan over medium heat, warm ¼ cup (60 milliliters) of olive oil. Add the onions and salt. Cook slowly until the onions are well caramelized, stirring to prevent burning. This will take about 20 minutes.

Set aside half of the caramelized onions. To the half still in the pan, add the cumin and *filfil mat'hoon*, followed by the squid and lemon juice. Increase the heat to medium-high and stir until the lemon juice appears to have evaporated and the squid has browned slightly. Set aside.

In a clean pot, warm 3 tablespoons of olive oil on medium-high heat. Add half the rice. Stir continuously until the rice has browned noticeably. This will take 5 to 10 minutes. Rice browns suddenly, so keep your eye on it and don't let it burn!

To the toasted rice, add the other half of the caramelized onions along with the remaining uncooked rice. Mix well, then pour in 4 cups (1 liter) of water. Add a pinch of salt and, if available, a few pearls of mastic, crushed first with a little salt.

When water boils, lower the heat and simmer slowly until the rice is *al dente*. Add a portion of the calamari and mix it into the rice. Remove the pan from the heat and allow the rice to rest for a few minutes.

Spread the rice over a serving plate and cover it with the remaining calamari. Garnish with slices of lemon and chopped parsley.

This is an extremely satisfying dish, with richly flavored rice and browned calamari. In the various cooking demonstrations we've done since this book was initially published, this recipe is probably the most unanimously acclaimed.

As in many of the rice dishes in this book, much of the flavor comes from the caramelized onions, so it is worth taking the time to caramelize them properly—stirring over a slow flame until they are brown and sticky.

To save yourself some time, look for pre-cleaned, whole frozen squid in the freezer section of your supermarket. Avoid precut squid rings, as they tend to be rubbery. Peeled shrimp may be used instead of squid.

Variation: Calamari in Tomato Sauce

Follow the recipe exactly but omit the rice, instead adding 3 to 4 peeled and finely chopped tomatoes (plus 1 tablespoon of tomato paste if you prefer a thicker consistency) to the calamari after they have browned. Cook this down a bit and serve with white rice or with Khubz Kmaj (page 100).

Saltaone Mashwi

Stuffed Roasted Crabs

Serves 3–4

12 large live male blue crabs (preferably "number ones"), at least 5½ to
  6 inches (12 to 15 centimeters) in diameter
4 tablespoons *Filfil Mat'hoon* (page 28)
3 tablespoons chopped parsley
2 teaspoons ground cumin
1 teaspoon salt, more for cleaning crabs
8 cloves garlic, crushed or finely minced
3 tablespoons extra-virgin olive oil

Preheat your oven to 400°F (200°C).

Prepare the crabs: You may want to place the crabs in the freezer first
to numb them. Cut the ventral nerve cord by stabbing the crab quickly
with an ice pick or a sharp knife in the center of its belly flap or between
the eyes. Remove the top of the crab shell, or carapace, by gently separating the top from the bottom by hand or with a paring knife. There
is a small crack where the carapace joins with the rest of the body; use
this as a starting point. Sprinkle the crabs with some salt and remove
any guts and organs. Pull off the feathery gills. Rinse well. Flip the crab
over. You will see a small triangular shape near the middle. Lift this flap
up and remove it. It should come off easily. Rinse away any organs. The
crabs are now ready for stuffing.

To make the stuffing: Using a mortar and pestle, mash the garlic well,
along with the salt. Combine the mashed garlic with the *filfil mat'hoon*,
chopped parsley, cumin, and 1 tablespoon of the olive oil. Place approximately 1 teaspoon of stuffing in each crab cavity. Arrange the crabs in a
pan and drizzle them all over with the remaining olive oil.

Cover with aluminum foil. Roast on the lowest rack for approximately
10 minutes or until the crabs turn pink. Uncover the pan. Move the oven
rack to the middle and set your oven to broil. Return the pan to the oven
for 5 minutes or until the stuffing is slightly browned.

Serve with lemon wedges, *Khubz Kmaj* (page 100), and an assortment of
other seafood recipes.

سلطعون مشوي

This was Laila's childhood favorite, always prepared by her father, who is
from Gaza City. Her mother, a native
of Khan Younis (which is not on the
coast), had never even heard of crab
before she met him, though they lived
only miles apart.

Try to choose heavy or "fat" crabs
nearing the end of their molt cy-
cle; they will be full of meat. You can
sometimes find them pre-cleaned
and hollowed out for stuffing, though
they'll never be as fresh. If you don't
like your food spicy, omit the *filfil
mat'hoon* and use mashed parsley
and garlic instead.

Zibdiyit Gambari

Clay Pot Shrimp

Serves 5–6

زبدية جمبري

Of all Gaza's delicacies, this recipe is the one visitors most frequently request. They encounter this dish at Gaza's seaport restaurants and are smitten. Our version was provided by Um Ramadan. If you plan to use larger shrimp (or prawns), reduce the quantity by half.

2 pounds (about 1 kilogram) small shrimp, peeled and deveined
2 hot green chile peppers (to taste)
2 tablespoons chopped fresh dill
6 cloves fresh garlic, chopped
3 tablespoons olive oil
1 large onion, finely chopped
4 tablespoons tomato paste
6 tomatoes, peeled and diced
1½ teaspoons ground coriander seeds
1 teaspoon ground cumin
¾ teaspoon ground cardamom
½ teaspoon allspice
½ teaspoon black pepper
1½ teaspoons salt, divided
¼ cup (20 grams) pine nuts or slivered almonds
2 tablespoons sesame seeds
2 tablespoons chopped parsley

Preheat your oven to 375°F (190°C).

Cook the shrimp in a dry pan over high heat for a few minutes. They will release some liquid: Pour this off and return the shrimp to the stove until the pan is dry again. The shrimp should be just barely pink. Set aside.

Coarsely chop the green chile and crush it in a mortar and pestle with ½ teaspoon of salt. Set aside. Rub the chopped garlic and dill together by hand, mixing well.

In the same pan in which you cooked the shrimp, sauté the onions in the olive oil on medium heat. When the onions are translucent, add the tomato paste and stir well for a minute or so, until the tomato paste has darkened slightly.

Mix in the tomatoes, spices, remaining salt, crushed chiles, 1 cup of water, and the dill and garlic mixture. Stir well. Simmer for 10 minutes on low heat, then stir in the shrimp.

Meanwhile, fry the almonds or pine nuts in 1 tablespoon of olive oil until they turn golden, stirring continuously to avoid burning, and set aside.

Pour the shrimp mixture from the pan into the *zibdiya*. (An ovenproof earthenware dish or individual ramekins will also do.) Cover it with the sesame seeds, nuts, and parsley. Bake for 10 minutes covered with aluminum foil, then remove the foil and broil for another few minutes until the top is crusty.

Serve with *Khubz Kmaj* (page 100) to mop up the sauce, and an assortment of pickles.

SWEETS AND BEVERAGES

Rural Gaza was never known for fancy desserts. With such splendid orchards as used to grow in the region, meals were generally concluded simply with fruit, nuts, and sage tea. Sometimes peeled cucumbers and carrots were also presented after the meal. In winter, rustic puddings like *haytaliya* or *halawit smeed* were occasional treats. Then once a year, Gazan villagers would go to the spring fair in El Majdal Asqalan, a village depopulated in 1948, and buy tins of fancy confections that would be savored for months. Urbanites, particularly those from Yaffa, enjoyed a more elaborate range of pastries made for special occasions, particularly for sharing at Ramadan. In this chapter, we present samples of both simple rustic desserts and the elaborate pastries generally made by commercial confectioners, as well as a variety of hot and cold drinks.

Qatir

Rose-Scented Simple Syrup

Makes 2½ cups of syrup (about 600 milliliters)

1 to 2 cups (225 to 450 grams) sugar
1 cup (240 milliliters) water
1 teaspoon lemon juice, strained of seeds and pith
1 teaspoon orange-blossom water *or* rosewater

Boil the sugar, water, and lemon juice vigorously on medium-high heat for 5 minutes. Reduce the heat and simmer for another 5 minutes uncovered, until the syrup forms a continuous stream rather than droplets when poured from a spoon. Remove from the heat and add the orange-blossom water or rosewater, if desired. Let the syrup cool completely at room temperature or in a refrigerator.

قطر

A basic syrup is used in many desserts. The appropriate ratio of sugar to water depends both on the recipe and on personal taste: We offer a suggested ratio in each recipe. A little lemon juice keeps the sugar from crystallizing. You can omit the rosewater if you like. In Gaza, the syrup is often made with the lemon juice alone, while elsewhere in Palestine, like Yaffa and Jerusalem, the scented waters are added.

Haytaliya

Palestinian Wheat Pudding

Serves 6–8

2½ cups (450 grams) hulled soft spring wheat berries, rinsed
6 or more cups of water (1½ liters), enough to soak the wheat
⅔ cup sugar (150 grams), adjust to taste
1½ cups (360 milliliters) whole milk
1 teaspoon orange-blossom water
1 tablespoon butter or ghee
Assorted mixed nuts, such as crushed pistachios, sliced almonds, and golden raisins

Crack the wheat in a food processor or with a heavy mortar and pestle. Don't be concerned if it appears to remain whole: the idea here is to release some of the natural wheat starch. If you own a high-powered blender, you may also pulse the wheat a few times inside. If necessary, add some of the water to the blender as you go.

Transfer the cracked wheat to a large bowl and add the water. Leave this to soak for at least 2 hours, preferably overnight.

Strain the wheat, pressing out as much moisture as possible. Reserve the water. The wheat itself will not be used in the recipe, so feel free to prepare it for breakfast as you would steel-cut oats or feed it to the birds!

In a pot over medium heat, combine 3 to 3½ cups (720 to 840 milliliters) or so of the reserved wheat water with the milk and sugar and stir continuously until the pudding thickens. Add the butter and stir to melt it, then add the orange-blossom water. Pour the pudding into small bowls and garnish with toasted nuts (and, optionally, golden raisins).

Serve warm or at room temperature, or cool if desired. *Haytaliya* can also be served with a drizzle of honey on top.

هيطلية

Back when the region was mostly rural, this luscious silken pudding was enjoyed during the wheat harvest, a more rustic but no less delicious version of the more common starch-based milk puddings of the modern-day Levant. It is altogether different from the Syrian pudding with the same name. Generally served at room temperature, it is also delicious chilled.

Halawit Smeed

Semolina Butter Pudding

Serves 4–5

A simple and delicious winter treat.

1½ *Qatir* (Rose-Scented Simple Syrup (page 300) with a 1-to-1 ratio of
  sugar to water
2 cups (360 grams) fine semolina
10 tablespoons (85 grams) butter or ghee
For the garnish: Dried coconut, slivered almonds, crushed raw
  pistachios, and golden raisins

Prepare the syrup and keep it warm.

Next, melt the butter in a skillet. Add the semolina, stirring continuously on medium heat until the semolina is deeply golden brown. Pay careful attention; it will brown very suddenly. Lower the heat and gradually
add the warm syrup while mixing vigorously for about 30 seconds. It
will be absorbed very quickly. The syrup will splatter, so take care.

Remove the skillet from the heat and transfer to several serving bowls
or one large platter. Sprinkle your garnishes on top. Serve at room temperature or slightly warm.

Um Ali

Bread Pudding

Serves 4

1 large round *Khubz Saj* (page 102), or use store-bought *lavash* or
   markook, cut into thin strips
2 cups (240 milliliters) whole milk
¼ cup (55 grams) sugar, to taste
1 tablespoon butter
½ teaspoon ground cinnamon
Assorted toasted unsalted nuts, such as pistachios and almonds, and
   golden raisins

Preheat your oven to 375°F (190°C). Separate the strips of bread, then place them in a baking dish. Transfer to the oven, then toast them until golden. Divide the bread into individual bowls or a single serving dish.

In a small saucepan over medium heat, bring the milk to a slow simmer. Add the sugar and cinnamon and mix to dissolve them for a minute or two. Stir in the butter and swirl until it has melted. Pour the milk mixture evenly over the strips of toasted bread. Set them aside to absorb the milk mixture for about 15 minutes.

Switch the oven to broil. Transfer the bowls or serving dish to the oven, then broil for just a few minutes to brown the top slightly. Remove from the oven, and garnish with chopped nuts and raisins.

أم علي

This Palestinian spin on the quintessentially Egyptian bread pudding *Um Ali*, or "Ali's mother," uses strips of whole-wheat griddle bread rather than puff pastry, as they do in Egypt. Several grandmas attest that it is more commonly served for breakfast during the winter than as a dessert, though it works nicely for either purpose.

Mhalabiya

Milk Pudding Parfait

Serves 5–6

For orange (or sour plum) pudding

4 cups (1 liter) orange juice or 4 tablespoon sour-plum jam diluted in
   3½ cups (840 milliliters) water
⅓ cup (75 grams) granulated sugar
3 pearls of mastic, crushed with 1 teaspoon sugar in a mortar and
   pestle
6 tablespoons (about 50 grams) cornstarch, dissolved in a little water or
   milk to make a paste

Bring the juice (or jam and water) to a gentle simmer on medium heat,
stirring it continuously. Add the sugar, crushed mastic, and cornstarch
slurry and stir to dissolve them.

Reduce the heat to low and continue stirring until the mixture thickens.
If you are serving the fruit pudding on its own, pour it into individual
bowls and allow it to cool. If you are preparing it for parfaits, only fill
the bowls halfway. Allow the pudding to cool to room temperature, then
refrigerate it for several hours or overnight.

For milk pudding

4 cups (1 liter) milk
⅓ cup (75 grams) sugar, to taste
3 pearls of mastic, crushed with 1 teaspoon sugar in a mortar and
   pestle
4 heaping tablespoons (30 grams) cornstarch or rice flour, dissolved in
   a little water or milk to form a paste
1 tablespoon rosewater
1 tablespoon orange-blossom water

In a medium saucepan, bring the milk to a gentle simmer, stirring it
continuously to avoid scalding. Add the sugar, crushed mastic, and
cornstarch or rice-flour slurry and stir to dissolve them.

Reduce the heat to low and continue stirring until the mixture thickens,
then stir in the rose and orange-blossom waters. Remove the pudding
from the heat. Immediately pour into individual bowls. Cover the surface with plastic wrap to prevent a film from forming. If you are preparing a parfait, pour a layer of this milk pudding over the already cooled
layer of fruit pudding. Allow the parfait to cool, then refrigerate it for
several hours. Decorate with pistachio nuts.

مهلبية

In Gaza, layers of tart *arasiya* (sour
plum) or orange pudding are added to
the classic Arab milk pudding *mhalabiya*. Here we give recipes for both
milk and fruit puddings, which in Gaza
are typically prepared together in a
layered parfait. Both fruit and milk
puddings are also delicious on their
own.

Namoura

Semolina Walnut Cake

Serves 12–15

3 cups (525 grams) coarse semolina
1½ cups (340 grams) sugar
½ cup butter (115 grams), melted
3 tablespoons powdered milk
1 teaspoon cinnamon
1 teaspoon baking powder
1 cup (120 grams) walnuts, finely chopped
Tahina or butter, for greasing
Blanched almonds
1 quantity *Qatir* (page 300), using a 1-to-1 ratio of sugar to water

Mix the semolina and butter well. Add cold water as needed to achieve a pliable but not wet dough, this will probably take a little under 1 cup (240 milliliters). Set aside for several hours or (preferably) overnight, giving the grains a chance to fully absorb the fat.

Meanwhile, prepare the syrup and allow it to cool completely.

Grease a round 12 inch (30 centimeter) baking pan or a 13 x 9 inch rectangular pan (33 x 23 centimeters) very generously with *tahina* or butter. Preheat your oven to 350°F (180°C).

Add the powdered milk, cinnamon, and baking powder to the prepared dough. With damp hands, spread and flatten two-thirds of the dough into the baking pan. Spread the walnuts over this layer and cover with the remaining dough.

Bake for about 40 minutes or until golden. Halfway through, quickly remove the *namoura* and score it into diamond shapes (drawing first vertical and then diagonal lines across: cut only the surface, not all the way through) and decorate each piece with a blanched almond. Return the pan to the oven and continue baking until golden.

Remove the *namoura* from the oven and douse it immediately with cold syrup. Allow the pastry to cool completely before serving it or attempting to remove it from pan, lest it fall apart.

Cut into diamond-shaped bars where you scored it and serve with *Shay bil Maramiya* (page 326).

نّمورة

This recipe is adapted from one given to us by the daughters of the famous Khan Younis confectioner, Abu Assi. Don't be tempted to swap Cream of Wheat for the semolina: the final result will not be the same.

The Tale of Jamil and Buthaina

While we were visiting one well-appointed Gaza City kitchen, our host's neighbor dropped by to visit. The elegant lady, Um Zuhair (Baraka El-Haddad), saw we were busy in the kitchen and, enthusiastic to take part, offered to show us how to prepare one particular dessert she was fond of making. Soon her jeweled hands were kneading dough for *hulba*, a fenugreek and olive oil cake.

While kneading and baking, she launched into a full recitation of "Jamil and Buthaina," a tale dating back to Umayyad Arabia. Rewritten innumerable times, it is still much loved and often recited today. It recounts the story of a star-crossed pair: the poet Jamil Ibn Ma'mar, of Medina, and his beloved Buthaina from a neighboring tribe. Her family impedes their marriage, considering his poetry a blot on her honor, and Jamil is left to wander the desert composing verses so tender they make the birds and the stones weep. He sets the standard for frustrated love transformed into literature. Along with the similar "Majnoun Laila," Jamil's poems probably filtered into Europe through Muslim Spain to inspire tales like *Tristan and Isolde* or *Romeo and Juliet*.

The culture shared in the kitchen is not only food-related. The hours spent chopping and stirring often double as a vital cultural space in which women neighbors and family members debate politics and exchange gossip, recount stories, and recite poems. The recipes themselves are kept alive and, with them, a whole civilization.

Sayniyit Hulba

Fenugreek Olive-Oil Cake

Serves 12–15

3 tablespoons fenugreek seeds, picked over and rinsed well
3 cups (720 milliliters) water
1½ cups (270 grams) fine semolina
½ cup (120 milliliters) olive oil, warmed
1½ cup (200 grams) all-purpose flour
⅓ cup (75 grams) sugar
1 teaspoon active dry yeast
1 teaspoon baking powder
1 tablespoon nigella seeds
1 tablespoon toasted sesame seeds
Pine nuts or blanched whole almonds, for decoration
Butter or tahina, for greasing
Qatir (page 300), using a 2-to-1 ratio of sugar to water)

صينية حلبة

This uniquely Palestinian confection is often made for nursing mothers as fenugreek is said to increase milk production. The seeds have a strong bitter flavor; soaking or blanching them, then discarding the water, removes some of this bitterness. Don't be surprised if your skin smells slightly of maple syrup after eating this irresistible sweet!

Soak the fenugreek seeds in a bowl of cold water for 30 minutes or overnight. If you are pressed for time, you may skip immediately to boiling the seeds.

Strain the fenugreek and discard the soaking water. Place the seeds in a saucepan along with 3 cups (720 milliliters) of fresh water and bring to a rapid boil. Reduce the heat and simmer, uncovered, for 5 minutes or until the seeds have expanded and are soft to the touch. Strain the seeds over a bowl. Reserve both the seeds and the strained fenugreek water. Set aside to cool.

Meanwhile, in a medium bowl, mix the semolina and the warm olive oil together well—using your hands works best—to ensure complete saturation of the grains. In a separate bowl, whisk together the flour, sugar, yeast, and baking powder, then combine this with the semolina–olive oil mixture, stirring well. Add the reserved fenugreek seeds, the nigella and sesame seeds, and just enough reserved fenugreek water to make a pliable dough (about ¾ cup or 180 milliliters).

Cover and set aside in a warm place for 1½ hours, or until the dough has risen slightly and is soft to the touch (it will not necessarily double in size). Meanwhile, make the *qatir* and set it aside to cool. Once it is cool, refrigerate it until you are ready to use it.

Preheat your oven to 350°F (180°C). Grease a 12 inch (30 centimeter) round baking pan or a 13 x 9 inch (33 x 23 centimeters) rectangular pan with tahina or butter. Spread the dough in the greased pan and flatten with the palm of your hand.

Traditionally, *hulba* is made quite thin, about ½ inch (1¼ centimeters) thick, which will require using two pans for this quantity of dough. We like to bake all the dough in one pan for a somewhat thicker cake (about 1 inch, or 2½ centimeters). Score the dough with a knife, making square or diamond-shaped pieces. Place a blanched almond or pine nut on each piece. Bake for 45 minutes or until golden.

Pour the cold syrup onto the cake as soon as it comes out of the oven. Set it aside to cool and fully absorb the syrup, then cut and serve it.

Mafrouka

Rustic Sweet Olive-Oil Bread

Serves 4–5

½ quantity *Khubz Saj* dough (page 102)
½ teaspoon anise seeds (optional)
½ teaspoon sesame (optional)
½ teaspoon nigella seed (optional)
High-quality extra-virgin olive oil
Turbinado or other coarse raw sugar, for sprinkling
Flour, for rolling

Prepare the *saj* dough. If you are using anise, sesame, and nigella seeds, knead them into the dough, then set aside to rest for 20 minutes.

Divide the dough into golf-ball-sized pieces, then set these aside to rest for an additional 10 minutes. Roll out each round to about ¼ inch (½ centimeter) thick. Dust them with flour to prevent sticking.

Gently place a round of the rolled-out dough onto a griddle or heavy-bottomed skillet. Grill it for about a minute, until it is just beginning to brown, then flip it over. Brush the toasted surface with olive oil, then sprinkle it with about a tablespoon of the sugar.

Leave the bread to cook on the griddle for another 3 to 5 minutes, or until the sugar melts and begins to bubble. Carefully remove the bread from the heat and place it on a platter to cool slightly. Repeat this procedure with each ball of dough. Here you have the option of serving the crisps whole or cutting them into wedges or strips (a pizza cutter works well for this).

Serve with sage-scented tea (page 326).

مفروكة

A delicious rustic pastry, very similar to (and some say the ancient cousin of) the Spanish *torta de aceite*. Traditionally, freshly made and still-warm *saj* bread was topped with sugar, then doused and rubbed well with olive oil until the sugar dissolved, hence the name "*mafrouka*," or "rubbed." Here we brush the rounds of *saj* with oil as they bake, resulting in a crispier pastry—but feel free to try the original method, too!

Ma'roota

Mtabbaq

Mabroosha

Bsees

Ma'roota

Date Spice Bars

Makes about 45 bars

5 cups (630 grams) flour
2 tablespoons ground anise seeds
1 tablespoon nutmeg
1 tablespoon cinnamon
1 tablespoon active dry yeast
1 tablespoon baking powder
½ teaspoon baking soda
1 teaspoon ground *mahlab*
1½ cups (360 milliliters) water
1½ cups (360 milliliters) olive oil
3 tablespoons nigella seeds
1 cup (145 grams) sesame seeds
2 quantities date filling (see *Ka'ik* recipe, page 314)

Mix together the flour, anise, nutmeg, cinnamon, yeast, baking powder, baking soda, and *mahlab*. Stir in the water and olive oil. Add the nigella seeds and sesame seeds and knead well. Form the dough into a ball and transfer it to an oiled bowl. Cover, and allow the dough to rise for about 1 hour.

Preheat your oven to 400°F (200°C).

Punch down the dough, then divide it into two equally sized portions. Roll each into a rectangular shape, ¼ inch (½ centimeter) thick.

Between sheets of plastic wrap or wax paper, roll the date filling into a sheet roughly the same size as the rectangles of dough. Place the rectangle of filling on top of one dough rectangle, then place the other dough layer on top. Press down lightly and cut this into equal sized bars.

Alternatively, you can roll *all* the dough into one large single layer and roll the filling out to the same size. Place the filling on top of the dough and tightly roll both up into a single log. Cut ½-inch-thick cross-sections of this log using a piece of dental floss (wrap it around underneath the log and then pull the two pieces of floss across the top of the log as though tying a shoelace) to create pinwheel cookies.

Bake on cookie sheets lined with parchment paper (or greased) on the middle rack for about 20 minutes or until lightly golden. Do not brown them or the cookies will be tough.

مقروطة

A variation on *ka'ik* that is slightly easier to make, and no less delicious. They freeze well, too.

Mtabbaq

Nut Parcels

Makes 10–12 parcels

3 cups (380 grams) pastry flour
2 tablespoons sugar
¼ teaspoon salt
1¼ cups (300 milliliters) water
1 cup (100 grams) almonds or walnuts, finely chopped
1 tablespoon sugar
1 teaspoon cinnamon
1 teaspoon orange-blossom water
¼ cup (60 grams) ghee or butter, as needed
2 tablespoons olive oil
Qatir (page 300, or use a simple syrup with a 1-to-1 ratio of sugar to
  water) or honey for drizzling

Preheat oven to 375°F (200°C).

Mix the flour, sugar, and salt, then gradually knead the dough in water just until it becomes elastic. Divide the dough into egg-sized balls and set them aside for 20 minutes on a greased cookie sheet.

Mix the nuts with the sugar, cinnamon, and orange-blossom water. Set aside.

Melt the ghee or butter and cool it slightly, then combine it with the olive oil. Dip your palm in the melted butter or ghee and, on a well-greased surface, flatten each dough ball into a very thin, almost translucent circle. Place a teaspoon of the nut mixture in center of the dough circle and fold the four sides to the center, pinching them together to create a square parcel. Flatten the pastry gently and, if you like, decoratively score the top. Brush the top with ghee and arrange the pastries side by side on a cookie sheet; they will not expand during cooking.

Bake for 8 to 10 minutes until lightly golden. Do not overbake or the pastries will toughen. Remove them from the oven and douse them with the syrup (or drizzle them with honey if you prefer your pastries less sweet).

In Gaza, this traditional pastry is typically filled with nuts; in the West Bank sweet cheese is used instead. Although the dough is unleavened, it needs a rest period to relax the gluten.

Mabroosha

Bitter Orange and Walnut Bars

Makes about 24 pieces

3 cups (380 grams) all-purpose flour
1½ teaspoon baking powder
1 cup (225 grams) sugar
Pinch of salt
4 tablespoon butter or ghee, softened to room temperature
¾ cup (180 milliliters) olive oil
2 eggs
1 tablespoon rosewater
2 teaspoons orange zest
1½ cup (160 grams) bitter orange marmalade
1 cup (100 grams) finely chopped walnuts
½ teaspoon cinnamon

Preheat your oven to 350°F (180°C).

Whisk together the dry ingredients (flour, baking powder, sugar, and salt). To this, add the butter, oil, rosewater, zest, and eggs. Knead together until they are well combined. The resulting dough should not be sticky. If the dough appears overly crumbly, add a little more rosewater. If it appears too wet, compensate by adding a little more flour. Divide the dough into two equal portions.

Using the palm of your hand, spread out one portion of the dough in a greased 12 inch (30 centimeter) round baking pan or a 13 x 9 inch (33 x 23 centimeters) rectangular pan. Spread the jam or marmalade evenly over the dough. Mix the walnuts with the cinnamon and top the dough with this nut mixture. Using a medium-sized cheese grater, shred the remaining dough and distribute it evenly over the jam and nuts.

Bake for 30 to 40 minutes or until the crumbs are slightly golden and the jam is bubbling out. Let it cool, then divide it into bars. Serve with sage-scented tea (page 326).

مبروشة

The name of this pastry means "grated." It can be made with any jam, although traditionally *imrabba khushkhash*—a homemade bitter orange marmalade—is used.

Bsees

Buttery Semolina Nests

Makes about 8 or 16 pieces

3 cups (410 grams) pastry flour
1 cup (180 grams) very fine semolina
3 tablespoons granulated sugar
¼ teaspoon salt
½ cup (110 grams) highest-quality butter
Powdered sugar for sprinkling or spring honey for drizzling

Preheat your oven to 350°F (180°C).

Mix the flour, sugar, and semolina, then slowly add water to form a dough that is elastic but not sticky. Let this rest for 10 minutes. Divide the dough into 8 lemon-sized balls for larger pastries or 16 smaller balls for small ones.

Roll out each ball into a circle ⅛ inch (1/4 centimeter) thick on a well-buttered surface, then spread a thin layer of butter over the circle (about ½ teaspoon). Fold two sides of the circle to meet in the middle and pinch them down, forming a shape like a flattened cannoli. Spread another thin layer of butter on top, then fold in the other two round edges, forming a square. Roll it out again to form a very thin circle.

Brush the surface of the circle with a little melted butter. Using a pastry wheel, pizza cutter, or knife, cut this into very thin strips, then gather and shape them into a circle on a well-greased baking tray. The pastry should look rather like a bird's nest. Gently compact it with the palm of your hand. Repeat this procedure for each ball of dough, filling the tray. Set these aside to relax for 10 minutes or so.

Transfer the pastries to a greased baking sheet. Bake for about 10 minutes, until lightly golden—but no more, lest the pastries toughen. Sprinkle with powdered sugar or drizzle with honey. Lately we have seen some confectioners use candied cherries to decorate the pastry, but why gild the lily?

بسيس

Gazan confectioner Fayeq Saqallah invented this now classic but difficult to find pastry, made in the springtime with the best quality butter. It should be eaten with one's hands: They say Saqallah would have it no other way and scolded customers who ate his *bsees* with a fork and knife. He also insisted the dough be patted out by hand, never with a rolling pin. You may cheat on this: Mr. Saqallah is not watching. But the man surely had his reasons.

Ordinarily dusted with powdered sugar, *bsees* is also irresistible with fresh spring honey and seasonal jam.

Ka'ik

Date-Stuffed Holiday Rings

Makes 5 dozen

1½ cups (270 grams) fine semolina
2 cups (480 milliliters) olive oil, warmed
½ cup (120 milliliters) orange-blossom water or rosewater
2½ cups (320 grams) all-purpose flour
2½ cups (325 grams) whole-wheat flour
1 tablespoon active dry yeast
2 tablespoons ground anise seeds
1 teaspoon ground *mahlab* (available at Middle Eastern groceries)
1 tablespoon nigella seeds
1 teaspoon toasted sesame seeds

Date filling

2 pounds (approximately 1 kilogram) date paste (available in Middle
    Eastern grocers) or 2 pounds (1 kilogram) pitted medjool dates
    kneaded to a paste
2 teaspoons ground cinnamon
1½ teaspoons ground cardamom
½ teaspoon ground nutmeg
½ teaspoon ground cloves
2 tablespoons softened butter

Mix the warmed olive oil with the semolina and rosewater or orange-blossom water and rub them together by hand until well combined. Set aside for 20 minutes so the semolina grains can absorb the liquid.

Meanwhile, in a separate bowl, combine the flours, yeast, anise seeds, nigella seeds, and *mahlab*. Combine this mixture with the semolina.

Add approximately 1 cup (240 milliliters) of water, a little at a time, to the dough, and knead it in an electric mixer (if available) until it is moist and pliable. If the mixture is too dry, add a little more water, a bit at a time. Fold in the sesame seeds. Cover the dough and set it aside in a warm place for approximately 1½ hours or until it doubles in size.

Meanwhile, prepare the date paste: Pull the paste apart from the package and warm it slightly in a microwave or over a stove. Knead the warmed paste together with the butter and spices until they are well combined.

Preheat your oven to 400°F (200°C) and set the rack in the middle of the oven. Divide the dough into golf-ball-sized balls, setting them aside on a greased cookie sheet. Divide the date paste into an equal number of balls, approximately half the size of the balls of dough. Take each ball of dough and roll it under the palm of your hand into a log approximately 1 inch (2 1/2 centimeters) thick and 5 inches (13 centimeters) long.

كعك

In Gaza, large batches of *ka'ik* are frequently made for holidays—Muslim or Christian—and distributed to friends, family, and neighbors. In light of the holiday character of these cookies, the recipe we provide is for about 5 dozen *ka'ik*. Feel free to divide the recipe proportionally for a smaller batch.

Exceptionally sweet red dates grow in Gaza, particularly in the Deir el Belah ("monastery of dates") district and, when not consumed fresh in their *khalal* stage, they are processed into date paste for local consumption. Check your local Middle Eastern grocer for date paste. It is much more laborious and expensive to make the paste yourself, so only do this as a last resort.

Using your thumb or pinky finger, make an indentation from one end of the dough to the other. Roll a date-paste ball into a little log slightly shorter than the diameter of the dough, and place it in the indentation. Wrap the dough up over the paste, using a damp finger if necessary to seal it closed. Seal the ends closed and roll the stuffed log out back and forth a few times to even it out, then loop one end over the other to form a ring. Pinch it closed with the tip of your pinky. Arrange the rings on greased cookie sheets, 1 inch apart, and bake for approximately 20 minutes. If you prefer crisper cookies, set the oven to broil for the last 2 to 3 minutes.

Serve with sage tea (page 326) and distribute to friends and family...if you don't eat them all yourself!

315

The Rafah Tunnel Trade

When Israel withdrew from the Sinai Peninsula in 1982, the city of Rafah was suddenly split between Egypt and Gaza, riven by an immense metal and concrete wall. Families found themselves divided by a high-security international border, though their houses often lay less than a hundred meters apart. Before long, some influential families moved their businesses underground, burrowing dozens of secret tunnels under the border fence. These were principally used for contraband: with border trade relatively open, there was no financial incentive for smuggling ordinary goods.

That all changed in 2005. When Israel disengaged from the Strip and sealed it to the outside world, the number of tunnels mushroomed. When the blockade began in 2007, the tunnels became a lifeline. For years, almost everything moved through Rafah's tunnels: medicine, fuel, much-sought-after construction materials (otherwise barred from entering the territory), computers, cars, livestock, even people (like Palestinians lacking the Israeli-issued ID card that would allow them to reside in Gaza with their spouses). It was a vast enterprise and paid five times the average annual Gazan salary in one month. The business was kept tightly within families for reasons of security as well as economy.

Once a top-secret black market, the Gaza tunnel trade had just gone above ground when we were doing the field research for this book in 2010. It was well regulated and tunnel imports were being taxed like everything else, to the considerable benefit of the ruling Hamas party. What had once been clandestine opportunism quickly had become an established multimillion-dollar industry with market fluctuations, shareholders, and dividends like any other major commercial concern, including stakeholders on both sides of the border, Egyptian and Palestinian. The tunnel trade created its own *nouveau riche* in Gaza over a very short time, while providing the besieged population with vital consumer goods—at a price.

But the heyday of the tunnel trade collapsed as quickly as it came. Since the Sisi regime took power, Egypt has been working aggressively to seal its border with Gaza—which it perceives as a political and a security threat—first destroying the tunnels and, more recently, imposing a wide buffer strip between the two sides of Rafah. Israel, anxious to stop the alleged smuggling of weapons to armed Palestinian groups through the tunnels, has energetically bombed them and flooded them with seawater in collaboration with the Egyptian government. The Palestinian Authority in Ramallah opposes the tunnels on the grounds that revenues from their operation support the Hamas government. Now few tunnels are still operating, and those that are seem to be dealing mostly in contraband.

For the people of Gaza, the loss of the tunnel trade is a mixed bag. On the one hand, many farmers and manufacturers in Gaza claim that when the tunnels were active cheap Egyptian goods forced prices down, competing unfairly with local products. On the other hand, the tunnels were a key means of subverting the stranglehold of the blockade, and their loss leaves ordinary people—both consumers and shopkeepers—entirely subject to the whims of Israeli border policies, with no recourse against shortages.

Knafa Arabiya

Walnut and Cinnamon Knafa

Homemade version

Serves 16–20

½ cup (120 grams) melted butter
½ cup (120 milliliters) canola or other neutral-tasting oil
1 cup (180 grams) coarse semolina
1 cup (200 grams) medium-sized bulgur, rinsed
2 cups (480 milliliters) hot water, as needed
2 tablespoons flour
2 tablespoons ground cinnamon
¼ teaspoon ground nutmeg
1 cup (225 grams) sugar
1 tablespoon baking powder
¼ cup (30 grams) powdered milk
2–3 cups (200–300 grams) walnut halves
Qatir (page 300); use 2 cups (380 grams) sugar to 1½ cups (360 milliliters) water
¼ cup (35 grams) pine nuts
2 tablespoons crushed raw pistachios

Combine the melted butter with the canola oil, then add to the semolina and mix well, rubbing it with your hands or whisking thoroughly so that the semolina fully absorbs the fats. Set aside for at least 1 hour.

Pour hot water over the bulgur and set it aside to rest for 30 minutes, covered. Drain it in a sieve, pressing down with the back of a spoon to remove the excess moisture.

Preheat your oven to 350°F (180°C).

Combine the flour, spices, sugar, baking powder, and powdered milk. Add this mixture to the semolina mixture. Mix well. Very gently, stir in the well-drained bulgur until it is just combined, using your hands to break any lumps apart.

Grease a large 12 inch (30 centimeter) round baking pan with butter or ghee. Divide dough into two parts, one twice the size of the other. Spread the larger part evenly on the bottom of the pan with your hand. Top with a single even layer of walnut halves, then spread the remaining dough on top of this. Pat down firmly, with the palm of your hand. Place the pan in the oven and bake for approximately 40 minutes.

Increase the temperature to 400°F (200°C) and bake for an additional 10 minutes, until it is browned from the edges. Remove the pan from the oven and carefully invert it onto a large serving tray (place the larger tray directly on top of the hot pan, hold firmly, then, in a swift motion, flip both upside down).

Of the many dessert pastries made in Gaza, none is as splendid—nor as uniquely Gazan—as *knafa arabiya*. Ordinarily purchased from sweets shops, *knafa arabiya* is rather difficult to reproduce at home. We provide the recipe used by the classic Gaza City pastry shop, Saqallah's Sweets, and an adaptation for home baking.

Pour cold syrup over the whole pastry and cover it for 3 minutes. With the *knafa* still covered, carefully drain the excess syrup. Uncover and let this cool for half an hour, then cut it into even squares and decorate each square with a pinch of pine nuts and pistachios.

Saqallah's Knafa Arabiya

Serves 20

2 cups (360 grams) fine semolina
1 cup (140 grams) pastry flour
2–3 cups (480–720 milliliters) water
¼ cup (30 grams) powdered milk
¾ cup (175 grams) butter or ghee, melted
1 tablespoon cinnamon
¼ teaspoon nutmeg
3 tablespoons (40 grams) sugar
2–3 cups (200–300 grams) walnut halves
Ground pistachios, for garnish
Qatir (page 300); use 3 cups (675 grams) sugar to 2 cups (480 milliliters) water
¼ cup (60 grams) high-quality butter

In a large bowl, whisk together the semolina and flour until they are free of clumps. In a blender, mix together the water and flours, starting with the water first, one cup at a time, until a thin, crepe-like batter is achieved.

Pour the batter onto a hot griddle in thin threads (use a sieve or a condiment squirt bottle) and cook it briefly until it browns from the bottom. Scrape these pancake-like strips off the griddle and allow them to cool. Mix the cooled threads with ½ cup (112 grams) of melted butter or ghee, then run them through a clean meat grinder (ideally) or pulse them in a food processor to attain a consistent breadcrumb-like texture.

Meanwhile, warm the simple syrup. Add ¼ cup (60 grams) butter and stir until it has melted. Keep this warm.

In a small bowl, combine the cinnamon, nutmeg, and sugar and set aside.

Spread the batter crumbs on a large baking pan and toast them in the oven until they turn golden brown, taking care not to burn them. Remove them from the oven and use a colander to sift, if necessary, to remove the larger, nonuniform pieces. Spray the toasted crumbs with a little water to soften them.

Grease a 12 inch (30 centimeter) round baking pan thoroughly with butter, then sprinkle on a ½ inch (1¼ centimeter) layer of toasted crumbs, covering the whole bottom of the pan. Pat this layer down with your hand.

Next, add an even layer of walnuts, followed by a generous sprinkling of the cinnamon-sugar mix. Press down firmly on this layer with the back of a pan. Sprinkle on another thin layer of crumbs, then "fry" the *knafa* on a gas range, rotating the pan frequently to distribute the heat evenly.

For those less inclined to wait and rotate, an alternative is to bake the *knafa* in a 400°F (200°C) oven. Once the edges begin to brown, carefully flip the whole pastry over into another tray (place the larger tray directly on top of the hot pan, hold firmly, then, in a swift motion, flip both upside down). If using the gas-range method, make sure to brown the *knafa* under a broiler for 2 minutes after the edges have begun to brown before inverting.

Pour the hot syrup generously over the whole pastry. Cover the *knafa* for 2 minutes, then uncover it and let it rest for 2 hours. Cut it into even squares, then decorate each of the squares with a generous pinch of pine nuts and ground pistachios.

Saqallah's Sweet Factory

Jundi Street is a broad avenue that runs through the center of Gaza City, its wide median a swathe of rare green space and fountains, mostly in disuse due to the water crisis. Nevertheless, on a summer evening the atmosphere is festive: The street fills up with families out for a stroll, enjoying the breeze that rises up from the sea. Vendors move through the throngs hawking roasted peanuts or *barad*, a phosphorescent yellow slushie of sorts that is a local obsession. A crowd forms around Saqallah's Sweets.

Saqallah's is a landmark in Gaza. The Saqallah family was already famous for its pastry shop back in Yaffa; soon after their flight from that city, they opened another one in Gaza City. Since then, they have expanded to several other locations around the Strip. Most are run by sons and grandsons of the original owner.

While doing our field research for this book we spent a morning with Abu Fakhri, then manager of the store on Jundi Street. He himself was not of the Saqallah family, though he had been working at their factory for almost fifty years.

He told us, "When I was just a boy, I would walk by Saqallah's just to smell the pastries. I was a refugee, poor, I couldn't afford to actually eat them. And I thought, "Wouldn't it be the most wonderful thing in the world to work in a sweet factory?" So I went in and asked for a job."

He stayed with them for the rest of his life. Sadly, since the original publication of this book, we have learned of Abu Fakhri's passing. He is lovingly remembered by all the store's employees for his passion and dedication to the business where he made his life and his living.

Just as that poor refugee boy imagined, the Saqallah factory is indeed a magical world in which sugar is spun into delicate clouds and dough spread to transparent thinness, the air perfumed with buttery syrup and toasting nuts. Amid sacks of walnuts grown in Gaza and pistachios imported (through the tunnels) from California, the shop's several employees showed us their handiwork with pride. They make classic baklava of all kinds, as well as house inventions like *bsees* and—more rustic but somehow more delicious than anything else on the shop's many gleaming round trays—*knafa arabiya,* Gaza's most characteristic dessert.

Atayif

Special Holiday Sweet Pockets

Makes approximately 25 atayif

3 cups (390 grams) all-purpose flour
½ cup (90 grams) fine semolina flour
½ cup (60 grams) powdered milk
1 teaspoon yeast
2 tablespoons (30 grams) sugar
¼ teaspoon salt
⅛ teaspoon turmeric
3 ½ cups (840 milliliters) warm water
1 teaspoon baking soda

In a large bowl, whisk together the flours, powdered milk, yeast, sugar, salt, and turmeric. In a blender, add 3 cups (720 milliliters) of the water, followed by the whisked dry ingredients. Mix well until smooth. You should have a medium batter, the consistency of buttermilk.

Cover, then set the batter aside to rise for one hour in a warm place or until it has doubled in volume. Stir to deflate it.

Mix the baking soda with the remaining ½ cup (120 milliliters) of water, then stir into the batter.

Warm a large ungreased griddle or heavy skillet to medium heat. Grease it lightly by rubbing the surface with an oiled paper towel. Using a ladle, or a funnel with your finger closing the end, pour about 2 tablespoons of batter onto the griddle from about a foot above the surface. The *atayif* should be only a few millimeters thick—slightly thicker than a crepe— and no more than 4 inches (10 centimeters) in diameter.

Once little bubbles form and begin to pop and the top of the *atayif* begins to dry out (it does not need to dry out completely), remove it from the heat and set it aside to cool on a towel.

Try a couple of test pancakes first. If the *atayif* seem too thick, mix 1 to 2 tablespoons of warm water into the batter and whisk well. The ideal *atayif* should be pale, pliable, and about ¼ inch (½ centimeter) thick. It should not be heavily browned on the bottom, or it will break when you fold it for stuffing.

Stuff these little pancakes with one of the fillings on page 323, as instructed.

قطايف

Atayif make their welcome appearance in the Muslim holy month of Ramadan. They are small pancakes stuffed with a filling of nuts or cheese that are then fried (or baked, for the health-conscious) and then doused with syrup. They have been favorites throughout the Middle East since medieval times.

The pancakes for *atayif* are sold ready-made throughout much of the Middle East, then stuffed and fried at home. In Gaza, vendors pop up on street corners just before *maghrib* time—sunset—which marks the time for *iftar*, the breaking of the Ramadan fast. This *atayif* recipe was acquired from one such vendor in Khan Younis, with some modifications.

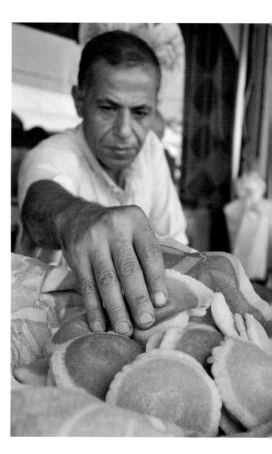

Atayif Stuffings

حشوة القطايف

Cheese stuffing

1½ cups (170 grams) shredded low salt or desalted white cheese, such as
    akkawi or *queso blanco*

½ cup (60 grams) fresh mozzarella, chopped (or an equivalent amount
    of shredded mozzarella, soaked in water and then strained)

2 tablespoons (30 grams) sugar

1 teaspoon rosewater or orange-blossom water

Strain the soaked cheese and pat it dry with a kitchen towel before using it. If you are using *akkawi*, de-salt it by soaking the shredded cheese in cold water and rinsing it several times. Crumble with a fork or your hand, then add remaining ingredients and mix well. Stuff as indicated below.

The traditional *atayif* stuffings are either some type of sweet cheese or crushed, spiced nuts. Laila's grandfather, rest his soul, preferred a milk-custard stuffing (*Mhalabiya*, page 303).

Nut stuffing

2 cups (200 grams) walnuts

2 tablespoons golden raisins

3 tablespoons (45 grams) sugar

1 teaspoon cinnamon

1 teaspoon rosewater or orange-blossom water

Mix all ingredients in a food processor until they are finely chopped, then stuff the pancakes.

To stuff

Gently fold the pancake in half and, starting at one end, pinch the edges with your thumb and forefinger to close it until you get about a third of the way up, making a sort of cone. Spoon in 1 teaspoon of the stuffing, then continue pinching the edges to close the pancake fully. Do not overstuff it, particularly if you are using cheese stuffing.

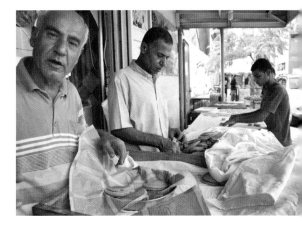

Atayif are traditionally deep-fried in hot vegetable oil until golden, then soaked in cold rose-scented syrup, but many modern health-conscious kitchens now prefer to bake them. We provide instructions for baking; if you prefer to fry them, just make sure you have enough oil to fully immerse the pancakes.

To bake

Preheat your oven to 375°F (190°C). Melt 2 tablespoons of butter or ghee. To this, add 1 tablespoon of canola or another neutral-tasting oil. Brush each stuffed *atayif* with the butter-oil mixture. Transfer to a greased baking pan. Bake for about 10 minutes. Flip the *atayif* over. Bake for an additional 10 minutes, or until golden.

Serve with a drizzle of honey or—more traditionally—by plopping the little pastries into a bowl of cold *Qatir* (page 300) as they come out of the oven.

Ramadan

Ramadan is the ninth and holiest month of the Muslim calendar, during which the Holy Quran is said to have been revealed. For thirty (sometimes twenty-nine) days, able and observant adults abstain from food, drink, worldly pleasures, and (ideally) any kind of immoral behavior or speech from dawn until dusk.

It is a month of re-centering and calibration, of freeing the body from the weight of the material to focus on the spiritual. It is also a time to feed the soul. The pious spend many hours into the night and early morning in prayer, devotion, and supplication. Those who are less devout still take advantage of the special character of the month to reflect and to spend more time with family and friends.

Despite the serious and contemplative spirit of Ramadan, it is also a season of feasting and celebration. Muslims the world over prepare for this special time by stocking up on seasonal foods. With the advent of satellite television, families across the Arab Middle East now watch the same month-long Ramadan miniseries with almost as much devotion as they dedicate to their fasting.

As for any holiday, there is the food. Throughout the region, many fasters eat a hearty predawn meal like *fool imdammas* before the fast. At sundown, you will often see people graciously handing out dates and little cups of water in the street to workers hurrying home to break the fast. In Gaza, lentil soup is often served for *iftar,* the evening meal, along with a salad like *fatt malaahi.* Then, through the evening, families enjoy a whole universe of special Ramadan sweets. Perhaps the most eagerly anticipated of these are the syrup-drenched *atayif.* Pop-up carts and stands appear all over the streets just before sunset selling the little pancakes used for making these delicacies. There are drinks, too: sweet tamarind and carob infusions, or an apricot concoction that is, sadly, prohibitively expensive now due to the war in Syria, where most apricots are produced.

As the month comes to a close, families invariably partake in cooking marathons, producing huge amounts of *ka'ik* and *sumagiyya* to distribute to friends and neighbors for the Eid holiday. These days in Gaza, both Ramadan and Eid have been stripped down to their bare essentials. Very few families can afford the luxurious ingredients that go into holiday dishes, and the scattered family members who might otherwise come together to celebrate can't do so because of the border closures. No fancy fare or dinner parties as one would find in more affluent countries, but a joyous and blessed month nonetheless.

Ahwa Sada

Bitter Coffee with Cardamom
Serves 20–30

1 cup (85 grams) Brazilian Arabica coffee beans, dark roast
12 cardamom pods, coarsely crushed in a mortar and pestle

Very coarsely grind the coffee beans in a mortar and pestle or in a grinder and combine them with the cardamom. Place both in a pot and cover with 8 cups (roughly 2 liters) of water. Boil for 2 hours on medium heat. Set aside for 5 minutes to allow the beans and pods to settle to the bottom of the pan, then strain out the solids and transfer to a thermos or an Arab-style coffee *dalla*, if you have one, to keep warm. Serve in small coffee cups with dates or other sweets.

قهوة سادة

At funerals and weddings, on holidays, and during religious ceremonies, there is always coffee. This kind of coffee differs from standard Arabic (also known as Turkish) coffee both in preparation and in taste: The beans are of a darker roast and must be very coarsely crushed and boiled for 2 hours. They are often roasted over an open flame. The resulting brew is strong and bitter and is served in very small portions, half the size of a traditional espresso, never with sugar.

Lamoonada bil Na'na'

Frothy Mint Lemonade

Serves 5

10 thin-skinned lemons or key limes, washed and scrubbed well
½ cup plus 2 tablespoons sugar (120 grams), adjust to taste
6 cups (1½ liters) cold water
1 teaspoon orange-blossom water
1 bunch mint leaves, stems removed

Chop the lemons or limes (with skins on) into small pieces. Combine them with the sugar and rub together by hand, making sure to squeeze out the juice and pulp as you go. Set aside for at least 15 minutes to allow the sugar to dissolve and form a light syrup.

Strain the mixture, pressing down on the limes with your hand to extract the most juice possible. Add the water to the strained mixture and stir well to dissolve the remaining sugar. Mix the juice in a blender with mint leaves and orange-blossom water until well combined and foamy. Pour the lemonade into cups with ice and garnish with mint leaves and lemon wedges.

ليموناضة بالنعناع

It was in a tenth-century Arabic treatise on farming that the lemon was first recorded in literature. Since then, there has been a long love affair between Middle Eastern peoples and the lemon: for cooking, for salads, for sweets, and in this case, as a perfectly refreshing drink. This thirst-quencher is served in all of Gaza's higher-end restaurants, but is also made at home and served to esteemed guests when in season.

Shay bil Maramiya

Sage-Scented Tea

Serves 5–6

3 teaspoons full-bodied loose black tea or 3–4 black tea bags
1 handful dried sage leaves
6 teaspoons sugar, adjust to taste
6 cups water

In a clean teapot, boil the water and sugar for 3 continuous minutes. Remove the teapot from the heat. As you do so, immediately throw in the sage leaves so they get one brief boil through (do not be tempted to boil them longer or a very bitter flavor will result). Add the tea bags, then cover and let them steep for about 5 minutes.

The tea should be an amber red color, not dark red, or it will be too bitter. Strain it and serve, preferably in clear glasses so the color of the tea is visible, with assorted pastries or to finish a heavy meal.

شاي بالمرامية

It is said that *maramiya*, or common sage, was named for the Virgin Mary (Maryam in Arabic) after she recommended it to soothe a sick child. Until this day, unsweetened sage infusions are used widely to treat stomachaches throughout Palestine and the diaspora. It is also an incredibly reliable remedy for menstrual pain.

Karkaday

Hibiscus Drink

Serves 7

1 cup (about 75 grams) dried hibiscus petals (also called "jamaica" or "sorrel" and available in Middle Eastern, Latin American, and African groceries)
8 cups (about 2 liters) cold water
1/2 cup (112 grams) sugar, adjust to taste

Soak the hibiscus petals in cold water for 30 minutes or up to overnight to maximize their flavor. Check the color: It should be a deep pinkish red. If the infusion is too light, add some more petals and continue steeping. Strain and sweeten with sugar or rose-scented simple syrup—making sure to dissolve well. Serve in clear glasses.

كركديه

Most popular during the holy month of Ramadan, *karkaday* has a tart and fruity flavor that does not have to be heavily sweetened to be enjoyed. It is also a popular remedy for reducing blood pressure. For a colorful variation, add ice and some mint leaves to the serving glass, or one tablespoon of rosewater, crushed ice, and pistachios.

Kharoub

Carob Juice

Serves 5

8 whole carob pods, rinsed
6 cups (1½ liters) boiling water
6 tablespoons (85 grams) sugar, adjust to taste

Crack the carob pods into small pieces: by hand, with a mortar and pestle, or with a heavy rolling pin. Combine the cracked carob pods and the boiling water in a bowl. Cover and let this steep for 15 to 20 minutes. Check the color: It should be an almost opaque brown. If the drink appears too light, add one or two more cracked carob pods and allow it to steep some more. The cracked carob can also be soaked overnight to maximize the infusion. Strain and sweeten. Serve chilled.

خروب

Nothing quenches thirst quite like an ice-cold cup of *kharoub* in the sweltering Palestinian summer. Colorful *kharoub* vendors donning red fezzes (*tarboush* in Arabic) and carrying great ornate pouring vessels decorated with carnations can be seen wandering through public marketplaces. Dried *kharoub* can be found in natural food stores or online. Don't be tempted to substitute carob powder: As one of the women we interviewed, Um Rami, discovered, the result is pretty dreadful.

Shay A'shab

Herbal Tisane

Serves 5

6 sprigs lemon balm (also known as melissa)
6 sprigs fresh mint
3 sprigs fresh *zaatar* (or substitute Greek oregano)
2 sprigs fresh or dried Jerusalem sage
2 sprigs fresh basil
1 sprig fresh rosemary

Combine the herbs in a pot and add the boiling water. Steep for 5 minutes or until the color is a pale yellow-green. Sweeten it if you like, though the tisane is perfectly refreshing unsweetened.

شاي الأعشاب

We had this bright, delicious herbal infusion at the Gaza Safe Agriculture Project organic farm, where the herbs were snipped directly from bushes buzzing with beneficial insects. Many families have these herbs growing in their courtyards and gardens, for both their sweet smell and their medicinal properties. The antispasmodic and antiseptic properties of *zaatar* make it a well-used remedy for coughs and colds.

PICKLES AND PRESERVES

Pickled vegetables and sweet preserves have always had an important role in Palestinian cuisine: Breakfast often includes white cheese and jam, while little bowls of bright pickles and olives accompany most meals. Large jars of pickles line the shelves of most kitchens and are exchanged among families and neighbors. These products have become even more important now, as a means of preserving any surplus crops in the absence of reliable refrigeration.

Imkhalal Ajir

Pickled Baby Watermelons

Makes 2 pounds (about 1 kilogram) of pickles

2 pounds (just under 1 kilogram) baby watermelons roughly the size
   of a golf ball, quartered *or* 2 pounds from the palest side of a slightly
   underripe watermelon, with rind, cut into 2 to 3 inch pieces
7 cups (1½ liters) water
6 tablespoons (110 grams) salt
¼ cup (60 milliliters) vinegar
½ teaspoon sugar

Sterilize your canning jars, then place inside each jar as many watermelons or pieces as will fit comfortably.

Mix the water and salt, then bring them to a boil in a large saucepan. Set aside to cool to room temperature. Mix the vinegar and sugar into the salted water.

Pour this pickling solution into each jar, making sure that the surface of the watermelons is completely covered. You may want to place a small saucer on top to weigh them down. Discard any excess solution.

Close the lids tightly and set the jars aside for at least two weeks before consuming.

Variation: Pickled turnips
Substitute 2 pounds of well-scrubbed turnips, sliced into ½ inch circles or half-circles, and follow the recipe as above, omitting the sugar. Peel and slice one beet. Distribute the beet slices evenly between canning jars. This will give the pickles a nice pink color.

مخلل عجر

Small, unripe green watermelons are a surprising favorite, especially in the southern part of the Strip. If you can't get your hands on unripe baby melons, you can use the palest side of a mature watermelon, rind and all, cut into small pieces.

334

Imkhalal Lamoon

Hot Stuffed Pickled Lemons

Makes 4 pounds (1¾ kilograms) pickles

4 pounds (approximately 1¾ kilograms) small lemons or key limes

Filling
1 teaspoon safflower threads
2 tablespoons *Filfil Mat'hoon* (see page 28)
1 tablespoon nigella seeds
1 tablespoon olive oil
½ teaspoon salt

Pickling brine
7½ cups (approximately 1¾ liters) water
6 tablespoons salt

In a large pot, submerge the lemons (or limes) in enough water to cover them fully, then boil them for about 15 minutes. Drain, discarding the water. Set the lemons aside to cool.

Gently crush the safflower threads between your fingers. Combine them in a medium-sized bowl with the *filfil mat'hoon*, nigella seeds, salt, and olive oil.

Separately, boil the water for the pickling brine in pot, then add the salt and stir to dissolve. Make sure the water comes to a full boil; otherwise the pickles will go bad. Set this aside to cool completely.

When the lemons are cool, make a deep lengthwise slice on one side of each one, from end to end. Stuff this with about ¼ teaspoon of the red pepper filling. When all lemons are stuffed, put them in a large container and cover them completely with the cooled brine. If the brine is not enough to cover them completely, make more (following the same ratio of salt and water).

Place a small plate on top of the floating lemons to keep them submerged, then close the container well and store it in a cool place for two weeks. When the lemons are soft, including the peel, they can be quartered and served with olives as a complement to all meals.

مخلل ليمون

The large yellow lemons generally available in supermarkets can be used for this recipe, but if you can find small, round, thin-skinned fruit—key limes or Mexican limes would do—the result will be much closer to the delicate pickles consumed in Gaza, which are made with the indigenous Palestinian sweet lime.

Slow Food in the Gaza Strip

The new wave of American artisan-cheese aficionados and rooftop farmers may be surprised to discover their inadvertent kinship with the people of Gaza.

All over Gaza, families are reviving old methods of farming, cooking, and conserving foods to survive the restrictions imposed by the siege and the persistent electricity cuts. Faced with massive unemployment due to the closure of the borders and the annihilation of the productive sector, Gazans have turned en masse toward small-scale agriculture: on plots of land if they have access to them, on rooftops and balconies if they don't.

Dovecotes and rabbit hutches flourish above the city. Electricity cuts make refrigeration unreliable, leading to a rediscovery of old conservation techniques: Pickles and jams proliferate, and drying racks can be found in many backyards. Without access to gas for ovens and stoves, many cooks are consulting their grandmothers about how to fire up the clay ovens that have lain abandoned for a generation.

This forced self-reliance is felt not only among ordinary people trying to get by, but also at a government level: recognizing Gaza's desperate water crisis, the government has announced strategic plans for large-scale wastewater recycling and the promotion of indigenous rain-fed agriculture.

The idea is not new. In the First Intifada, during the 1980s, the key word in Palestinian politics and daily life was *sumud*, or steadfastness. Rather like the Gandhian *swadeshi*, this was a coordinated political push, eagerly taken up by the grassroots, to achieve self-reliance and move toward economic, social, and psychological independence from Israel.

Israel retaliated, at that time, by providing incentives for growing cash crops for export and by massively recruiting workers for Israeli agriculture, causing many to abandon their small farms in Gaza for more lucrative wage labor.

A generation later, with the borders now closed, young people are returning to the land as a last recourse, tapping the agricultural knowledge of their elders to do so.

Imkhalal Bitinjan

Pickled Eggplant

Makes 2 pounds (1 kilogram) of pickles

6 cups (1½ liters) of water
4 tablespoons (75 grams) salt
½ teaspoon sugar
2 tablespoons white vinegar
10 cloves garlic
3 tablespoons *Filfil Mat'hoon* (page 28)
2 pounds (just under 1 kilogram) baby eggplants, stems removed

Sterilize your canning jars, then set them aside.

Boil the water for the pickling brine, then add the salt and sugar and stir to dissolve. Make sure the water comes to a full boil to prevent spoilage. Let it cool to room temperature. Stir in the vinegar.

In a mortar and pestle, pound the garlic with a pinch of salt until it is coarsely crushed. Transfer it to a small bowl. Add the *filfil mat'hoon* to the garlic and mix well.

In a large saucepan, submerge the eggplants in water and boil them until they are partially cooked, 5 to 7 minutes. Strain, discarding the water. Once the eggplants are cool to the touch, make a 1 inch slit down the side of each one and gently stuff with ½ teaspoon (or more) of the garlic-*filfil* mixture.

Stack the eggplants neatly in the sterilized jars, pressing down to make more space if you have to, then cover them completely with brine. Discard the excess brine (or pickle something else, like watermelon or turnips!).

مخلل باذنجان

This is a quick and simple recipe for pickling one of Gaza's most prominent summer crops. It uses tiny eggplants, the first of the season, no larger than a few inches. Indian eggplants of a similar size will do splendidly. This recipe was given to us by Um Hani, who makes jars to distribute to each of her married children every year.

Na'ema and the Backyard Farm Revolution

Arriving at the Khan Younis Union of Agricultural Workers, we stumble into a large room where women of all ages are crowded together around a conference table, very attentively listening to a class on bookkeeping. Na'ema Al-Daghma hustles us into her office next door, where she and her colleague Hanan Shahin shower us with information, interrupting each other in their enthusiasm, the conversation about agriculture and economics peppered with recipes for sweet eggplant jam and pickled okra.

Together they run the Union's program for women, serving the large (by Gazan standards!) agricultural region of the Eastern Villages. The women in the classroom, they explain, are learning all different ways to make their tiny family plots more efficient, from bookkeeping to strategies for composting and recycling wastewater to techniques for drying and conserving what they produce.

The region, they say, used to be agriculturally stable: Much of the land was planted with rain-fed crops like olive trees, date palms, and wheat, and each family had a small backyard garden for horticulture and small animals. With the uprooting of trees and reduction of farmland, some have tried shifting to intensive horticulture, but the water required for irrigation is too expensive: Pumping requires fuel, and the water that comes up is often too saline to use. That leaves just the

back-yard scale of production, traditionally the domain of women. Na'ema and Hanan are out to teach rural women how to maximize the productivity of these tiny plots, and empower themselves—within their families and communities—in the process.

With delight they recount their success stories—how, by pooling resources and sharing ideas, whole neighborhoods have managed to rise out of total dependence on aid. Participants in their workshops have collaborated to raise small animals like chickens, ducks, and rabbits as well as the fodder to feed them; they've build shared drying racks to conserve seasonal vegetables like tomatoes, okra, eggplant, and *mulukhiyya*. They've held canning parties to preserve pickles and jams, teaching each other a whole range of recipes and techniques. Together they have worked to generate markets for these products, providing these women with a small but important income. This turns the tables not only on families' food security, but also on power relations within the family.

Not content just to sit and talk, Na'ema squeezes into our car and whisks us off, first to show us her own verdant backyard farm, with its flocks of ducks and chickens roaming freely under trees heavy with fruit, and then to drop in on several of the "graduates" of their program.

Mrabiya Arasiya

Sour-Plum Jam

Makes about 5 pounds of jam

3 pounds (about 1½ kilograms) arasiya plums or any other small very tart plums, such as sloe

3 pounds (1½ kilograms) sugar

Wash the fruit well and remove the stems. Combine the plums and sugar in a large bowl and set them aside for 30 minutes. Transfer them to a pot and cook on low heat for about 1 hour, skimming any froth that rises to the surface.

The jam should be thick: you will know it is ready when a drop of syrup forms a ball when dripped into a dish of water. Allow the jam to cool, then transfer into sterilized jars. Serve for breakfast or for a light supper with *Khubz Kmaj* (page 100) and white cheese.

مربى القراصيا

Arasiya are small greenish-purple plums native to Gaza. They are too sour to be enjoyed fresh, so they are used to make a much-loved jam, very thick and tart. For Gazan Palestinians in diaspora, a jar of *arasiya* jam is a treasured gift. With tree populations (located mostly in the hills along Gaza's border) quickly dwindling due to systematic Israeli land clearing, the plums are becoming a costly rarity. Our attempt to procure these plums and cook them into jam in the summer of 2010 was a two-week-long comedy of errors, ultimately ending with the power shutting off just as we were ready to photograph our prized find (see photo on page 119).

As a substitute, slightly unripe Empress plums, sloes, or other sour wild plums work nicely.

This same basic jam recipe is used by many families to process the massive quantities of strawberries Gazan farms produce for export, which otherwise would rot in the sun waiting to cross the closed border.

Halwit il Ari'

Pumpkin Conserve

Makes about 7 pounds (3 kilograms) of jam

1 medium-sized sugar pumpkin, butternut squash, or other orange gourd
¼ cup (32 grams) calcium hydroxide (also called hydrated lime, pickling lime, or slaked lime)
4 pounds (about 2 kilograms) sugar
Juice of one lemon
1 tablespoon toasted sesame seeds

This addictive conserve is sought out in Gaza City's public markets in the fall, from the few remaining vendors who still make it by hand. Soaking the pumpkins in limewater helps them retain their shape and gives them a slight crunch; skip this step and you will end up with mush.

Dissolve the pickling lime in 5 cups (approximately 1 liter) of boiling water. Cover this and set it aside overnight. Two layers will form: the calcium water and the solids. Use the water and discard the solids.

Chop the pumpkin into bite-size pieces, or shred it using a cheese grater. Soak it in the limewater for at least 16 hours. Drain the limewater solution and rinse the pumpkin. Re-soak the pumpkin in fresh water for 1 hour.

Strain the pumpkin and combine it with the sugar in a pot. Set aside for 5 hours.

With a slotted spoon, remove the pumpkin from the sugar, which will have turned syrupy, and set it aside. Add the lemon to the sugar and boil for about 10 minutes. Return the pumpkin to the syrup and simmer for an additional 30 minutes, or until a drop of syrup dripped into a bowl of water forms a small ball that keeps its shape.

Pour the pumpkin and the accompanying syrup into sterilized jars, mixing in the roasted sesame seeds. Seal safely.

Variations
• *Candied Carrots: Use 4 pounds (2 kilograms) of large carrots instead of pumpkin.*

• *Eggplant Conserve: Use small whole eggplants or larger eggplants cut into small pieces. Add 3 cloves and 1 cinnamon stick to the boiling syrup.*

• *Fig Conserve: Use fresh figs and add raw walnuts or almonds to the syrup before sealing the jars.*

Imrabba Balah

Stuffed Date Jam

Makes 2 pounds (just under 1 kilogram) of jam

2 pounds (roughly 1 kilogram) fresh red dates (yellow Barhi dates in the *khalal*—or crunchy—stage may be substituted)
3 cups (570 grams) sugar, more as needed
Blanched almonds, equal in number to the dates
1½ teaspoons citric acid
1 tablespoon whole cloves
2 cinnamon sticks

Fill a large pot with water and bring it to a boil. Blanch the dates in the boiling water. Strain them over a bowl, making sure to reserve the water, and transfer them to an ice bath to cool. Peel the dates by rubbing them between your fingers; the peels should come off easily.

Measure the reserved date water, then return it to a large pot and mix in 2 cups of sugar for every cup of water (450 grams of sugar for every 240 milliliters of water). Add the citric acid, cloves, and cinnamon sticks. Boil vigorously for about 10 minutes, or until a syrup forms.

Meanwhile, make a small slit in the side of each date and squeeze out the pit. Place a blanched almond in place of the pit.

Once the date water and sugar have formed a syrup, gently add the stuffed dates and reduce the heat to low. Simmer for about 1 hour, partially covered, then can in sterilized jars (following safe canning procedures).

This delicious conserve is made with Gaza's famous red dates. As of October 2015, farmers have finally—after a fifteen-year ban—been allowed again to export them to the West Bank.

When in season, there are more of these dates than anyone knows what to do with; what is not turned into date paste or consumed fresh is often made into *imrabba balah*.

On Irrigation

The water situation in Gaza has been grave for a long time. After 1948, with the arrival of the refugees, the already limited natural resources of the Strip, which relies on a network of shallow aquifers, began to be overstretched.

In the 1980s, when the Israelis were in control of both the civil and military administration of the Strip, they built their settlement right on top of the best water sources and overdrew from the coastal aquifer for intensive greenhouse horticulture projects. Then, when the Palestinian Authority took over after the Oslo Accords in 1994, they had neither the force nor the mandate to control drilling and pumping. When the Israeli borders closed at the beginning of the second Intifada in 2000, hundreds of thousands of newly unemployed people returned to subsistence farming in Gaza, leading to a major crisis of overdrilling for irrigation.

Part of the problem has to do with the division of land: People inherit lands that are divided into smaller and smaller lots, and they try to divide the water resources. Part of it has to do with what is being grown: Historically there was a lot more rain-fed agriculture—olives, dates, almonds—but much of that has been destroyed by successive Israeli incursions and politically driven agricultural policies over the years. Since those trees take a long time to grow back, many Gazans choose to cultivate irrigation-intensive garden vegetables instead.

Until the full-blown siege began in 2006, there were strong incentives for growing value-added fruit, vegetables, and flowers for export by way of Israel, especially strawberries, cherry tomatoes, and carnations. It seemed to make sense at the time: if you're a tiny territory with limited resources, no possibility of self-sufficiency, and a major employment crisis, what you can do is produce labor-intensive cash crops for export to energize the local economy.

Now, due to the blockade, those products generally can't leave Gaza, though the possibility of a momentary shift in policy keeps farmers growing them. Despite efforts to take advantage of these crops (massive household production of strawberry jam, sundried tomatoes, and so on), they mostly go to waste. The carnations are fed to donkeys.

From a hydrological perspective, according to Gaza Hydrology Group expert Bashar Ashshour, Gaza shouldn't have any agriculture at all, much less for export. It can't afford to "export" water, its most precious and scarce resource. The population grows and grows and the aquifer is already insufficient for basic consumption needs. Saline water from the sea is seeping into the aquifer at an alarming rate.

Others, like Rafeek al-Madhoun from the United Nations Development Program, insist that there could be plenty of water for agriculture if it were managed better. There could be systems for rain catchment and wastewater treatment for irrigation, he says, if it were not for the byzantine structure of different and conflicting donor organizations at work in Gaza, which give priority to short-term projects with immediate visible results rather than long-term infrastructural investments.

Index

347

Acknowledgments

This book owes so much to so many people: to the backers who supported the initial Kickstarter campaign which funded our fieldwork; to Laila's parents, Moussa and Maii, for covering child care and more while we raced all over Gaza, as well as for many later consultations and fact-checking errands; to all the many NGO workers, farmers, and professionals in Gaza who facilitated contacts and interviews; to the friends who helped with the transcription and translation of hundreds of hours of interviews. We also thank our publisher, Helena Cobban, for taking a chance on us, the reviewers who took the time to look into this obscure little publication, and the notable figures in the food world—Claudia Roden, Nancy Harmon Jenkins, Yotam Ottolenghi, Èdouard Cointreau, and others—who very graciously have promoted this book and helped it along. Many thanks also to Yassine and Juan for their continual enthusiasm and support for this project at every step of the way.

Above all, our gratitude goes to all the women who invited us into their homes and their lives, so generously sharing their stories and their tables with us. They are the heroines of this book.

Resources

We are frequently asked by readers what they can do to help. This is not always an easy question: Debates rage over both how to improve everyday life for Palestinians in Gaza and how to impel a change in the greater political context. We offer these suggestions for getting started.

Inform

Stay abreast of news in Gaza and Palestine. Here are some reliable sources of more in-depth information:

United Nations Office for the Coordination of Humanitarian Affairs (ochaopt.org)
Gisha—Legal Center for Freedom of Movement (gisha.org)
Institute for Middle East Understanding (imeu.net)

Educate

Find opportunities to educate others. This could be as simple as a conversation with a neighbor, a cooking club, or a community event. There are great resources available for starting informed and productive conversations about Palestine in schools and elsewhere. Check here:

Peace Research Institute in the Middle East (vispo.com/PRIME)
Voices Across the Divide (voicesacrossthedivide.com)
Council for Arab-British Understanding (caabu.org)
Choices Program (choices.edu)

Advocate

If you want to go a step further, advocate. Demand accountability from your elected representatives, or participate in grassroots solidarity efforts such as the global boycott, divestment, and sanctions (BDS) movement. Check:

Palestinian BDS National Committee (bdsmovement.net)
US Campaign to End the Israeli Occupation (endtheoccupation.org)
Palestine Solidarity Campaign (palestinecampaign.org)

Donate

While charity is more a palliative than a solution, donations do make a huge difference in the daily lives of millions of Palestinians and drive many projects such as the ones we highlight in this book. Here are a few of the reliable organizations that work in Gaza:

United Palestinian Appeal (helpupa.org)
American Near East Refugee Aid (anera.org)
Middle East Children's Alliance (mecaforpeace.org)
United Nations Relief and Works Agency (unrwa.org)
CARE International (care-international.org)
Palestine Children's Relief Fund (pcrf.net)
Medical Aid for Palestinians (map-uk.org)
Kinder USA (kinderusa.org)

Visit

There are a number of organizations that now offer guided educational trips and solidarity volunteer camps in Palestine:

Interfaith Peace Builders (ifpb.org)
Green Olive Tours (toursinenglish.com)
Alternative Tourism Group (atg.ps)
Israeli Committee Against House Demolitions (icahd.org)

Buy

Sources for fair-trade Palestinian products:

Hadeel Fair Trade Palestinian Products (hadeel.org)
Zaytoun from Palestine (zaytoun.org)
Yaffa Palestinian Products (yaffa.co.uk)
Canaan Fair Trade (canaanusa.com)
Palestine Fair Trade Australia (palestinefairtradeaustralia.org.au)